BLOOD AND BRONZE

PADDY DOCHERTY

Blood and Bronze

The British Empire and the Sack of Benin

HURST & COMPANY, LONDON

First published in the United Kingdom in 2021 by
C. Hurst & Co. (Publishers) Ltd.,
New Wing, Somerset House, Strand, London, WC2R 1LA

Printed in the United Kingdom by Bell and Bain Ltd, Glasgow

Distributed in the United States, Canada and Latin America by Oxford University Press, 198 Madison Avenue, New York, NY 10016, United States of America.

A Cataloguing-in-Publication data record for this book is available from the British Library.

ISBN: 9781787384569

This book is printed using paper from registered sustainable and managed sources.

www.hurstpublishers.com

This book is dedicated to Ekang,
a victim of the British Empire
who never received justice

CONTENTS

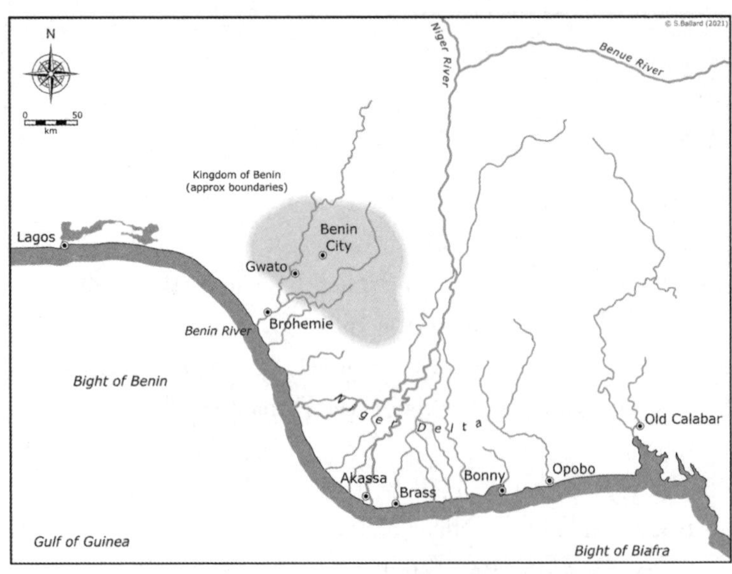

Niger Delta region in the late nineteenth century

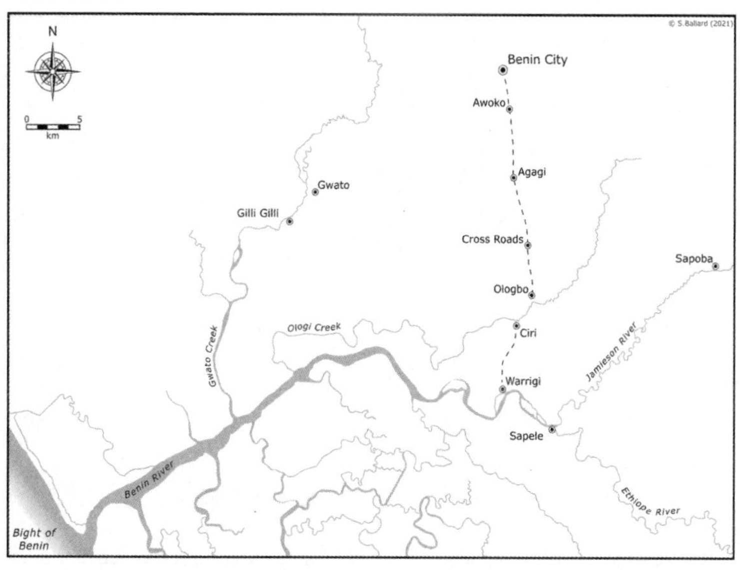

Advance of the Benin Punitive Expedition, February 1897

ACKNOWLEDGEMENTS

Many thanks to the staff of the National Archives in Kew, and to Ruth Loughrey and Scarlett Dennett at Unilever Art, Archives and Record Management in Port Sunlight. Particular thanks go to Jerry Rudman, archivist at Uppingham School, for his generous help with material on James Phillips. I am also grateful to Anne Jones at Companies House archives, Katie Barrett at the Cheltenham College archive, the archivists at Liverpool Record Office, and Sam Sales at Special Collections in the Bodleian Library.

My gratitude goes to the Society of Authors for their support during the writing of this book. Thanks to Charles Walker at United Agents, Michael Dwyer at Hurst Publishers, and Farhaana Arefin for her dedicated editing. Posthumous thanks to my late father, Robert Docherty, who drew the illustrations for this book in the last year of his life. Aita Ighodaro deserves an honourable mention for accompanying me on that visit to the British Museum, and I thank Olly Hyde-Smith, Julia Popescu, and Kate & Gunnar. Special thanks go to Markéta Mojžíšová.

This book began life as an effort to tell the full story of one episode of colonial wrongdoing; it was researched and written with a growing sense of horror and shame as I learnt more about the extraordinary violence of the British Empire in what is now

Nigeria. The vast majority of the victims died anonymously and uncounted, but we are able to put a name to Ekang, the woman who suffered one of the most shocking colonial crimes that I uncovered in the archives. She stands in for all those harmed by the British Empire with no hope of justice, and I dedicate this book to her.

PROLOGUE

'The Master's Tools Will Never Dismantle the Master's House'

Audre Lorde[1]

The first time I laid eyes on the Benin Bronzes was in the spring of 2007. I had recently begun a relationship with a young British Nigerian woman, who identified strongly with her family links to Benin City. Being dimly aware that the British Museum held a collection of magnificent artworks from the historical Kingdom of Benin—in what is now southern Nigeria—and that they remained unfamiliar to both of us, I took her to see them on one of our earliest dates. This illustrates the particular but largely unacknowledged advantage of romantic involvement with a historian.

Inside the sprawling neoclassical complex of the British Museum, the African collection is downstairs, in a gallery named—for financial reasons—after a British supermarket magnate. Down some shiny stone steps and through heavy swing doors, it is a cool space of marbled calm, offering some respite from the echoing bustle of the Great Court crowds above. The displays mix a number of pieces of contemporary art from Africa with a great many historical artefacts, some beautifully decorative, others of largely academic interest. Almost all were obtained, one way or another, during the long period of the British Empire.

At the western end of the long gallery is the room housing the collection of works from the Kingdom of Benin. Enter the room, turn left, and immediately you are struck by the grand array of Benin plaques, surely the most famous of all the artworks from the kingdom. Suspended on slim rods, a grid of at least fifty of these dazzling pieces—each roughly the size of a large book—fills the room, floor to ceiling. Lit gently, almost reverentially, as befitting their pricelessness, they dominate the room, filling it with the glow of their chocolate colouring.

The 'Benin Bronzes' is a collective term used loosely to refer to artworks made not only in bronze but also in brass and similar alloys, alongside other Benin pieces in ivory and various woods. The plaques are cast in brass but are no longer shiny, having aged over the centuries into tawny browns with reddish hints, as if dusted by cocoa powder. In intricate detail they show dozens of scenes from the history and myth of the Kingdom of Benin: kings and courtiers, soldiers and celebrants, monsters from imagination and merchants from abroad. The complex high-relief casting—showing figures almost emerging from the surface—is evidence of superlative skill and, on this scale, of highly organised production; the plaques on show here are merely a tiny fraction of the Benin body of work.

Most striking perhaps is the highly stylised rendering of human features: boldly abstracted, with angular geometry, seemingly modern in style centuries before European Modernism. Faces are shown with large nostrils, eyes wide and heavily rimmed, staring intensely. In almost all plaques, the figures depicted look directly outwards, as if at the viewer, giving them an immediacy and special connecting power.

Focusing on one plaque almost at random among the dazzling array, one might see a central figure dominating the scene—a great general, or perhaps the king himself. His skull, jaw and neck are clad tightly in a helmet and raised collar patterned in a way that represents coral beading, showing high status. He wears a necklet of leopard's teeth, pointing outwards aggressively. His bare chest is crossed by a thick bandolier of coral beads, and he wears broad armlets of the same precious material. His body bears a series of marks, either tattoos or perhaps decorative scarification. A wrap around his waist is intricately patterned and may be edged with coral.

In his right hand this striking figure brandishes a sword with an extravagantly wide, curved blade in a shape reminiscent of a fish. He is flanked by two bearded warriors, shown slightly smaller and both dressed similarly: tall helmets that remind one of British Grenadiers of the eighteenth century, and what seems to be armour on their chests. Both soldiers carry short spears with lengthy, decorated blades. They look like stabbing spears, but does the fact that both warriors hold them pointing down mean that they were meant to be thrown? In a curious gesture, the king or commander also grasps one of the held spears in his left hand.

Set beside the main figures are two smaller ones, servants or musicians who are shown roughly half-size, denoting their status. This mix of scales is a clever use of perspective and, beyond that, is powerfully representative of rank. They are naked, with bodies covered all over in a neat pattern that might be tattooed or painted, resembling a harlequin suit. Other characters, even smaller, seem to float about the heads of the main military figures.

Giant flowers are etched into the surroundings, conveying the impression of a rich, fecund environment, though much of the background surface of the plaque has broken off around the figures, giving it ragged edges. With deep and problematic symbolism, the background that remains carries in two places the catalogue numbers of the British Museum, clearly marked in white paint on the tawny brass surface.

Another plaque shows a king sitting side-saddle on a horse, elaborately helmeted and richly decorated everywhere with coral. He grips the arms of two supporting figures, pages on either side, one of whom also carries a staff surmounted by a great bird, wings outstretched. I certainly wouldn't have known this at the time of my first visit to see the Benin Bronzes, but this represents the 'bird of Oro', which features especially in the Ugie Oro ceremony that commemorates the great Benin king Oba Esigie and his victory in defiance of portents in a battle in the sixteenth century.

Once again playing with perspective and deftly presenting rank, the unknown artist has shown a groom holding the reins of the horse in the corner of the plaque, reduced almost to insignificance.

In a rather different piece, a cattle sacrifice is displayed. Five figures, dressed as pages or servants, hold an outstretched bullock while a central character is seen in the act of cutting its throat. In a virtuoso display of casting skill, the design is especially intricate and the high relief notably pronounced: with all four legs splayed, the animal is lifted clear above the surface of the plaque. Other figures, shown much smaller for communicating perspective, complete the scene. Due perhaps to minor differences in alloy composition and to the accidents of human handling over the centuries, the metal here is a notably rich hue, the colour of roasted coffee beans, and has been burnished in places to a beautiful lustre.

In yet another plaque from this splendid array, a battle scene is depicted. A soldier in the centre bears a formidable sword, undecorated, with an irregular blade weighted heavily towards the point—a weapon for fighting, not for ceremony. He wears a distinctive crocodile hide helmet, a necklet of protruding leopard's teeth, and the chest bell that proclaims his role of warrior. Behind him is a group dressed similarly, perhaps under his command. The dominant figure wields his great sword in his right hand while in his left he clutches the arm of a horseman who seems to be lurching forward in the saddle, impaled on a spear blade. This figure bears facial scarring and a helmet of very different form, coding him clearly as a foreigner. The plaque may thus represent an important victory against outsiders.

The grand array of plaques dominates the room, but the British Museum cabinets hold many other valuable artworks from the Kingdom of Benin (and only a fraction of the total is on public display). Among the most readily recognised of the other Benin pieces are the Queen Mother heads, cast in brass and bearing the distinctive hairstyle known as the 'parrot's beak'—a tall spike of hair covered in a mesh of coral beads. The earliest of these heads, made in the sixteenth century, are gently curved, sinuous and lifelike in their appearance, and are cast in rich, dark and lustrous metal. More recent heads, dating from the eighteenth century, have become more highly stylised, with angular, geometric features and exaggerated proportions. These heads are altogether larger, stouter in frame and generously decked in coral regalia, the brass aged now to a deep mahogany.

Small statuary pieces show kings, musicians, priests or even visitors from European kingdoms. Straight-sided bells are cast in brass and decorated with geometrical patterns with animal faces, leopards or crocodiles. There are iron swords, highly decorated and for ceremony only. There are masks, some in ivory, some cast in bronze, many of which are too small to wear on the face and are intended to be used as pendants. Ivory is also carved into figurines, and into bracelets with delicate fretwork showing kings and crocodiles, inlaid with metal. Entire elephant tusks are carved all along their length in figures and stories drawn from the store of Benin myth and legend. Many cabinets are full of such fascinating pieces.

The British Museum therefore holds an extraordinarily rich and comprehensive assemblage of artworks from the Kingdom of Benin: not merely a handful of items but hundreds of artefacts. This fact alone is enough to provoke curiosity, given the relative size of the historical kingdom. One might speculate that the extensive collection represents a significant portion of the Benin cultural patrimony, and perhaps think it odd to find it on display in a gallery far away in another country. This is, of course, the salient fact of the controversy of the Benin Bronzes, and it is explained—as far as it goes—in the British Museum labelling.

Museum artefact signage can be a delicate matter, especially when it comes to contested or controversial pieces. For its Benin collection, the British Museum attempts to solve the quandary with brevity: what it says is largely factual, but it avoids detail. It tells us that in 1897 the British sacked Benin City in retaliation for the killing of British representatives, and that thousands of artworks were seized as 'booty'. Such vocabulary is frank, almost confessional, and to that extent is commendable. However, the fleeting treatment of what sound like historical events of great magnitude raises many questions. Why exactly were British forces in Benin late in the reign of Queen Victoria? Who were the representatives in question, and how did their deaths warrant the sacking of a city? Most pertinently, perhaps, if these artworks were taken as booty, why are they still in London today?

My first visit to the Benin Bronzes therefore left me with a profound impression of their great beauty and the exceptional skill behind their creation, but also a deep curiosity about how they actually came to be in the British Museum. Sadly, the relationship that prompted my first sight of the Bronzes did not last, but that inquisitiveness lingered for years. Life is generally never as tidily organised as one might hope, so it took me some time finally to be able to answer those questions from that spring day years ago; this book is the result.

PROLOGUE

In seeking to understand the removal of the Bronzes from Benin in 1897, my research naturally expanded to consider the British presence in West Africa at that time. The British Empire entity that launched the invasion of the Kingdom of Benin was the Niger Coast Protectorate, now part of Nigeria; to comprehend its intrusion into Benin properly, it is essential to consider the Protectorate's genesis and development, and the goals of its officials. Moreover, given the stated reason for the 1897 action—avenging dead representatives—it is necessary to examine the moral claims and standing of the Niger Coast Protectorate itself: was it possessed of a legitimacy that might give it the authority to demand retribution? It made claims (as did the Empire more broadly) to be spreading civilisation; was it? How did the Empire measure up, according to its own avowed standards? Was it everything that it claimed to be, and that was claimed of it by politicians, supporters and allies in the popular press?

Addressing such questions in a specific case can (indeed, must) force a reckoning with British imperial history more widely. On the whole, Britain still lives in a state of denial about its empire's legacy, especially since there has never been a decisive break with the imperial era, such as a revolution, comprehensive military defeat or wholesale reconstitution of the state. The utter destruction of the Nazi regime in 1945 marked such an historical turning point for Germany. Less dramatically, the collapse of the Fourth Republic in France in 1958, during the crisis of the liberation war in Algeria, marked at least an opportunity to restructure and rethink, even if colonial attitudes persisted into the Fifth Republic. Britain has had no such moment of forced reflection and reorganisation: we have shed an empire but otherwise the state remains largely unchanged, despite devolution and a bit of tinkering with the House of Lords.

For many British people, the institutional continuity between the days of empire and the present means an implied transfer of the moral authority of our present government (such as it is) to this previous era. The fact that we still inhabit the state and society that ruled an empire has allowed us to feel an inappropriate national ambivalence about the realities of the imperial project, and we have not adequately addressed the moral horrors of the colonial era. I am quite certain that many readers will even have been offended at my use of the word 'horrors' in connection with recent British history, despite there being no other honest way to describe many episodes from the British Empire period. This includes colonial violence and oppression that happened during the very lifetimes of some people currently reading this paragraph.

This ambivalence is often simply the unconscious and quotidian result of living in a society that has not taken care to handle its past with frankness. Witness, for example, the routine consumption of cultural products which erase or excuse the colonial exploitation underpinning our wealth: relentless remakes of Jane Austen novels on television and in cinemas, with almost no recognition that the lives of luxury enjoyed by the characters depicted were very often paid for, at least in part, by the labours of enslaved African people toiling on Caribbean sugar plantations. Much worse than this cultural complacency is the recent use of feel-good empire rhetoric by politicians on all sides—even prime ministers—in their bids to flatter the electorate into surrendering their votes. This direct refusal to engage with our imperial past is a failure of leadership that helps explain how Britain has come to develop a 'newsreel memory' of the colonial period, recollecting only the photogenic parts, after the story has been edited to remove anything that might spoil the upbeat narrative or dampen the national mood. Thus, we sometimes manage to celebrate the British involvement in ending the slave trade after 1807 without ever recognising that Britain was for decades the leading slave trading nation in the world.

In asking the simple question of how the Benin Bronzes came to be in London, I was thus drawn into considering much broader questions surrounding the morality of empire and colonialism. The story of the Niger Coast Protectorate and its 1897 invasion of the Kingdom of Benin became a case study of the operational methods of the British Empire on the ground and—unavoidably—its moral claims. In telling the tale of the conquest of Benin, therefore, this book also seeks to examine the nature and legitimacy of the British Empire itself. Before we look at the British in Africa, however, we must go back to the emergence and flourishing of the powerful kingdom once known as Great Benin.

1

THE KINGDOM OF BENIN

In the origin myth told by the Edo people of the Kingdom of Benin, the universe emerges spontaneously into being with a man floating on his back, mute and unmoving on calm water. There was no knowledge, no meaning and no history; all was yet to be created. Suddenly a voice from nowhere commanded, 'Open your eyes,' and his eyes snapped open. His body remained completely still.

This order was the only time the voice sounded outside the man. Having awoken him, it entered him and became his. 'It is dawn,' the man declared, rising to a seated position. Nothing yet existed; all was emptiness except for the water on which he sat. Then a long pale whip appeared beside him, and a snail shell on the other side. The man picked up both, and on turning over the snail shell saw a stream of fine brown silt fall onto the water. Each grain was both a complete universe and an individual man, and as they hit the surface of the water it disappeared, solid earth taking its place. With firm ground around him, the man stood for the first time.

Raising his whip, he cracked it into the haze that surrounded him, and on the horizon a point of light appeared, growing swiftly and becoming the bright, golden orb of the sun. In the new light and warmth that it gave, the man saw the earth beneath him and the sky above, and he was happy. He walked for the first time, moving forwards then backwards, to one side then the other, in doing so creating the act of counting. With counting now in existence, time began, and with the beginning of time, knowledge became necessary.

The man again raised his whip and this time struck the earth before him. Immediately, the world was filled with forest—trees, bushes, greenery of every kind surrounded him everywhere, save for the clearing where he stood. Surveying his creation, the man was pleased but not yet satisfied. As he struck his whip again, the jungle was suddenly filled with all manner of animals, springing into being in a cacophony of calls and cries. One by one, they approached him in their gratitude. The leopard hailed him, then the deer, the adder, the hawk. Each one greeted the man as creator-king, announcing its name before departing to take up its allotted place in this new realm. This went on until every last creature had paid homage.

The new creator-king cracked the whip, bringing a village into being in the clearing where he stood. From within the buildings, human voices could be heard. One figure stepped out, declaring, 'I am Okpia, as a man I worship you, my lord,' as he kneeled in obeisance. Then another emerged and fell to the ground before the king, announcing, 'I am Okhuo, and as a woman my loyalty to your majesty is through my husband.' Finally, a third figure, an infant, appeared and declared, 'I am Omo, my friend, and as a child I worship you with my innocence.' By this time the clearing had filled with people and the active life of the village, and the creator-king looked upon his new universe with joy. After a moment, he saw that at the opposite end of the clearing stood a grand building, greater than any other, a fine construction that stretched all along one side of the village, a palace fit only for a king. In front of this impressive dwelling thronged a great crowd, waiting patiently but with anticipation.

The creator-king set off on a slow, dignified walk across the clearing to the magnificent building, bearing his whip in one hand and the snail shell in the other. The respectful crowd parted to allow him through, as he continued his stately procession to his rightful home. The intended goal felt both incredibly near and impossibly far away, but always right and fitting. As he stepped into the great palace, the crowds cheered, crying, 'Welcome home, Lord from the Sky!' The creator-king nodded in recognition both of their applause and of his own deep feeling in having arrived.

Looking out at his people, he came to understand his power, and the extent of his dominion over man, woman, beast and plant. Deciding to introduce order to his realm, the king called forward some members of the crowd and gave them instructions: some would dress him, some would cook for him, others would do work of different kinds. All were happy with their allotted tasks.

Then the king ordered that a mound of earth be formed in the courtyard of his palace, and that it be painted white. When it was completed, he slowly approached the mound and with great dignity knelt beside it, placing the handle of his whip into the earth and laying the snail shell beside it. Turning to the gathered crowd, he announced that this would be the shrine of Osa, the Almighty King in the Sky, and that henceforth he would be known as Osanobua. He appointed an elderly man as priest of the shrine and commanded him always to wear white. With the permission of the king, the priest spoke to the crowd and told them of the duties of reverence and respect that they owed to the king. Everyone showed their satisfaction.

By this time, the sun was setting, and the moon was about to take its place in the sky. With all humans and animals assigned their place in the realm, the creation of the world was complete.

* * *

Thus goes the Edo origin story as told by Professor Iro Eweka in his volume of folk tales from the Kingdom of Benin.[1] Significantly, Eweka was a prince of the Benin royal family and grew up among members of the court who had come of age in the pre-1897 era and were familiar with the traditional culture: he thus provides a direct link to the chain of oral transmission reaching back centuries. This is of especial value because until the twentieth century, Benin was not a literate culture, all history, legend and practical knowledge being passed on by word of mouth from generation to generation.

This single fact provides the greatest challenge to any historical study of the Kingdom of Benin. History is typically reliant on written materials, documentary evidence being prized above other forms; historians value nothing more highly than a bulging government archive compiled over the years by diligent bureaucrats who wrote everything down. In the absence of such sources, other forms of knowledge (e.g. archaeology and linguistics) become all the more important, and this is one reason why the Benin Bronzes—especially the brass plaques—are of such exceptional value, being the repository of Edo history, myth and social customs. Crucially, however, where history is reconstructed from oral traditions and the analysis of cultural artefacts, precise dating is impossible, and there remains a lively debate about chronology within the study of Benin.

From archaeological and linguistic evidence, it seems clear that the Edo people separated from the related ethnic groups of the Yoruba and Igbo in the region of the Niger-Benue confluence approximately 3,000 to 6,000 years ago.[2] Gradual migration southwards from the savannah zone saw them penetrate the southern forests and forest swamplands west of the lower Niger River, meaning that the Edo appear to have occupied their present location for almost 4,000 years. It is intriguing to think that, in the creation myth summarised earlier, the stately walk across the clearing by the creator-king may well represent this slow and steady migration of the Edo into their present homeland, as transformed by a mythologising oral tradition operating over the centuries.

Little is known about the early period of Edo settlement, but the kingdom likely developed from multiple villages and microstates established around the beginning of the second millennium: archaeological remains show a network of several thousand miles of earth boundaries from the period, suggesting numerous minor centres of power.[3] Benin City itself may have originated as a religious site, and by c. 1300 it was the centre of a modest kingdom based around a system of chiefly tribute. A new dynasty came to power under Oba Ewekpa from c. 1320, and over the following two centuries, the kingdom was transformed through conquest into a highly centralised imperial power.[4]

Evolution of the system had begun even before the dynastic change, with the introduction of the Onijie system of hereditary village chiefs, who were granted tributary rural fiefs in a manner roughly analogous to European feudalism. Oba Ewedo (ruled c. 1374–1401) worked to further separate himself as king from the powerful Uzama nobility, principally through means of a standing army. Development of this coercive authority allowed the king to exert direct control over tribute payments from the Onijie, and to increasingly centralise power in royal hands. Under Oba Oguola (ruled c. 1401–1428), redistributive demands increased, especially due to the king's establishment of specialised communities of metalworkers and brass casters. This marked the beginning of the great tradition of Benin art, which was fundamentally courtly—and thus political—in origin. A crucial enabling factor for this expensive development was the dramatic expansion of trade over this period, along with direct royal control of trade routes.

It was, however, under Oba Ewuare (ruled c. 1455–1482) that the Kingdom of Benin was transformed into an empire, when he further expanded the military capacity of the state and launched a series of wars of conquest. Annexations were, in particular, aimed at the north–south trade routes that carried commerce between Benin and the regions beyond the Sahara.[5] Alongside this military expansion, this period saw a significant development of state bureaucracy and witnessed numerous internal rebellions, not least because of the increasingly national character of the polity: by the end of his reign, Ewuare seems to have incorporated the majority of Edo-speaking peoples of the region into the Kingdom of Benin. His successors Oba Ozolua (ruled c. 1482–1509) and Oba Esigie (ruled c. 1509–1536) continued the expansionary efforts to control the north–south trade routes, including through the establishment of new military outposts. Additionally, Benin City was fortified with formidable ramparts sometime in the period between 1450 and 1550,[6] further illustrating the capacities and military nature of the state.

This era therefore saw the extension of Edo rule over a vast network of trade routes and tribute-paying towns and villages, making the Kingdom of Benin dominant in the region and providing it with great wealth. This was the high point in Edo imperial expansion, and for their success in conquest, these kings—especially Oba Ewuare and Oba Esigie—are frequently depicted in Benin artwork. Their achievement in creating this powerful, centralised state also meant that the first European visitors to Benin, who arrived in this period, were highly impressed with the richness and sophistication of the kingdom.

The Portuguese, who had been edging their way along the coast of West Africa for much of the fifteenth century, were the first Europeans to venture to Benin City, under the navigator João Afonso de Aveiro in 1485. A measure of their regard for the kingdom is that they returned to Lisbon with an Edo visitor—a chief of Gwato—who thus became the first West African ambassador to Europe.[7] The Portuguese were soon followed by the explorers and traders of other European nations, who were attracted by the commercial possibilities of the organised trade of the Kingdom of Benin. That the Europeans arrived to a highly developed economic and governmental system seems to be confirmed by the fact that the Oba of Benin (likely Oba Esigie, but this is not confirmed by the European records) sent a second embassy to Lisbon in 1514 to complain about the conduct of European traders on the Benin River.[8] They also requested a consignment of firearms. This embassy was followed by another in 1516, and yet another in 1540,[9] demonstrating a developed governmental capacity with international reach. Similarly, a Portuguese embassy was established in Benin City, certainly by 1516, as attested by letters written home to Manuel I.[10]

Although the primary aim of European traders in West Africa was at first to obtain a source of gold, the slave trade gradually increased in importance until, over the decades, it eventually became the principal activity of outsiders in the region. As a growing empire with captives aplenty, the Kingdom of Benin was a ready supplier of enslaved people in the early period of European contact. However, demonstrating the requirement for slave labour in the kingdom itself (not least for military purposes), Oba Ozolua introduced some restrictions on the export of male slaves, which soon became a total ban lasting until around 1725; female slaves, though, could be exported freely.[11] While the transatlantic slave trade was not therefore a critical factor in the economic rise of Benin, it did later have a negative impact on the kingdom through enabling the development of competing centres of power on the margins of its empire.

This development was to take place some time in the future; of more immediate concern were internal tensions and the disruptions they caused. As we have seen, throughout the fifteenth and sixteenth centuries, Benin was an expansionary kingdom, tightly centralised around a monarch who was not only militarily powerful but regarded as a god. Divine kingship—as embodied in much Benin art—was an important factor in statecraft, and from the earliest period of contact, Portuguese visitors recorded the awe in which the Edo beheld their kings.[12] An important aspect of this concept of divine rule was the power that the Oba wielded over life and death itself, displayed most graphically through the practice of human sacrifice. A royal prerogative (and only occasionally granted to certain chiefs), the sacrifice of slaves, war captives or other people was held to be a duty of the king in his role as supreme mediator with the divine realm; as highly public evidence of his coercive power, it naturally also had a political value. Although some of the earlier European reports from Benin revelled in descriptions of this practice, it seems that the scale of human sacrifice increased in response to mounting outside pressures on the eve of European colonialism; it is clear that it was highly valued for propaganda purposes by the imperial powers, who also exaggerated its incidence.[13] Nonetheless, human sacrifice was a significant cultural reality in the kingdom, and it is a regular feature of Benin artworks.

The development of ritual and of the religious importance of the king would in itself prove a danger: over time, and in the context of the growing power of rival chiefs, the Obas of Benin became increasingly the captives of ceremonial.[14] This change in the nature of kingship was relatively swift: Oba Ewuare and Oba Esigie in the late fifteenth and early sixteenth centuries had marched around the region conquering at will, but by the early seventeenth century the king was ritually restricted to the palace in Benin City, from which he emerged only once or twice a year for the most important public religious ceremonies.[15] The king had largely fallen under the control of his own military, and of the great chiefs who commanded it.

This growing power of the chiefs—especially the Iyase, the most senior 'town chief'—intersected with succession crises to make the seventeenth century and much of the eighteenth century a deeply troubled period for the Kingdom of Benin. The death of Oba Ohuan in c. 1630–41 prompted a succession crisis, which marks a significant turning point and the beginning of decline.[16] Outright civil war is reflected in European accounts from 1696 until well into the 1730s, and the Iyase was at times the leader of rebellion against the king. Indeed, the nature of Edo kingship could become a weakness: it seems from the oral traditions that Oba Ewuakpe ordered so many human sacrifices on the death of his mother (likely in the 1690s) that the people rebelled and he was forced to flee into the countryside.[17] Accounts of European travellers also allow us to infer that the casting of the brass plaques ended around 1700, implying serious deterioration of royal systems of patronage and production.[18] However, Oba Ewuakpe later played a crucial role in re-establishing the foundations of the monarchy through the introduction of primogeniture and a settlement with the nobility, demonstrating that the story of the Kingdom of Benin in this era was not a simple one of decline. Moreover, his son Oba Akenzua further restored the power and reputation of the monarchy through reconquest of rebellious areas, becoming one of the strongest and wealthiest of all Benin kings.[19] It was likely under Akenzua that a treaty was signed with the Dutch in 1715,[20] indicating a sufficiently stable central apparatus of government once again to be able to conduct international diplomacy.

These outside forces also had a destabilising impact. Over time, the transatlantic slave trade stimulated the appearance in the coastal regions of new collaborative elites, who emerged to benefit from the inflows of wealth (in the form of trade goods) from the European purchasers of human beings. These revenues allowed the development of alternative centres of power, and new microstates began to emerge on the fringes of the Benin Empire in the Niger Delta.[21] In some areas of the great river system, the Kingdom of Benin had never extended its rule, notably the coastal strip inhabited by the Ijaw people, who were from an altogether different linguistic group and thus less susceptible to the proto-nationalist Edo imperial project. In other parts, the suzerainty of Benin—at one time enforced, or at least claimed—came under challenge as emergent polities took advantage of the weakness and distraction of the royal regime in the interior to fight among themselves for access to slave trade revenues.

This centrifugal dynamic can be seen in the autobiography of Olaudah Equiano, an enslaved African who eventually purchased his freedom, became successful in business and settled in England. An Igbo from the south-east of the Niger Delta, Equiano was born in 1745 and at just eleven years old was kidnapped into slavery in the West Indies and then Virginia, before serving for some years as the personal slave of a Royal Navy officer. Writing in 1789, Equiano gives a description of his home region at that time. Referring to the various kingdoms in West Africa, he reports:

> Of these the most considerable is the kingdom of Benin, both as to the extent and wealth, the richness and cultivation of the soil, the power of its king, and the number and warlike disposition of its inhabitants.[22]

Crucially, he records that he was born in a 'remote and fertile' province of the kingdom, but that 'our subjection to the king of Benin was little more than nominal', mentioning that the business of government was conducted by their own chiefs and elders.[23] Equiano thus describes part of the gradual process by which an empire might lose its hold on frontier regions if the central machine does not work continually to maintain and enforce its control; during the long period of internal dissension in the kingdom and consequent neglect by the central authority, some regions on the fringes of the empire would have been obliged to take on the responsibility for governmental functions even if they had no aspirations for independence.

Despite this degree of decline, the reign of Oba Eresoyen (ruled c. 1735–50) appears to have been relatively peaceful.[24] With the issue of royal legitimacy finally settled, he focused on strengthening the spiritual basis of Edo kingship, an important part of the increasing transformation of the Obas into divine kings, largely removed from the daily business of rule. Such an evolution is reflected in the resurgence of brass casting in the period, which was becoming strikingly political, indeed propagandistic, in the claims it made about royal occult powers.[25] This development in the nature of the Edo monarchy continued into the nineteenth century, and the Kingdom of Benin would never more have warlike, conquering kings.

It was in this period that the minor states of the Niger Delta were able to develop, freed from the pressure of Benin imperial power and funded by the revenues of the European slave trade. Given the reliance on waterborne communications in what was a fundamentally riverine region, the typical pattern was for each tributary of the great delta to evolve a separate economic system and the accompanying governmental structures. Thus political formations gradually appeared at Bonny, Brass and especially at Old Calabar on the Cross River, where the Efik people developed two rival power centres, at Duke Town and Creek Town. The Itsekiri people spread from the Forcados River to dominate the trade on the Benin River too, as the Kingdom of Benin gradually lost its purchase. In the complex politics of the Niger Delta of this era, inextricably interlinked with European trade, new political units would on occasion rise and fall, such as New Calabar and, much later, Opobo.

Besides the gradual loss of influence over the fringes of its old empire, in the nineteenth century Benin would also suffer from the long period of civil wars in the Yoruba kingdoms to the west, which disrupted valuable trade flows and severed certain eastern Yoruba areas that had previously been subject to the kingdom.[26] Additionally, European traders stopped using Gwato as a port, preferring the Itsekiri-dominated lower Benin River, which further damaged the economy of the kingdom. Nor had internal political ructions been ended altogether: Oba Osemwende (ruled c. 1816–1851) had to fight rivals to secure the throne and endured much dissent.[27]

Despite this measure of decline, however, on the eve of the West African colonial period, the Kingdom of Benin remained a highly organised, sophisticated political entity with a rich and complex culture. We must remember that the British accounts of the kingdom from the nineteenth and early twentieth centuries were typically refracted through the requirements of the British Empire project, and often aimed at justifying expansionary policies. Evidence of human sacrifice or other cruelties was highlighted instead of the abundant proof of developed political structures and exceptional artistic traditions. On occasion, British accounts would reveal the sophistication of Edo culture almost despite their best efforts to conceal or diminish it. For example, the 1825 account given by Captain Fawckner of his visit to Benin City was summarised by Charles Read and Ormonde Dalton of the British Museum in a way that suggests a certain reluctance to describe the features of what was in fact a thriving, organised political culture and developed urban life:

> The city of Benin was a large and rambling town, surrounded, like many Yoruban cities, by a mud wall and a ditch, and divided by broad avenues. The more important buildings comprised numerous courtyards, and covered a great amount of ground. As in other African towns, there were large market-places, where all buying and selling

> was done, and in these the inhabitants spent a great deal of their time... The King's 'palace' resembled in general construction other large houses, but was of greater extent and distinguished by certain particular features. It had one or more pyramidal towers, which in Fawckner's time were built of wood.[28]

This is, however, leaping ahead. Before we consider the relationship between the Kingdom of Benin and the British Empire, it is essential that we step back and look at the reasons why Britain came to be in West Africa at all.

2

WEST AFRICA AND THE BRITISH INTRUSION

No message having returned from Lagos, I determined in conjunction with Lieut. Commander Stokes, Dr Henry and Captain White to visit the city of Great Benin, whose King in times gone by was the most powerful sovereign of Yoruba.

Richard Burton, HM Consul for the Bight of Biafra,
26 August 1862

So far as I can ascertain there has been very little previous correspondence respecting the establishment of British protection or jurisdiction over the Oil rivers (the mouths of the Niger) or the neighbouring districts.

Augustus W. L. Hemming, Colonial Office, 3 May 1883

The original sin of the British Empire in Africa was slavery; long before colonies and protectorates became the means of seizing the territory of West Africa, Englishmen were seizing its people and kidnapping them across the Atlantic in slave ships. This 'triangular trade'—Britain, West Africa and the Caribbean forming its three points—became one of the principal foundations of the wealth and power of modern Britain.

Among the first English slave traders was Captain John Hawkins. Commissioned as a privateer by Elizabeth I, he sailed to what is now Sierra Leone in 1562 and acquired several hundred enslaved African people, transporting them across the Atlantic to be sold in the Spanish Caribbean. His efforts proved so lucrative that in 1565, after a second African voyage, Hawkins was awarded a coat of arms by Queen Elizabeth befitting his wealth and success. Demonstrating the importance of the grisly trade to his life and fortune, the Hawkins arms are surmounted by an enslaved African, securely bound against escape.

Despite the potential profits to be had from trading in enslaved human beings, however, English trade with West Africa was for decades dominated by commodities such as gold, ivory and pepper; it is of course significant that modern Ghana was for centuries known by Europeans as the Gold Coast. The shift to slavery for English merchants came during the seventeenth century, as English settlers and absentee owners developed sugar plantations in the Caribbean and thus demanded a ready supply of cheap and profitable labour. By the 1680s, thousands of enslaved people were being carried across the Atlantic every year by the Royal African Company—a chartered corporation that for a time held the monopoly on African trade with Britain and was headed by the Duke of York, who was later elevated to the throne as James II. The fact that the English slave trade was led at this time by a future king leaves no doubt about the social acceptability of the gruesome business in Restoration England.

The Royal African Company lost its monopoly on trade with Africa by the end of the century, and through the eighteenth century many private merchants began slaving as demand soared. The authoritative Trans-Atlantic Slave Trade Database[1] estimates that of the astonishing total of 12.5 million enslaved Africans who were taken across the Atlantic during the entire period of European slave trading, fully 3.3 million people were carried in

British slave ships. In the eighteenth century alone, over 2.5 million enslaved people were kidnapped across the Atlantic by British commercial interests, the dominant slave traders of the century. The fact that even greater numbers were transported by Portuguese slavers throughout the colonial period (principally to Brazil, which has forced something of a rethink of the dynamics of the transatlantic trade) does not change the fact that Britain played a key role in the enslavement and exploitation of Africans.

This crucial point is something that many British commentators of the early years of the twenty-first century still seem keen to overlook. They often focus instead on the 1807 Slave Trade Act, which abolished the trade in slaves within the British Empire (though not slavery itself). Thus, the act's bicentenary in 2007 was full of public self-congratulation for ending the trade without the same degree of attention being paid to the salient fact of British domination of slavery for the preceding century. Numerous articles, television features, and even films celebrated the 1807 Act as a humanitarian triumph (even though the institution of slavery was left untouched in British territories until the Slavery Abolition Act of 1833). In the wake of this bicentenary fanfare, Prime Minister David Cameron felt able to give an address to the Britannia Naval College in Dartmouth in which he credited Britain with having 'swept the evil of slavery off the high seas'[2] without mentioning a single one of the 3.3 million Africans who had been cruelly enslaved onto British vessels.

Although there are some understandable reasons for seeking to avoid the issue in this way (shame, fear of reparation demands, ignorance), they are wholly inadequate and do a disservice to the historical facts. There is no doubting the profound (and continuing) impact that slavery had on Britain itself, and it must be recognised and explored. The economic historian (and first prime minister of independent Trinidad and Tobago) Eric Williams argued in his landmark work *Capitalism & Slavery*[3] that the profit earned from transatlantic slavery (via Caribbean sugar plantations) played the crucial role in enabling the Industrial Revolution in Britain itself. In this analysis, therefore, without the slave trade, Britain would have been an also-ran in economic development, rather than the dominant global economy for a sustained period of the modern era. Even if one does not accept the full implication of the Williams thesis, profound economic benefits can readily be tracked in eighteenth- and nineteenth-century Britain. The leading port cities of the time owe their wealth to the triangular trade: Liverpool and Bristol especially, also London and Glasgow. Such development was not limited to ports. Kehinde Andrews, Professor of Black Studies at Birmingham City University, has written powerfully of how his hometown of Birmingham was built on the manufacture of the firearms and manacles that were essential tools of slavery.[4] Entire industries arose from—or expanded greatly because of—the triangular trade, from shipping and insurance to banking and finance.

Directly as Britain (and other European countries) grew wealthy from slavery, West Africa suffered. While a small number of Africans—middlemen traders and elite groups—benefitted from the trade, the region as a whole was devastated by depopulation, endemic warfare resulting from slaving raids, and lasting social dislocation. The consensus view among Africanist scholars is that the slave trade stunted West African population growth so significantly that the impact continues into the present era.[5]

One of the most searing analyses in this vein was developed by the Guyanese professor of history and political activist Walter Rodney. In his classic 1972 text *How Europe Underdeveloped Africa*,[6] Rodney located the period of the slave trade within a longer history of European exploitation of Africa, forming a continuity with the colonial occupations that began in earnest in the late nineteenth century. The lasting impact upon Africa of slavery and colonisation, and the continuing financial benefits enjoyed by Britain and other European countries, thus bring the issue firmly into the twenty-first century.

* * *

An important continuity that Rodney and others have explored derives from the palm oil trade. During the long years of the campaign to abolish the slave trade, especially from the 1780s in Britain, the merchants of Liverpool, Bristol and elsewhere faced the prospect of an abrupt end to their business, should abolition come to pass. Many slavers therefore sought to diversify into 'legitimate commerce': West African products that could make up for the loss of income. Palm oil—a valuable vegetable oil native to the region, with a variety of uses—proved the most lucrative. Even before the abolition of the trade in enslaved people, many merchants had therefore developed interests in palm oil, and after the 1807 Slave Trade Act, all those who wished to remain in business in West Africa had little choice but to follow suit. The big slave merchants thus became the leading palm oil traders, and growth was swift. In 1807, British imports of palm oil stood at 2,233 cwt; by the 1840s they had risen to an average of 426,000 cwt per annum.[7] Palm oil had swiftly replaced slavery as a highly profitable business for British merchants and as the primary British strategic concern in West Africa. It would also, as we will see, become a factor in the downfall of the Kingdom of Benin.

Besides the ongoing operations of British companies and individual traders, there is another much more insidious continuity. As Walter Rodney and several other scholars have identified, the 1807 Act and the switch to palm oil effectively meant a relocation of the site of exploitation: rather than crossing the Atlantic to work on Caribbean sugar plantations or American cotton fields, slave labour was employed within Africa to harvest the large volumes of palm oil newly required for sale to British buyers.[8] The end of the slave trade on British vessels had, unsurprisingly, also forced adaptation upon West African elites—the kings and chiefs who had previously benefitted from the sale of human beings—many of whom responded by entering the palm oil trade, replacing one commodity with another. Slaves thus continued to be exploited within Africa for the ultimate benefit of British commerce and industry, with such practices persisting in various fashions and under various pseudonyms ('domestic servitude' being a favourite) even during the colonial era. Neither the 1807 abolition of the trade nor the 1833 abolition of the institution of slavery within British territories were therefore quite the landmarks that numerous newspaper articles of the early twenty-first century, and not a few public speechifiers, would have us believe.

A focus on 'legitimate commerce' did, however, suit the prevailing narrative of the early and middle years of the nineteenth century, when Britain self-consciously (and self-interestedly) promoted the liberal doctrine of free trade. Having decisively defeated the French and Spanish navies at the Battle of Trafalgar in 1805, the Royal Navy obtained for the British Empire a global supremacy at sea that was barely challenged until the end of the century. This salient advantage—allied with the crucial intellectual contributions of David Ricardo, Adam Smith and other free-trading economists and philosophers—was the enabling factor that allowed Britain to spread (and quite often impose at gunpoint) free trade and British investments around much of the world.

* * *

This period—when the British Empire was arguably at the height of its powers—brings us to an important consideration for the way that we think about the nature of imperial expansion and the definition of 'empire'. For many decades from the late nineteenth century, people in Britain and all over the Empire were used to looking at a map of the world on which all the parts under formal British rule were shaded in red ink, giving them a pinkish colour. Such maps were ubiquitous in school textbooks and certain parts of the popular press, and 'the pink bits on the map' were universally recognised by British people as somehow 'ours'. In time, around a quarter of the world map would be coloured in this way, stretching across the chart from Canada in the top left, through Africa, the Middle East and India, all the way to Australia and New Zealand in the bottom right. Presented simply thus, such that the entire world is either pinkly British or it isn't, the map creates an impression that the real boundaries of the British Empire were neatly coterminous with those of the areas in pink; an interested observer might be forgiven for assuming that the limits of the British imperial project therefore matched those shown on the map. This would be mistaken; imperialism must be understood as the exercise of power over—and the extraction of advantage from—another region or country, regardless of the particular legal relationship between the two parties concerned. Lack of formal submission through a treaty or other arrangement does not make the extension of influence, or even the imposition of control, any less real.

Known as 'informal empire', this key concept was famously set out in the landmark 1953 article 'The Imperialism of Free Trade', written by Professors John Gallagher and Ronald Robinson.[9] In the middle of the twentieth century, the conventional approach among historians of empire was to interpret the nineteenth century as dividing into two periods, according to the expansion of the formal British Empire, as charted clearly on the map. Thus, the early and middle years of the century—during which few 'pink bits' were added—were typically viewed as an anti-imperial age in which Britain showed little appetite for expansion. The later nineteenth century—when the British Empire joined enormous swathes of territory to its claims, especially in Africa—was conversely interpreted as avowedly imperialist. By focusing especially on the formal empire represented on the map, historians therefore typically saw a divide in enthusiasm for the Empire between early and late Victorians.

Through extending their analysis to include informal empire, Robinson and Gallagher demonstrated a fundamental continuity across the era, thereby upending the study of imperial history. Far from being reluctant to impose themselves on the world, the free-trading Brits of the early and mid-nineteenth century were just as aggressive in their expansionary energies as their countrymen of later decades. As Robinson and Gallagher deftly analysed, the difference was only in the precise nature of the methods used. If informal techniques of influence and control are considered alongside formal empire, the continuity becomes clear.

Informal empire comprises a battery of techniques for exercising influence over a foreign polity, sometimes executed consciously and sometimes merely the accidental result of pursuing other goals. In the case of the British imperial project, consideration of such methods allows us to look at areas of the world that were never part of the formal British Empire and to analyse the degree of power wielded over them by Britain. Consider, for example, the continent of South America, which from the late fifteenth century was appropriated and colonised largely by the Portuguese (in Brazil) and the Spanish (almost everywhere else). By the early nineteenth century, the Iberian powers had declined so profoundly that they were unable to retain their American colonies, and by 1830 they had lost all their territories in the region (with the exception of the Caribbean islands of Cuba and Puerto Rico).

During this period of Spanish and Portuguese decline, and especially after South America had achieved independence in the shape of new republics and kingdoms, Britain was steadily increasing its influence around the continent. Using its naval power to help persuade the emerging countries to grant commercial privileges to its own traders and manufacturers, Britain broke up what had been a Spanish trade monopoly and sought to secure an informal supremacy for itself. Under Foreign Secretary (later Prime Minister) George Canning in the mid 1820s, therefore, Britain threw her considerable diplomatic clout—and latent military potential—behind the recognition of the independence of the new Latin American states. With access to these markets thereby assured, British capital and expansionary energies flowed into the continent, into everything from Brazilian railways to Argentine cattle farming. By 1913, over a quarter of all British investment outside the British Isles was in Latin America. Importantly, this investment had flowed into a region which lay entirely outside the formal British Empire, besides the small colonies of British Guyana and British Honduras (existentially both outgrowths of the British Caribbean possessions). Thus, through extensive investments, a network of trade treaties, active diplomacy and the ever-present threat of force via the Royal Navy, Britain had developed a predominance over much of a vast region in which it never sought formal rule.

Given the obvious British willingness to seize territory worldwide and claim it as their own, the absence of empire-building in South America may seem surprising. Why did Britain not seek to gain formal possession of regions that it evidently found commercially attractive? The answer, put simply, is that it did not need to, since it was able to get what it wanted out of the polities of the continent without going to the trouble and expense of undertaking formal rule. This is the crux of the Robinson and Gallagher thesis of informal empire. Throughout the nineteenth century, British expansionary aims remained broadly unchanged, varying only in method: 'By informal means if possible, or by formal annexations when necessary, British paramountcy was steadily upheld.'[10]

Thinking in terms of informal empire thus corrects any misapprehension, derived from the map, that the British Empire was neatly and solely composed of the areas in pink. To gain a more accurate picture of the true extent of the Empire, we need to imagine a map that also includes a series of less clearly defined pink zones spreading over areas such as South America, waxing and waning continuously as political shifts take place and investment levels rise and fall. Visualised in this way, empires can be understood as fluid and ever-changing, gaining and losing purchase over territories in a way that is not fully recognised in the politico-legal landmarks of treaties and formal annexations.

Similarly, the ubiquitous map of the British Empire also misleads by suggesting a homogeneity in imperial formations, since almost all British possessions were coloured in the same pink. Only occasionally were some territories represented differently, to indicate special political status, perhaps in pink and grey stripes (the 'Anglo-Egyptian Sudan', or UN mandates after World War Two). Generally, though, the typical map gives the impression that all the pink bits were of the same legal status and were ruled in the same way. This obscures a reality that was much more complex: the British Empire comprised a wide range of legal forms and political arrangements, which frequently evolved over time as circumstances changed both on the ground and in Britain. Colonies of settlement (the 'white colonies') such as Canada and New Zealand were in time granted degrees of self-government as 'dominions'. The British intrusion into India was, for over two centuries, carried out by a commercial enterprise under royal charter, and was additionally divided into 'British India' and dozens of princely states, which were nominally independent but controlled by British officials. Part of Hong Kong was held outright after being ceded by China in 1842 following the First Opium War, while another part was held from 1898 on a ninety-nine-year lease (which decided the timing of the return to China of the entire colony in 1997).

Other legal forms were also developed, such as the 'protectorate', a somewhat nebulous relationship of frequently contested meaning and barely a step up from informal empire. A protectorate sometimes grew into the more substantial 'Crown colony', which implied a closer relationship with London (though without guaranteeing a significant commitment of money and personnel). The chosen form of imperial connection would depend on a wide variety of factors, from the desirability of the territory and its natural resources to the level of opposition from local people and the availability of local collaborators. A substantial consideration was the strategic value of the area in question, particularly its utility in assisting the defence of existing British possessions. New forms could be invented as necessary, according to local requirements and the imagination of imperial officials.

This raises an important point about the nature of the British Empire: very often, the legal structures were improvised and the organisation on the ground somewhat makeshift, even threadbare. Colonies were frequently under-resourced in men and money (especially those judged to be less important), at times seriously hampering their capacity to carry out the responsibilities they claimed, and making an improvisational approach essential for many harried colonial officials. The ramshackle character of much imperial power might surprise a modern reader, trained by television re-runs of *The Jewel in the Crown* to imagine empire as comprising smart uniforms, marbled interiors and arrogant certainties.

The systemic enthusiasm for protecting the imperial budget where possible relates directly to the Robinson and Gallagher analysis: if informal means were sufficient to obtain the results Britain required, the Empire would naturally prefer to avoid the expense of implementing formal rule. This valuable insight also furnishes us with a useful tool for tracking shifts in power; since avoidance of invasion or annexation was desirable on cost grounds, instances of conquest may thus indicate that Britain was unable to get what it wanted by other means. If it could not obtain its goal (whether market access, material resources or strategic security) without taking over, that suggests a loss of power, whether local and limited or global and significant. As we will see, this dynamic played a crucial role in the British advance into Africa in the late Victorian period.

* * *

The factors that determined the extension of British influence or rule in any given geography were often many and varied. In the Niger Delta region, however, it was the palm oil trade that alone drew in British officials in the mid-nineteenth century. Though frequently vocal in celebrating their independent agency and autonomous ways, the palm oil ruffians of the Oil Rivers were very willing to call upon the assistance of government when necessary and available. Such occasions—and the delicate interplay of British traders and consuls with local rulers, palm oil middlemen and possible opponents—demonstrate the possibilities, limits and uncertainties of informal empire.

Take, for example, the visit to the Oil Rivers in the spring of 1862 by the British consul for the Bights of Benin and Biafra, Richard Burton. The famous soldier, explorer, translator and spy had recently married and, in need of a stable income, had accepted the unglamorous post in the Spanish-held island of Fernando Po. In April 1862, Burton received word that an Englishman had been assaulted in the Old Calabar area, and he accordingly set off to visit. In his despatch home to the Foreign Office, Burton reveals in passing something of the frontier nature—for European visitors—of the Oil Rivers even in this period: 'The River is chartless, buoyless, and without pilots. We were nearly wrecked off Tom Short's Point by a shipmaster who had volunteered to pilot us, and we anchored off Duke Town, on Sunday the 4th May.'[11]

Burton's visit to Old Calabar demonstrates some of the available techniques for exercising informal influence, as well as illustrating the status of the representative of the British Empire even in an area outside British territory. He records that he was presented with petitions by a series of white traders (meaning requests for his intervention or assistance) and then heard complaints from Sierra Leonean traders. He agreed with the British traders to establish a 'Court of Equity', a forum for settling business disputes between Europeans and local traders. This amounted to a significant claim of jurisdiction and a challenge to the authority of the local ruler; a court under British auspices (and chaired by the consul) naturally gave British traders a degree of extraterritorial protection. King Archibong was unenthusiastic (Burton calls him 'uncooperative')[12] but eventually signed a treaty providing for it. Though one must remember that Burton had something of a tendency for ripe language, he made lurid claims in explaining the Court of Equity to the Foreign Office:

> Some such measure is called for by the present state of the River, which has literally been managed by the revolver for the last six months. Certain articles may appear to press heavily upon the natives of Duke Town, but I can hardly treat them otherwise. The murders and torturings and the abominable crimes which prevail among them render the place an African Sodom and Gomorrah.[13]

This, then, is classic informal empire in action: the extension of a measure of official protection to British subjects (in practice, all Europeans) without incurring the costs of establishing an administration, and imposed solely through the force of reputation. Archibong assuredly judged it better to agree a treaty rather than risk a visit by Royal Navy gunboats. Moreover, the treaty provided for the 'opening up of the River to the white traders and the missionary',[14] so European influence was being forced further inland up the Cross River.

The most striking act of Burton's visit to Old Calabar, however, was what seems to be an entirely opportunistic coronation:

> [O]n the 8th May I proceeded with Commander Perry RN, accompanied by the supercargoes of Old Calabar, to inspect the several markets on the Cross River. Passing by Creek Town I called upon the friendly old Chief Tom Eyo, and with the approval of all the missionaries and supercargoes placed upon his head a footman's gold laced hat which converted 'Father Tom' into King Eyo Honesty IV.[15]

An intervention of this kind into the politics of the independent states of the Oil Rivers is a remarkable demonstration of the willingness of a British consul to exercise powers—or to accrue new ones—that derived solely from his status as the local representative of the distant hegemon. No treaty or other legal agreement gave Burton authority to crown kings in this way, but the standing of the British Empire and the capacities of its navy allowed him to do so. Besides serving as a public demonstration of British power, the coronation of King Eyo Honesty IV also served British ends in a more insidious way: by setting up a king in Creek Town to rival King Archibong in Duke Town, Burton was providing for the adoption of a strategy of divide and rule if desired in the future.

Given that he was originally summoned to Old Calabar merely because of an assault upon an Englishman, it is interesting to note that Burton came away with a new Court of Equity, European access to the Cross River, and a new and friendly monarch on the Oil Rivers. This illustrates the extempore nature of informal empire, as well as the improvisation involved in the job of imperial official; note that these actions were taken without the direction or authorisation of London.

* * *

Later in the same year, Consul Burton also travelled to Benin City, on a trip once again occasioned by a British trader seeking help. In July 1862, an English trader named Dr Henry arrived in Fernando Po to report that his factory on the Benin River had been attacked by local people and was still being occupied; he requested Burton's assistance in recovering his property. Interestingly, Burton reported to the Foreign Office that the urgency of the case led him to set out to attend to it, despite his view that the Benin River more properly came under the jurisdiction of the Colony of Lagos. This demonstrates both the independence of action of a consular officer of the period and the poorly defined and *ad hoc* nature of his responsibilities.

Having at his disposal the gunboat HMS *Bloodhound*, under the command of Lieutenant Commander Stokes, Burton set out to steam from Fernando Po to the mainland. Arriving at the Benin River on 3 August, he assembled the white traders and the local chiefs for a palaver. In agreement with the British traders, he then ordered that the river be closed to trade until a local chief named Akabwa—said to be responsible for the attack on Dr Henry's trading post—was surrendered. With only limited means available to him to enforce this edict, it is not clear whether Burton succeeded in blocking trade; he reported to the Foreign Office on the 'thoroughly disorganised state of the River'.[16]

After sending a letter to the governor in Lagos, Burton then spent some days travelling to Warri, taking the opportunity of surveying the route between the town and the Benin River (all such mapmaking would be of great value for the future should a forward policy be adopted or an armed intervention required). On arrival back at the mouth of the Benin River, he found that no answer had yet been received from Lagos, so he decided with Lieutenant Commander Stokes and Dr Henry 'to visit the city of Great Benin, whose King in times gone by was the most powerful sovereign of Yoruba'.[17] In this description, Burton captures something of the former power of the Kingdom of Benin, though he seems to conflate the Edo people with the (linguistically related) Yoruba people to the west, no doubt having been led astray by the mythical claims of a royal Edo connection to Ife.

The party travelled by canoe to Gwato (which Burton reports took seventeen hours of rowing) and then marched through the bush to Benin City over a bad path, arriving on 19 August. Though a highly experienced explorer and a multilingual student of other cultures, in his first impressions of Benin Burton nonetheless displays a naïve relish in the evidence of human sacrifice in the city. He records it in lurid detail, and this report was to feature in later attempts at justifying British violence towards the kingdom:

> When the usual preliminary visit had been paid to the 'Captain of war', the dignitary next in rank to the King, we were led to the quarters assigned to us—One of the first objects that met our sight was a negro, freshly crucified after the African fashion, sitting on a stool with extended arms, lashed to a framework of poles. I fear it was in honor of our arrival... We then marched over the space before the King's palace. It was strewed with human skulls and bones, like pebbles... Our first visit to the palace showed us the body of a fine young woman fastened to the top of a tree—a fetish for rain... During the night I heard the voice of the 'Spirit Oro', and next morning we found close out doors, the corpse of a man, with broken shin bones, and a gashed throat... Walking to the market we remarked a pool of blood where another victim had been slaughtered.[18] [*sic passim*]

In 1862 the king of Benin was Oba Adolo, and Burton describes being given a friendly reception. It is clear from this report that the kingdom was then in a state of crisis, having been through internal ructions and facing the commercial competition of their Yoruba neighbours:

> Lieut Commander Stokes and I waited twice upon the King who appeared much pleased to see us in uniform. He is a fine looking

> man, still young, and of peculiarly prepossessing appearance... His palace is in ruins like the City, the effect of the diversion of the trade to Lagos, the abolition of slave exporting and a chronic civil war with a younger brother who has established himself near the Niger. He received my present with great affability, and promised to send a messenger to Benin River threatening a stoppage of provisions, if the Chief Akabwa was not given up. He appeared most anxious to renew trade, but I could make no promises.[19]

Burton's gift to the king was bolts of silk costing £22–6d, about the value of a horse in England at the time. It is also notable from this report that Oba Adolo still regarded himself as having some form of suzerainty over the lower reaches of the Benin River, even though in practice this power had been lost many years before.

After two nights in Benin City, Burton and his colleagues returned to the coast, well pleased with their reception. That this was Burton's only visit to the Oba during his two years as consul in Fernando Po illustrates something of the makeshift nature of British informal imperial influence; a handful of officials might be stretched thinly over a vast area, with one or two gunboats to share between them, and be left to uphold British interests as best they could.

* * *

In highlighting the improvisational and opportunistic character of much of the British imperial presence on the ground, these visits by Consul Burton to the Oil Rivers and to the Kingdom of Benin also demonstrate a crucial fact about the British Empire as a whole: there was no grand plan behind the growth and direction of the British imperial project. No single, shared vision determined when and where Britain would extend its territory or annex altogether new areas, or indeed withdraw and retrench. On the contrary, a multiplicity of agendas competed both locally and nationally, as varied interest groups—military officials, traders, missionaries, politicians, bankers, etc.—promoted their own ideas for the future direction of the Empire. Certain axioms were widely accepted—the absolute necessity of defending India easily being the leading one—but even then, there were often disputes as to how best to attain such ends. With such a variety of parties seeking to influence the decision process (sometimes in contradictory directions), imperial policymaking could appear somewhat haphazard.

Take, for example, the select committee established by Parliament in 1865 to consider the future of the British territories then held in West Africa. Speaking in the House of Commons to propose the committee, Charles Adderley MP said that he wished to determine whether the British possessions in question were 'well ordered and regulated, and whether they attained their object'.[20] This avowedly rational process culminated some months later in the committee submitting a report which recommended the abandonment (on strict cost–benefit grounds) of the Gold Coast, Gambia and Lagos, and the retention only of Sierra Leone, which was valued as a naval base. This radical proposal was not implemented, not least because of the challenge of assuaging public opinion, but it is striking that such a bold policy of retrenchment should originate from the very centre of British power in an era generally characterised as expansionary. Imperial policy did not therefore follow a single vision, but rather it emerged from a contest of rival plans and impulses, promoted by a wide variety of interest groups and individuals.

In West Africa, the most powerful force drawing in British influence was that of coastal commerce, primarily the palm oil trade. Although business interests were often against formal annexations to the British Empire in their reluctance to incur new taxation and regulation, they were at the same time keen to avail themselves of government assistance when necessary; there were some problems that could only be solved by a consul, backed with the threat of action by the Royal Navy. Accordingly, as palm oil interests grew in importance during this period, the British consul for the Bights of Benin and Biafra was permanently relocated in 1872 from the island of Fernando Po to Old Calabar on the mainland. Thereafter, this small palm oil–trading town was to become the centre of British power over the Niger Delta and its valuable trade.

Similarly, and further illustrating the vanguard role that commerce often played in the expansion of empires, George Goldie arrived in the Niger basin in 1877. After a brief military career and much time spent travelling in Africa, Goldie (later Sir George) conceived a bold plan to use commercial means to extend British rule over the middle reaches of the Niger River, far inland from the Oil Rivers. From his arrival in the region, he worked assiduously to amalgamate all the British trading companies on the main stretch of the Niger; by 1879 he had succeeded, and the United African Company was born. Through this vehicle and his daringly aggressive vision for the region, Goldie became one of the most significant forces determining the trajectory of British expansion in West Africa.[21] Moreover, his activities up the Niger were a central factor in the European diplomatic flurry of the 1880s that became known as the Scramble for Africa.

* * *

In the early years of the 1880s, a new concern can be found in British official documentation dealing with West African affairs: the fear of European competitors. For several decades, Britain had enjoyed a supremacy at sea that ensured domination of the coastal trade with Africa; untroubled by maritime also-rans, the Royal Navy even thought of itself as the magnanimous protector of the legitimate commerce of other nations. By the 1870s, however, commercial pressures had grown and, more troublingly, the French were expanding eastwards from their colony of Senegal, threatening to reach the Upper Niger. Under the aggressive General Brière de l'Isle, the final pacification of Senegal was achieved, and significant advances were made by the French towards the great river. Plans were laid for a Dakar–Niger railway, and exploratory military strikes were launched into what is now Mali.

A direct response to these growing competitive pressures can be seen in the British discussion of regional policy. A key advocate of a more bullish British approach was Edward Hyde Hewett, who arrived as consul at Old Calabar in September 1879. Although Foreign Office file notes reveal that officials in London were privately impatient with his exceptionally lengthy and often confused despatches, Hewett nonetheless played an important role in Britain's advance in the region during the 1880s (though more as dogged executor than intellectual inspiration). By early 1882, Hewett had become so concerned about what he judged to be the relative weakness of the British position in West Africa that he formally proposed to the Foreign Office a bold advance: the annexation of the entire coastline between the Colony of Lagos and the French territory of Gabon. Hewett was not much concerned about the precise choice of imperial form, being agnostic between the creation of a colony or protectorate, or indeed handing it all over to a chartered company; the salient goal was only to prevent European rivals from claiming it for themselves.

The Colonial Office was not entirely enthusiastic, and it seems to have been caught by surprise. Augustus Hemming, a long-serving Colonial Office administrator who later became Sir Augustus and governor of Jamaica, noted the lack of previous discussion: 'So far as I can ascertain there has been very little previous correspondence respecting the establishment of British protection or jurisdiction over the Oil rivers (the mouths of the Niger) or the neighbouring districts.'[22] Now that the matter was being forced upon them, Hemming naturally also appreciated the key issue facing Britain: 'Mr Hewett stated very fully the grounds for the view he took, and pointed out the importance of these countries to British trade and the danger of their falling into the hands of a foreign power.'[23]

This was the central dilemma: how to square a reluctance to take on additional costs with the danger that a rival nation could move first and annex some or all of the territory themselves. The process of attempting to resolve such issues could generate surprising results. Note, for example, the strange policy leap that Hemming took in March 1882 in his own effort to reconcile these contradictory impulses:

> Looking at the matter from the point of view of the advantages to British trade, the maintenance of peace and order, and the spread of civilisation, there can be little doubt of the benefits which would accrue from our occupation of this territory—and as the above are the only reasons, so far as I am aware, for which we hold any Colonies on the West Coast of Africa at all, and there would seem to be no other grounds on which their retention can be defended, it appears to be a logical conclusion that the larger area over which we extend our influence the better ...
>
> Personally, I wish the policy recommended by the House of Commons' Committee in 1865 could be carried out, and that we could retire from the West African Colonies, keeping up only one or two small posts, as it were, of observation. As this, however, is a scheme which the opposition raised even to the exchange of the Gambia, shows to be impossible, I think we ought, under the circumstances, to pursue the opposite course and develop and extend, by every means in our power, the influence and commerce of Great Britain.[24]

Colonial Secretary Lord Kimberley was not supportive of this expansionary attitude. Showing greater concern for his ministerial budget, in a minute on the Hewett proposal Kimberley illustrates that interdepartmental politics could certainly intrude on imperial policymaking:

> It is very natural that the Foreign Office should wish to hand over to us the troublesome duty of managing our relations with the Oil Rivers, but I am certainly not in favour of Mr Hewett's proposals ... Such an extensive protectorate as Mr Hewett recommends would be a most serious addition to our burdens and responsibilities. The coast is pestilential; the natives numerous and unmanageable. The result of a British occupation would be almost certainly wars with the natives, heavy demands upon the British taxpayer, and at best another and more extensive Gold Coast Protectorate, with all its dangers and difficulties ...
>
> At the same time I am not by any means prepared to tie myself to the doctrines of the Committee of 1865, or to adopt their recommendations en bloc. If we were to retire from our West African Settlements, and retain one or two small posts of observation, we should deal a fatal blow at our very important West African trade. The posts we abandoned would be soon occupied by other European Powers, who would endeavour to exclude our trade, as the French do wherever they go.[25]

Lord Kimberley therefore declined to support the Hewett plan because of the potential liabilities (both for his own department and for Britain as a whole), nor would he support the annexation of any territory on the coast in question at that time. He was, however, evidently sufficiently concerned about the threat from European rivals to avoid altogether ruling out preemptive advances. This concern was to become overriding through the decade ahead, during which virtually the entire continent of Africa was seized and hurriedly dismembered by the European imperial powers.

3

'THE RUSH FOR AFRICA HAS BROKEN UP THE LITTLE FAMILY PARTY'

THE SCRAMBLE OF THE 1880s

Here, as in other parts of the world, Germany is determined to share with us the trade.

Alfred Moloney, Governor of Lagos, April 1888

That the present chaotic condition of the Protectorate cannot long continue without grave evils arising, is, I think, disputed by no one...

Vice Consul Harry H. Johnston, 26 July 1888

As the fateful decade of the 1880s began, Britain had made some tentative advances beyond the coastline onto the mainland of what is now Nigeria. The British consul was headquartered at Old Calabar, and from there he exercised a significant degree of influence over the Niger Delta despite having no formal authority; the distant prospect of Royal Navy gunboats gave him an undeniable power even if laws and treaties did not. George Goldie had united the trading companies on the Niger River beyond the Delta and was gradually pushing north, signing proforma treaties with dozens of chiefs and local rulers as he advanced his area of commercial operations. These developments were merely an evolution of the centuries-long British intrusion into West Africa. What marked a step-change, however—and which is clearly seen in the official documents of the time—is the new concern about European rivals. With the French advancing on the Upper Niger from Senegal and German traders becoming increasingly active in the Cameroons and on the coastline to the west of the Colony of Lagos, British officials were experiencing an unfamiliar feeling of uncertainty.

At the Colonial Office in the spring of 1883, Augustus Hemming was also becoming concerned with the French threat on the Niger River from the maritime side. Having been lobbied by senior representatives of Goldie's firm (by now renamed as the National African Company), he was urgently trying to obtain from the Foreign Office a commitment to defending British trade in the region. Illustrating the way in which European interference in one part of the African continent could redound upon other regions through zero-sum paranoia, Hemming referenced the acquisitive activity of the French explorer Pierre de Brazza on the Congo River in his memorandum to a senior colleague, Sir Robert Meade:

> It would have been, perhaps, desirable if the Foreign Office had given us some inkling of their opinion ... I have, however, ascertained privately that they are inclined somewhat strongly to the view that it is advisable for this country to take some action without delay in respect to the Lower Niger, with the object of preventing any repetition there of De Brazza's tactics on the Congo ... Whether they propose a protectorate of the territories at the mouths of the Niger, or merely to secure by treaties with the native Kings and Chiefs the freedom of the river, I do not know.[1]

Urging upon his colleagues the need for the foreign secretary, Lord Granville, to take action to secure British interests on the Niger, Hemming expressed alarm about the 'very serious blow which would be struck at British Commerce in that part of the world if the Oil Rivers and other places with which our trade is extensive and important were to be brought under the sovereignty of France'.[2]

This shows the ongoing official dilemma at the heart of imperial power: how best to secure British interests while spending as little money as possible. The Colonial Office documents also illustrate the process—and the inevitable frictions—of decision-making across departments, each of which had their own priorities and strategic goals, which might sometimes be contradictory. In responding to Hemming, Sir Robert Meade expressed this with just a hint of exasperation:

> I do not see what else we can say. The fact is this is a Cabinet question which the Departments concerned cannot settle. The view of the Foreign Office, which was pressed on Lord Kimberley, was that England should annex all unoccupied territory between Lagos and the French settlement of the Gaboon [*sic*]. Now this would be a tremendous undertaking. We could not annex it without making ourselves responsible for peace and order there. This would mean a task as heavy as governing the Gold Coast in a country and climate still severer. We should have to obtain a revenue which could only be obtained by levying customs dues, and I doubt English traders wishing for this [*sic*] ...
>
> To checkmate French aggression it would be necessary to go a long way up the Niger. We should have great difficulties in getting treaties with the various Kings and Chiefs, and from whatever point we left off we may be sure the French would carry on similar tactics up to the source in the vicinity of which they are already operating.[3]

This memorandum also contains something quietly tragic. In discussing his concern about French advances, Meade (who went on to run the Colonial Office as permanent under-secretary in the 1890s) forecasts precisely the political dynamic that would shortly lead to European countries seizing virtually all of Africa by the end of the century:

> I think, moreover, it would be bad policy to imitate the French proceedings in the Congo. They would retaliate somewhere else, and we should see the very unimproving spectacle of each country grabbing what it can, not because it wants the territory but to keep the other out. There would be no end to this, and I am sure the country would not tolerate it.[4]

There is something of a frustrating pathos in the fact that the senior echelons of British power were well aware of the negative possibilities of this tit-for-tat mentality, but that they nonetheless embarked upon a leading role in the 'unimproving spectacle' in the years ahead, at the cost of the lives and freedoms of millions of African people.

There was, of course, nothing inevitable about the descent into retaliatory annexations and pre-emptive advances. At this time—when Africa was still largely independent of outside empires but when European interlopers were increasingly establishing footholds—there were British officials still willing to take a nuanced, strategic view that avoided territorial acquisitions. Concerned about French moves on the Congo River (and about the vast Congo Basin being thus denied to British commerce), the British response was initially to agree to place the enormous swathe of territory and its valuable waterway into the control of Portugal. As the original European intruder into Africa in the modern era, Portugal had been established in what are now Angola and Mozambique since the fifteenth century. By the nineteenth century, however, it had declined in power and its empire had gone to seed; it still maintained possession of its territories, but it was largely without expansionary energy or capacity. It was precisely this quality that Britain found valuable: since Portugal could never be a threat to British interests, Britain proposed that the Portuguese take possession of the Congo, on condition of guaranteeing free trade access to all other countries.

As the hegemonic power, Britain would be more equal than others by virtue of its maritime strength, this latent capacity providing it with the confidence to cede any claim on the territory. To this end, much Foreign Office energy was dedicated to negotiating a draft treaty with Portugal that would have seen the Portuguese territories of Angola and Mozambique linked together in a gigantic new transcontinental bloc. Though agreed in principle in February 1884, the Anglo-Portuguese Treaty was never ratified.

The failure of this subtle strategy—which would have maintained British interests while another country paid the costs of administering territory—was due in part to the opposition of commercial interests, magnified through the press. As the national paper of record, *The Times* had long had a disproportionate influence on the political direction of the country, including its imperial policy. During the diplomatic negotiations over the Congo, it reported on the energetic protests against any such treaty, declaring the danger of handing over 'this important district to the inadequate, feeble, and corrupt administration of Portugal.'[5] Moreover, the newspaper declared an implacable, wholesale opposition, on grounds largely imaginary: 'Such an annexation must assuredly cripple British trade in Equatorial Africa, prevent the development of new markets, and probably lead to troubles with the native tribes, to anarchy and outrages which would drive away a commerce that is now peaceful and flourishing.'[6]

By the time that the draft treaty with Portugal was prepared in early 1884, the animosity of *The Times* had not diminished. Following the publication of the proposed text, the newspaper insisted in a leading article that 'the Treaty will be a calamity to all concerned, an unpardonable and irreparable mistake on the part of a British Government, and the greatest sufferers will be the manufacturers of Great Britain.'[7]

This kind of press agitation demonstrates that public opinion had a significant role to play even in the semi-democratic political system of late-nineteenth-century Britain. It also indicates the absence of a single grand imperial plan, as well as the difficulty of keeping all elements of the British Empire aligned behind an official strategy.

* * *

One important factor behind growing anxiety among British West African traders at this time was the long decline in the value of palm oil. Throughout the 1860s and 1870s, the prices they were able to command for their principal product had been falling. The early 1880s saw another major slump, and it would continue: by 1887, the price of palm oil—at £19/ton—was only half the level of 1861.[8] In these conditions of stress, businessmen naturally sought all available means of protecting their livelihoods and profits, and of obtaining an advantage over their competitors. Such circumstances tended to make even the most individualist of free traders more inclined to embrace government involvement in the marketplace.

Over the decades, the commercial dynamic of the palm oil trade had also been transformed by a profound structural change: the development, from 1852, of a regular steamer service between Britain and West Africa. Before this time, palm oil traders would gather their product by sailing a vessel to their preferred station on the Oil Rivers, anchoring in place, and then gradually filling up the ship over several months, as middlemen traders brought cargoes of palm oil from the interior down to the coast. When the vessel was full or they had run out of barter goods to trade, they would raise anchor and sail home. Until the 1850s, therefore, the palm oil trade was largely ship-borne for the Europeans, who would remain onboard while African chiefs and traders handled everything ashore. When the African Steamship Company began its monthly mail steamer from Liverpool to West Africa in 1852, the structure of the business changed swiftly.[9] Being able to send cargoes on the regular steamer service, palm oil traders could save on the cost of buying and maintaining their own vessels. This prompted a move onshore and the establishment of 'factories'—warehouse depots—on dry land. The reduction in barriers to entry also spurred fierce competition in the industry, which helps to explain the price declines of the following decades. Thus, a distant commercial innovation was one of the key factors that drew British interests onshore in the Niger Delta.

By the early 1880s, an added worry for British commercial interests was the fear of European rivals as their activity in West Africa grew. Having secured the relocation of the British consul to the Oil Rivers over a decade before, by 1884 British traders were lobbying for the appointment of additional consular officers so that they were never left without access to assistance during periods of consular leave or travel. In petitioning the foreign secretary in early 1884, the Manchester Chamber of Commerce made their reasons very clear: 'the advent of the Merchants of other countries during the past few years, require that British interests there should at no time be without adequate representation on the part of Her Majesty's Government.'[10]

Notably, this kind of pressure for greater government involvement was coming from a wide variety of business segments, independently of one another. The specific expression of their concerns reflected the nature of their businesses and the vulnerabilities they perceived. For example, the coastal traders of Liverpool were particularly exercised by the maritime Germans annexing territory in the Cameroons:

> The African Trade Section have good reason for supposing that the Germans are taking measures to divert the trade of these places to Hamburg, and that it will not be long before unequal duties are imposed or other means taken to extinguish British Trade.
>
> In these circumstances I am requested on behalf of this Section of the Chamber to protest against these seizures of territory which threaten to rupture treaty arrangements already made with this

> Country, and to ask your Lordship to consider how the privileges granted to the British by the treaties named can best be preserved and the interests created by trading in these parts be protected.[11]

Quite separately, Goldie's National African Company was concerned largely with the threat posed by the overland French, who were still advancing from their colony of Senegal. Lord Aberdare, chairman of the company, wrote to the foreign secretary to urge him:

> To arrange with France that she will undertake not to acquire or exercise any political rights or influence on the rivers Niger, Binue [sic], or their affluents (and in countries adjacent thereto) between the mouths of the Niger and some points such as, e.g., Timbuctoo [sic], to be agreed on, England being left to acquire in such countries such political rights as circumstances may hereafter suggest to be desirable.[12]

From different angles and a variety of sources, therefore, elements of the vast and complex British Empire were feeling the pressure of foreign competition. Moreover, in writing to Lord Granville, Lord Aberdare implied that France was becoming sufficiently powerful in the Niger region to frustrate British ambitions altogether: 'There is every reason to believe that, if not obstructed by the political action of foreigners, this great and important development of British trade will progressively advance.'[13]

All of these factors—business stresses, foreign competition, structural changes in the palm oil trade—were therefore combining to draw Britons in West Africa, both official and commercial, into taking a firmer footing onshore. Notably, of course, the Kingdom of Benin was not yet a strategic consideration for Britain, given that it no longer had any purchase over the littoral zone to which European interlopers still largely confined themselves. Indeed, in a general sense, African polities and their inhabitants were a marginal factor in European calculations, if they were considered at all. British officials could demonstrate remarkably selective vision when it came to looking at maps of Africa, often avoiding recognising African political entities because they did not sufficiently resemble the European template. Moreover, this partial sight extended to African people themselves; a remarkable Foreign Office memorandum of 1884 even defines as 'uninhabited' those parts of Africa not yet occupied by European empires.[14]

This attitude—the gross symbolic erasure of Africans from the political landscape—combined with rising international rivalry in preparing the ground for the Scramble for Africa. The most important precondition, however, was a decline in British power, and the spark that ignited the rush for Africa was a signal British political failing: the occupation of Egypt in 1882.

* * *

India was, above all, the most valuable British colonial territory; without India, a unique source both of great wealth and immense manpower, the British Empire would likely never have achieved its global dominance. For this reason, much British anxiety was generated by the need to protect India from threats internal and external, and the necessity of defending the routes to the Subcontinent at almost any cost was one of the few unchallenged axioms driving imperial policymaking.[15] This was the principal determinant of the British occupation of various territories that lay on the routes east, including in the South Atlantic, South Africa, Aden and British Somaliland.

Egypt had, in contrast, long provided a shortcut to India without necessitating occupation. Formally still a part of the Ottoman Empire, it had been largely independent since the early nineteenth century, and both Britain and France conducted separate diplomatic relations with the ruler of Egypt, the Khedive. As long as free passage could be obtained across Egyptian territory (linking the Mediterranean to the Red Sea even before the Suez

Canal was opened in 1869), the situation was satisfactory and neither Britain nor France sought occupation. For one thing, on the chessboard of international politics, both European powers wished to avoid weakening the Ottoman Empire against Russia by severing Egypt from its formal control. Indeed, in the 1850s Britain and France had allied to fight the Crimean War precisely to stave off Russian pressure on Constantinople. For some decades, therefore, the two Western European powers had developed a stable *modus vivendi* in Egypt, and by the 1870s this amounted to a 'dual paramountcy' as their investments in Egyptian railways, government debt and the Suez Canal mounted.

By 1876, the growing debt of the Khedive was becoming unsustainable, and Britain and France stopped lending. Forced to raise taxes to service interest payments, the Egyptian government provoked internal dissension that by 1881 led to a nationalist uprising by the army under Arabi Pasha. Having seized control of the country in September 1881, this distinctly modern revolt against European influence directly threatened British access to the most efficient routes to India. Although extremely reluctant to acquire new territory, Prime Minister Gladstone therefore finally assented to the invasion of Egypt in July 1882, partly in an effort to hold his fractious Cabinet together, and the House of Commons voted in support by the end of the month. In August a force was landed, and on 13 September it routed the Egyptian army at the Battle of Tel El Kebir: Egypt was in British hands. Although the Cabinet had at the time regarded occupation as a temporary expedient, it would last several decades and prove highly troublesome, not least to British diplomatic relations in Europe.

The fact that Britain judged it essential to undertake the occupation of this highly sensitive area reflects, in the first instance, the overriding importance attached to India in British imperial calculus. At a more profound level, it also reflects the growing relative weakness of the British Empire; it was no longer able to get what it wanted out of Egypt without going to the trouble and expense of taking it over. The liabilities that might arise from such an action—both financial and political—were impossible to calculate, but even this level of risk was regarded as preferable to the loss of access to routes east. This was a defensive advance, and not made from a position of strength. For this reason, the 1882 occupation of Egypt must be regarded as a landmark in the long and gradual decline of the British Empire.

The rival power which benefitted most immediately from Britain's new exposure in Egypt was Germany. Having been united in 1871 by the ruthless and strategic chancellor Otto von Bismarck, Germany was industrialising swiftly and beginning to compete with Britain in some markets around the world, including in West Africa. Although Bismarck had no real interest in Africa itself, he was always quick to utilise anything that might give him leverage over an opponent, and the occupation of Egypt was an excellent opportunity to drive a wedge between Britain and the disgruntled French. By the early 1880s, Bismarck was also ready to allow greater freedom to German advocates for African colonies, in order further to pressure Britain.

It was in these circumstances of stiffer European competition that British officials were working to secure the Anglo-Portuguese Treaty respecting the Congo, and the situation also prompted a significant change in British strategy in West Africa. The British government had declined the bold proposal by Consul Hewett for the extension of British territory in the region in the spring of 1882. A dogged character, however, Hewett tried again only a year later, and this time met with a different reception. As the Foreign Office head of Africa noted, 'On the 17th of May 1883 Consul Hewett arrived in England and informed us that a great number of the principal chiefs on the Oil Rivers District were begging for British protection.'[16]

Following consideration by the Foreign Office and the Colonial Office, in November 1883 the matter was placed before a Cabinet committee, which accordingly recommended the establishment of an expanded consular administration in the region, along with treaties of protection and the annexation of a small district in the Cameroons. This commitment would represent a substantial forward movement (meaning financial outlay) and required the assent of the Treasury, whose approval was not granted until May 1884, illustrating the sometimes cumbersome nature of imperial decision-making.[17] Hewett departed for West Africa just four days later, and from the middle of June he was busily engaged in signing treaties of protection with all the chiefs and local rulers whom he could find in the Niger Delta region. On occasion, he was able to press into service passing Royal Navy officers. Hewett's written instructions to one such officer give a flavour of his approach to the task:

> I suggest that you make the object of your mission as little known as possible at Brass. You can tell the British Traders, who will pay you a visit on your arrival, what you have come about, and that you would like to consult with them as to the best mode of proceeding. You should impress upon them the necessity for secrecy and expedition in negotiating with the Kings and Chiefs.
>
> Be pleased to explain to the Kings and Chiefs that the Queen has no wish to take away their country from them: that the proposed Treaty leaves them to govern their own Country and people according to their own laws—that it does not interfere with their custom of possessing a plurality of wives, or their right to own slaves.[18]

Even with such assistance, Hewett was unable to cover all ground in the time available. In a significant development, he lost out to German representatives in his planned territorial annexation on the Cameroon River; this was one of the factors driving British traders to lobby for greater government assistance around that time. That German officials were beginning to make claims on African territory was one unintended consequence of Britain's occupation of Egypt. Another indirect consequence was the defining event of the Scramble for Africa (which with accidental symbolism happened outside the very continent it concerned): the Conference of Berlin.

* * *

While Hewett was aboard ship and heading for West Africa in June 1884, the Foreign Office received notification from the German government that it could not assent to the Congo being ceded to Portugal.[19] Bismarck had evidently spied another opportunity to insert himself between other European powers, as he latched on to what had originally been a Portuguese proposal for a conference. When the formal invitation came from Prince Bismarck in October 1884, the vague suggestion of a conference with Portugal had been transformed into a multi-nation summit, in Berlin and under German auspices, that would aim to settle a range of issues of contention in Africa. Bismarck had already worked to reassure France of his cooperation in their various points of friction with Britain.

With the Conference now looming, the treaties that Hewett had been frantically signing around the Niger Delta were suddenly all the more important. In another stark indicator of Britain's declining power and prestige, it would—like all other countries—have to provide evidence of its influence in West Africa to satisfy the Conference of its claims; such a requirement would have been unthinkable a generation before. Thus, as the Berlin gathering approached, the Foreign Office was preparing its case and assembling the arguments for why the British position on the River Niger must be recognised by the other powers. As head of the African department, Percy Anderson noted that:

> the trade from the Benin river to the Cameroons is exclusively British: there is not a single foreign establishment on the coastline:

> moreover the British Consul has been for years the authority in disputes among the natives which the Courts of Equity, under his supervision, have settled trade matters; and we have now concluded Treaties along the whole line by which the territory is placed under British protection.
>
> ———
>
> This being so it seems incontrovertible that, though as regards the Congo, we can appear at the Conference as one of many Powers interested, as regards the Niger we should take our seat as the Niger Power, the one Power at present concerned in the trade of the Lower Niger and Oil rivers.[20]

In the same memorandum, Anderson hints towards the customary British arrogance of imperial power, but in turning it into a question he appears suddenly hesitant, as if reflecting a loss of national confidence:

> If we prefer to cancel our Treaties have we lost the right to insist upon them—i.e. to preserve our position as the Niger Power,—until we are satisfied as to the conditions on which we could consent to withdraw them? I mean, that instead of appearing in the Conference to listen to what France & Germany have to say should we not appear for them to listen in the first instance to what we have to say? Should we not explain that, as regards the Niger, we must share our decision after hearing what is proposed?[21]

This uncertain tone reflected the realities of a changing world in which Britain was no longer able to have its way untrammelled. At the Berlin Conference—the full proceedings of which lasted from November 1884 until February 1885—Britain achieved its goal of being recognised as the paramount power on the Niger but had to surrender any claims to disposing of the Congo to its preferred ally. Instead of the Congo Basin going to Portugal, it was made over as a personal fiefdom to King Leopold II of Belgium.

The settlements reached in Berlin were not, however, absolute. The agreed demarcations of African territory were dependent on the power concerned undertaking 'effective occupation', a condition that was left deliberately vague in the Berlin articles.[22] For Gladstone's Liberal government—generally keen to avoid taking on expensive imperial commitments where possible—this presented something of a dilemma. A secure defence of British interests in the Niger region required the declaration of a protectorate and the active management of the territory, but this was not entirely what the Cabinet had agreed to in its reactive decision process before Berlin. In the discussions of early 1885, therefore, one solution stood out as a thrifty means of spreading the Union Flag up the River Niger: subcontract George Goldie and his National African Company to take on the administration of the territories in which they were already doing business. While some in the Foreign Office argued strongly—largely on legalistic grounds—that rule over the Niger must be imperial and direct,[23] others embraced the potential cost savings and available speed if the task was farmed out. Thomas Lister, the assistant under-secretary, was firmly in favour of empowering Goldie:

> The [National African] Co has steamers & Agents, the chief of whom Mr McIntosh is British—It is perfectly able and willing to discharge the duties of administration for which HMG have become responsible, and unless it should be considered necessary that this country should go to the great expense of setting up the machinery of Govt. upon the two rivers where the Co. now rules supreme, there seems to be no other course open, and certainly no better one, than that of legalising & affirming the position of the Co. and placing the business of administration into its hands ...
>
> I have only to point out that the action of England on the Niger will be jealously watched by France and Germany and that any failure to assume as quickly as possible the duties imposed by the Conference and accepted by HMG will probably be seized upon with avidity as

> proof of weakness in the claim which has been maintained at Berlin to our supremacy in the basin of the Niger.[24]

The appeal of this cost-effective solution for the region beyond the Niger Delta was enough to override the concerns of legal purists, and accordingly, a protectorate over the Niger Districts was officially declared on 5 June 1885.[25] This brought a vast area formally into the British Empire, including Goldie's area of operations up the Niger and Benue rivers, as well as the Niger Delta rivers already under a degree of consular influence. For the immediate future, the precise status of this extensive region was left somewhat vague. The National African Company and the Liverpool-dominated coastal traders confined themselves largely to their respective areas and formed two quite distinct economic systems, making separate evolution likely, though all details were yet to be determined.

For the ambitious Goldie, the next step was the award of a royal charter, the legal device that would give his company the powers of a government. Though he had been denied a charter in 1881 (when Gladstone was still able to quash anything that appeared overly expansionary), the radically changed circumstances of 1885 argued for granting one; at least the fiction of imperial administration had to be maintained in order to satisfy the stipulations of the Berlin Conference. The negotiations dragged on for some time, not least because Goldie was demanding significant powers, but the charter was finally agreed. It was approved by an Order in Council of 25 June 1886, when the company became the Royal Niger Company Chartered & Limited. Although the charter award formally prevented the company from exercising a monopoly on trade in the chartered territories, it was widely understood that Goldie would implement one anyway, and since the Royal Niger Company was also its own regulating authority, there was essentially nothing to stop him.[26]

Unsurprisingly, the charter award upset the Liverpool traders, who saw a rival commercial entity not merely receive government assistance but fully acquire the powers of a government, including the capacity to run a monopoly market virtually with impunity. Although the two trade systems maintained largely separate areas of operation, there were occasional complaints about incursions. Indeed, as early as December 1886, the African Association of Liverpool—representing most of the African trading companies in the city—was lobbying the foreign secretary over 'the encroachment of the Royal Niger Coy Chartered & Limited into the territories over which the Coy has no jurisdiction by their charter'.[27]

This friction between the British Delta traders and the Royal Niger Company continued in the years ahead. Early in 1887, the Foreign Office's Percy Anderson summarised the changed circumstances in the Niger region in a way that characterised the Liverpool companies as out of date and struggling to cope in the brave new world post-Berlin:

> Till recently the trade in this part of Africa was carried on in a loose sort of fashion by houses doing, individually, no large trade. They worked through the coast middlemen who barred them from the interior markets. With them the traders sometimes stood in, sometimes wrangled, settling disputes in a patriarchal fashion through mercantile courts under the fatherly casual superintendence of Consular officers. There was no publicity so few questions were asked.
>
> The rush for Africa has broken up the little family party: and the rich and powerful Niger Co on the one hand, the Germans on the other, have broken through the middlemen crust and forced their way to the interior markets. The Liverpool men are fighting the battle of the middlemen ... Their object is to reform the broken crust. Were they to succeed they might benefit till it was broken again, which would not be long delayed, and would stifle the brilliant prospect, for trade generally, of free access to the comparatively civi-

> lized Mahometan tribes of the interior. Their demand is now as complete an anachronism as would be a petition for the restoration of mediaeval guilds.[28]

This captures something of the state of flux—crisis, even—found in the Niger Delta palm oil trade during the 1880s. In this new era, British traders were facing a variety of challenges to their profits and position.

* * *

With palm oil prices continuing to fall, and without the advantage of the monopoly enjoyed by the Royal Niger Company, the coastal trading firms were increasingly distressed. Adaptation to the new conditions was ever more necessary, and this need was becoming evident even to the conservative Liverpool traders. Not long after Anderson had noted their efforts to preserve things as they were, another British official reported that foreign rivalry was making itself felt:

> Here, as in other parts of the world, Germany is determined to share with us the trade ... The rival importance of the port of Hamburg has awakened us from our passive indifference, making itself at last felt among our commercial classes.[29]

In these new circumstances, the one obvious change in business strategy was for the coastal traders to leave their comfortable berths on the coast and venture inland to deal directly with the palm oil markets of the interior; by cutting out the local middlemen, profit margins might be improved. This was no easy prospect, however. For one thing, such a strategy would require significant investment in the capacity—enormous numbers of porters, river boats and so on—required to transport large volumes of cargo through hundreds of miles of jungle.[30] For another, the middlemen chiefs were a considerable obstacle, being naturally keen to hang on to their lucrative trade; many were organised and willing literally to fight for their position.

At that time, easily the most formidable of the middlemen traders was King Jaja of Opobo. An Igbo by origin, Jaja was enslaved as a boy in the 1830s and sold in Bonny, where he was put to work in the trading houses. An individual of extraordinary talents, the young Jaja rose swiftly to a valued position in the Bonny trade, earned his freedom, and came to head one of the principal trading houses. He became a wealthy and powerful man. By the 1860s, faction fighting in Bonny threatened civil war, and Jaja reacted by making a bold move: since as a freed slave he could never be king of Bonny despite his obvious capacities, he decided to establish his own kingdom. In 1869, therefore, he quit Bonny and founded a new town at Opobo in the nearby Imo River, where he made himself king. European traders followed, and it was not long before Jaja had made Opobo the leading trade centre in the region. By a treaty of 1873, the British government even formally recognised his rights and status as king of Opobo.

However, by the late 1880s, which saw changed circumstances for British traders, King Jaja and his domination of the inland trade in his region of the Delta had become a problem. At the Foreign Office, Percy Anderson was continuing his efforts to push British trade inland, which meant that Jaja had become the main obstacle:

> Jaja is a resolute and able chief: his policy is directly opposed to ours: we are determined to penetrate to the inner markets and under any circumstances must succeed sooner or later: he is resolved to keep us out of them as long as possible. In a war the markets would be paralysed and he would play a waiting game better than the Liverpool merchants.[31]

Though this statement by a senior government official demonstrates a clear imperial impulse, it is also a tacit admission of the very limited concrete meaning of the declaration of the Niger Districts Protectorate, for though the region had been formally 'British' for two years by this time, there was almost no impact on the ground. Britain still relied only upon the personal capacity of an individual consul to influence and persuade the powerful kings and chiefs of the region (with the occasional call upon a Royal Navy gunboat being the ace up his sleeve). The formal change in the status of the region made no practical difference, especially under a somewhat haphazard factotum like Consul Hewett.

This changed, however, when Harry Johnston took over as consul in April 1887, while Hewett went on sick leave.[32] Finally, an imperially minded and energetic officer was in place, one who seemed determined to give meaning to British claims over the Niger Delta, even if it meant using nefarious tactics.[33] Trained as a painter, Johnston was already famous as an African explorer when he was appointed as vice consul in Old Calabar in October 1886; amongst other travels in the continent, he had met Henry Morton Stanley in the Congo in 1883 and had journeyed up river beyond Stanley Pool, one of very few Europeans to have done so at that time.

Johnston had not long been in charge at Old Calabar when he had just the opportunity he needed to flex British colonial muscles. In June 1887, a number of Liverpool traders complained to the Foreign Office that King Jaja was preventing them from accessing interior markets. In response, London instructed Johnston to 'proceed at once to Opobo and do your utmost to remove obstacles'.[34] Over the next two months, Johnston worked to manipulate the situation with Jaja into a crisis that he could resolve by force. Certainly, the description Johnston gave of his new enemy is revealing in its high praise, despite his best efforts to attack his character:

> No doubt Jaja is no common man. Though he is in origin a runaway slave, he was cut out by Nature for a King and he has the instinct of rule, though it not infrequently degenerates into cruel tyranny. His

> demeanour is marked by quiet dignity and his appearance and conversation are more impressive than in the case of his civilised neighbour, King George of Bonny, though the latter wears well-cut London-made clothes, gums his moustache to a fine point, smokes cigarettes, scents his handkerchiefs with the newest essence, dilates on the acting of Ellen Terry and Henry Irving, and criticises the comic operas of Gilbert and Sullivan; while King Jaja may present himself with a fathom of cloth around his loins, strings of coral beads on his sinewy neck, a smoking cap on his head, and talk to you simply of trade matters or the manner and customs of his people. Nevertheless, I know King Jaja to be a deliberate liar who exhibits little shame or confusion when his falsehoods are exposed. He is a bitter and unscrupulous enemy of all who attempt to dispute his trade monopolies. And to the five British firms whose trade he has almost ruined during the past two years, his engaging manners, quiet conversation and entertainments to Naval officers are a poor compensation for heavy monetary loss.[35]

Labelling King Jaja a liar is a notable case of projection, for Johnston himself had an extensive history of deceitfulness, and indeed his chosen method of dealing with Jaja involved outright trickery. By September 1887, Johnston had decided to overthrow the Opobo king and engineered a contretemps. Reporting later in a lengthy despatch to the Foreign Office, he set out his reasons for taking action:

> I made up my mind that I must do my best with the little force at my disposal, especially as I knew that delay was dangerous, that Jaja was preparing to escape to a district where fifty gunboats could not catch him, and that once escaped he would paralyse the Opobo and Bonny trade and keep the country in a disturbed state for an indefinite time. Moreover the Bonny men were clamorous for protection at their own markets where Jaja was beginning to harass them ...
>
> Jaja, who may be anything but a formidable enemy in open fight to a power like England, would with his cannon, rifles, and war canoes, his four thousand fighting men, and his own personal

> courage and tactical skill become a mighty conqueror among the peaceful, timid peoples at the back of Opobo. At present these tribes are without any cohesion—they are not led by any great chief—and they are consequently more readily open to the influence and rule of Great Britain.[36]

Having decided to take action, Johnston proceeded to Opobo in the Royal Navy gunboat HMS *Goshawk*, which was able to anchor off the town. King Jaja was invited to a meeting on 19 September 1887; when he requested a British hostage as insurance against his safe release, Johnston declined but gave a guarantee of free passage. Accordingly, at eleven o'clock on the agreed day, Jaja and around 700 followers gathered at the appointed meeting place in the town. The *Goshawk* then prepared for action and turned its guns on the king and his retinue. Johnston arrived with the commander and officers of the ship and read King Jaja an ultimatum: if he did not surrender himself to be taken into exile, his town and his people would be mercilessly destroyed.[37] Having been promised safe conduct, Jaja had made no military preparations, and Opobo was entirely at the mercy of the four guns of HMS *Goshawk*. In what appears to be a decisive act of statesmanship, Jaja swiftly and quietly agreed to give himself up in order to save his subjects, and within half an hour he was under arrest on the British vessel. Johnston reports that the episode remained entirely peaceful, 'although it was made patent to all that the "Goshawk" was ready for action and would instantly bring her guns in to play if the crowd of natives attempted any violent intervention'.[38] Thus King Jaja was deposed by force and taken into exile in the Gold Coast; even Prime Minister Lord Salisbury admitted privately that this was tantamount to a kidnapping,[39] but the action was nonetheless approved.

* * *

The forced and thus destabilising removal of King Jaja by Consul Johnston drove home to many on the British side the unsatisfactory nature of the administration of the Niger Delta. Indeed, a serious contradiction had been exposed: Jaja was one of the many local rulers to have signed a treaty of protection with Consul Hewett in 1884, only to find himself toppled at gunpoint three years later. This blatant evidence of British imperial hypocrisy was liable to have a serious impact on the calculations of other rulers in the supposed protectorate and must surely have weakened the British claim to authority. In the aftermath of the deposition of Jaja, Consul Hewett himself—living in South Kensington, London while home on sick leave—remonstrated with the Foreign Office. Percy Anderson reported that:

> Consul Hewett points out forcibly the anomalous position of the Protectorate of the Oil Rivers which is at present administered in a haphazard way by a small consular staff and is liable to be plunged into serious difficulties by such a matter as the Jaja affair.[40]

Around the same time, Anderson elsewhere noted 'the urgency of establishing a fixed British administration'[41] on the Oil Rivers, but given the gradual workings of the British Empire when no crisis arose to concentrate minds, little was done at that time. By the summer of 1888, no decision had yet been made about the preferred methods of British rule, and discussions were still under way. Harry Johnston was, by July 1888, back in London on leave and wrote an extensive despatch on the current status of the Protectorate, and the various options for future British administration. Although he shows no self-awareness about his own role in creating unstable conditions, Johnston had some interesting observations on the local rulers in the Niger Delta:

> Considering what very slight benefit has as yet accrued to them from our rule, it is surprising what loyalty the chiefs of the Oil

> Rivers have shown towards the British Government. 'In spite of all temptations to belong to other Nations' they have invariably inclined towards our English rule, even at a time when our policy was most unsympathetic and vacillating. They have been cheated by British merchants, bombarded by British captains, and fined by British consuls, and yet they like us, and stick by us, and are proud of being 'all same Ingilis man' and of speaking our language fluently if unclassically.[42]

Writing more in the style of his popular books on African exploration than for a typical Foreign Office report, Johnston is perhaps unintentionally revealing about the nature of British rule. He makes clear the value of power and prestige in attracting supporters, even when the British were not delivering a form of rule advantageous to the local people. Johnston goes on to summarise the increasingly universal view among officials that the confused state of affairs meant that something must be done—even if he does rather casually elide the salient fact that he had himself just been in charge of the Protectorate for a full year:

> That the present chaotic condition of the Protectorate cannot long continue without grave evils arising, is, I think, disputed by no one: but all are not equally agreed on the subject of the permanent form of Government which is to replace the present vague, unsustainable rule of the consular authorities.[43]

This period exemplified the transition from informal empire to formal imperial rule, and as often happened behind the scenes, there was much disagreement over the best way forward; the path was not obvious, and many interest groups had opposite preferences. The biggest complicating factor was that British official administration was unavoidably tied up with commercial structures. This was most obviously the case with the Royal Niger Company; as a chartered company it was both a profit-seeking private enterprise and a formal arm of the British Empire. These two identities were inherently contradictory, and complaints about the Company were unsurprisingly numerous. In the autumn of 1888, Hewett reported from the Protectorate on its rapacious behaviour:

> On the East as well as on the West side of the river Niger the Company has been enlarging its sphere of operation to such an extent, as to interfere very seriously with the trade of our Merchants who have for many years had trading establishments in the rivers Brass, New Calabar and Benin... The Company has already nearly entirely destroyed the trade of the Brassmen by having taken within its jurisdiction all of the markets on the Niger where the Brassmen used to get most of their oil, and by the imposition of import and export duties. It now seeks—or appears to seek—to do the same to the trade of other rivers.[44]

The contradictions that enabled this efficient exploitation would not be resolved until the charter was finally wound up at the end of the century (although the legacy advantage continued for what became simply the Niger Company, and eventually part of Unilever plc). In the immediate term, however, decisions had to be made about how to administer those parts of the region outside the charter. The Oil Rivers of the Niger Delta had been formally claimed by Britain at Berlin, but with no real thought as to what to do with them; the issue had been avoided for too long already, and something had to be decided.

From all the official discussions and outside lobbying, four principal options had emerged: extend the charter of the Royal Niger Company to include the Delta; turn the region into a new British colony; add it to the existing Colony of Lagos; or simply reinforce and develop the existing consular system of *laissez faire* administration. Senior officials in the Foreign Office were keen to be rid of the region, and they did not much care how: extension of the charter would place responsibility for the area and its costs with Goldie, while either of the colony options would bring it under the remit of the Colonial Office. That the priority was to free the Foreign Office of the Delta burden seems to be confirmed by the fact that over just six days in October 1887, Percy Anderson could argue that the 'logical step would then seem to be to make it a colony',[45] express the hope that the Company would take it over,[46] and also suggest 'that with a little pressure we may induce the Col. Office to add the Oil Rivers District to the Lagos Protectorate'.[47]

Goldie had been keen to take over the Niger Delta region during the charter negotiations of 1885–86, but this would require a merger agreement with the Liverpool traders. Although the two sides were by this time sworn enemies, much of 1888 was spent in renewed talks, which even showed some promise of success; if the Liverpool merchants had access to the advantages of the charter, they might even be able to live with the overbearing Goldie.

There was, however, much opposition to the prospect. Missionary interests, their backers in the press and such African parties as were allowed a voice (meaning only a small number of favoured chiefs and traders) were adamantly opposed and wanted the region to become a colony, imagining it to be a safer option than aggressive Company rule. This was, however, opposed by the Liverpool traders, who associated colonies with taxation and higher customs duties; if they could not have the advantage of coming under the charter, they would prefer low-cost consular rule.

There was, therefore, no easy solution available. In order to chart a way out of this quagmire of conflicting interests, in late 1888 the Foreign Office hit upon the idea of arranging for a senior official to travel to the region, investigate thoroughly and make a recommendation. Accordingly, in December of that year, Major Claude MacDonald was appointed as HM Special Commissioner in the Niger and Oil Rivers Districts; his letter of appointment states that he was 'to inquire into certain questions affecting Imperial & Colonial interests on the West Coast of Africa & into the position of the Royal Niger Co.'[48] In more detailed orders issued in January 1889, he was instructed to form a judgement on the complaints levelled against the Royal Niger Company and on the question of whether their charter should be extended to include the Oil Rivers. If he concluded that a charter extension was unwise, he was to make a recommendation on whether the area should be absorbed into the Colony of Lagos, be given a separate colonial administration or remain under consular jurisdiction.[49] MacDonald sailed for West Africa on 6 February 1889.

This appointment heralded the arrival of the most important figure in the imposition of British control over the Niger Delta, and thus one of the most consequential actors in the formation of what eventually came to be Nigeria. Claude Maxwell MacDonald had something of a classical British Empire background, being born in India to a major-general in the British Army, going to boarding school in England and then attending Sandhurst. He was commissioned into the 74th (Highland) Regiment of Foot in 1872 and participated in the invasion of Egypt in 1882. He returned to Egypt in 1884 to serve as military attaché to Sir Evelyn Baring, and then went to Zanzibar as consul general in 1887. By the time of his appointment to West Africa, therefore, MacDonald had had a thorough grounding in the techniques of enforcing British claims to power, especially in the context of informal empire.

MacDonald is a complex and interesting character. Though he was generally seen as aggressive in manner (particularly by his Foreign Office colleagues, as he was very firmly an imperial soldier in the guise of a diplomat-administrator), he writes well and his despatches show a clear intelligence and self-deprecating wit; his extravagantly cultivated moustache seems proof all by itself that he had a healthy sense of humour. Moreover, he seems to have made strenuous efforts always to administer the rule of law fairly, including with local African people in disputes with Europeans, and was a genuine free-trader at a time when for many the term was merely a convenient label for hypocrisy; he was against the practical monopoly held by the Royal Niger Company on grounds of principle.[50] His many despatches and letters do not contain the overt racism of many others from the era, and he writes fondly of his wife (or 'Lady Mac' as he later called her, following his elevation to knighthood). However, none of these positive qualities alter the fact that MacDonald was, above all, a dedicated servant of the Empire, and his very first act on arriving in the Protectorate was an outrage that ought to be famous for its brutality: the blockade of Opobo.

Since the violent deposition of King Jaja in 1887, British traders had continued their competition with the middlemen of Opobo for access to the interior markets. The consul (Johnston, then Hewett when he returned from sick leave) would assist where possible, through browbeating the Opobo chiefs and threatening force as and when necessary; Jaja still being alive in exile, no king had replaced him and his people still hoped for his return.

By February 1889, in the face of complaints by British companies that the well-armed Opobo men were blocking their access into the creeks, Hewett was keen to take active steps. He wrote to the Foreign Office, urging that it was of 'great importance that energetic action should be taken and Opobo severely punished ... an effective blockade would very quickly force Opobo to submit'.[51] Hewett proposed to lay siege to the town (which lay on a riverine island, making naval blockade possible) until they surrendered all their weaponry and paid a fine. Disarming Opobo in this way would be the next major step in removing a rival source of power and authority in the south-east Delta. In emphasising the likely effectiveness of his strategy, Hewett also made clear the degree of severity that it entailed:

> The opinion is that the Chiefs would give in in less than ten days if a strict blockade of the town were enforced, and that it would not be necessary to adopt any other measure, except perhaps firing at and seizing an occasional canoe that might try to run the blockade—because the supply of food would fail.[52]

Indeed, Hewett later wrote that the express goal of the blockade was 'to starve the inhabitants into a state of submission'.[53] Given these harsh tactics, Commander Harrison of HMS *Bramble* felt unable to undertake them without instruction from superiors, and so he telegraphed to the Admiralty accordingly. At the same time, the Foreign Office instructed Hewett to delay any action since MacDonald was onboard ship for Africa and would arrive shortly.[54]

No action was therefore yet taken. On 2 March, MacDonald reached the Bonny River, where he was met by Rear Admiral Wells, the commander of the West Africa Squadron.[55] Proceeding to Opobo, they anchored offshore and met Hewett; together, the commissioner, admiral and consul decided to enforce a blockade on Opobo until it gave up its weaponry.[56] The operation began on 12 March, with Royal Navy vessels being supplemented by steam launches lent by British traders. After a good number of arms had been surrendered, the blockade was raised on 5 April.

British sources for this period record very little about the episode besides the nuts and bolts of enforcement. We learn from Hewett that during the blockade, he summoned the chiefs of Opobo to meet him, threatening to shell the town if they did not come; he also reports that, having taken an Opobo chief hostage as security, he then announced to the people of the town that their chief would be hanged if anyone fired upon the British vessels.[57] We know these outline details from the Foreign Office records, but we have very little information about what happened inside Opobo during this period of blockade. Such considerations were not something that Hewett bothered to record, and since Opobo was a pre-literate culture, its own governing authorities did not keep bureaucratic records in any way that would serve as an archive for future historians. Nor are there contemporary written accounts from people inside Opobo at the time. In the official British account, it was a successful operation to disarm a rival power, and several weeks later Hewett wrote in self-congratulatory tones about the results of the action:

> I have no doubt our influence will be very greatly increased, not only at the markets but much further in the interior. The removal of Ja Ja, but more particularly, as I learnt, the confiscation of Opobo's war canoes, guns and rifles has gained for us much influence among the natives at the markets, who give 'the Consul', and nobody else, the credit of emancipating them from the tyranny and oppression of a Power they had considered invincible.[58]

Given the archival asymmetry, this might have been all that later generations came to know about the impact of the Opobo blockade, were it not for a chance remark by Major MacDonald himself in a report written six years later. In discussing the practicalities of disarming local people, he accidentally revealed the effect of the 1889 operation on the town of Opobo:

> The desirability of disarming the native tribes has been suggested; as to the desirability of so doing there can be no two opinions, the practicability of so doing is however another question. It was tried in Opobo in 1889, by blockading that town, the result being that many women and children died of starvation or were drowned in trying to escape from the starving town.[59]

It is notable that MacDonald slips into the passive voice when describing a decision that he had himself made; perhaps this amounts to an admission of his own guilt. Without any sources, we have no way of knowing just how many women and children of Opobo (and surely a number of men, too) died due to British actions in the spring of 1889. We can be sure, however, that there were numerous other episodes of imperial cruelty and injustice that were successfully obscured through omission from the official records. What other outrages have been hidden from history?

4

'VERY BAD INDEED'

CONSUL ANNESLEY IN THE OIL RIVERS

Truly the Consul has killed as much as he could and burnt Aquetté and did everything there as would please him.

Statement by the Bonny chiefs, Grand Bonny, August 1891

It will be a good thing if Annesley retires. There are some very nasty stories about his proceedings in the Oil Rivers which are getting about outside.

Eric Barrington, Foreign Office private note, November 1891

The creation of knowledge about the history of the British Empire has, in many respects, been a one-sided affair. The official documents of the imperial system (preserved largely in the National Archives in London) often provide the principal sources for historians of the subject, despite capturing only what British administrators regarded as interesting or useful, along with their own preferred internal narratives. Even without any malign intent, such a collection of materials will naturally reflect British priorities and value judgements, only sporadically featuring the concerns and opinions of local people, typically as war or crisis forced them into attention.

Moreover, given that government archives were kept secret for several decades, and especially since some colonised peoples lived in pre-literate societies—with no written records or publishing cultures—it was a fairly simple matter for imperial officials to prevent certain information becoming public knowledge. To put it bluntly, they could cover up wrongdoing relatively easily. With very little in the way of competing sources of written information coming out of West Africa, for example, the British had an effective monopoly of knowledge about events in that region for those outside it. This epistemological brute force helps explain sometimes surprisingly positive British views of the British Empire project, even well into the twenty-first century.

A direct beneficiary of this control of information was George Annesley, who served as British consul in the Oil Rivers for eighteen months from December 1889. The imperial system had no difficulty hiding his atrocious misdeeds in the Foreign Office archives before they did any damage to public perception, which is why he is now largely unknown instead of being a famous exemplar of British colonial wrongdoing.

* * *

During 1889 the British protectorate over the Niger region continued in a state of flux. Major MacDonald was engaged in his work throughout the year, investigating complaints against the Royal Niger Company and gathering material in order to form a view on the administrative future of the Niger Delta. Additionally, he was charged with the task of settling the border with German territory in the Cameroons.[1] Even while MacDonald enquired into its methods, George Goldie—by this time Sir George—continued the aggressive expansion of his company north of the Delta; the fact that the boundary between the territory of the

Royal Niger Company and the rest of the protectorate claimed by Britain had not yet been definitively fixed was a source of friction. Meanwhile, Consul Hewett soldiered on in the laborious and somewhat improvisational task of trying to administer his enormous district and all its rivers essentially single-handed.

Even though all concerned were looking to the recommendations of Major MacDonald to bring clarity to the governmental future of the region, commerce was not standing still. The principal trading companies of the Oil Rivers had expended much effort since 1887 on negotiations with both Goldie and the government over the question of extending the Royal Niger Company charter to absorb the operations of the Liverpool firms.[2] By 1889 these efforts had failed, and in response, in May of that year the leading traders (with the exception of Alexander Miller, Brother & Co of Glasgow) formed the African Association Ltd,[3] merging their Niger Delta operations into a single, powerful company. This new entity would go on to apply unsuccessfully for its own royal charter, but it nonetheless became the dominant force in the palm oil business of the Oil Rivers in the following years. As will be seen, it also played a minor role in the downfall of the Kingdom of Benin.

It was in the middle of this state of uncertainty that Consul Hewett fell ill. He wrote to the Foreign Office in August 1889 complaining of swellings in his legs, arms, hands and even face and requested permission to take the next mail steamer for Madeira.[4] Admitting that 'he is apparently very ill indeed', the Foreign Office telegraphed Hewett granting him leave.[5] The internal discussions on this issue, however, illustrate the makeshift nature of much of the machinery of the Empire; commenting on Hewett's request for a leave of absence, one official noted archly, 'It cannot be refused: but we might ask him whether he proposes to leave anyone in charge'.[6] Hewett managed to quit his post in September but caused some confusion in London by appointing two consular agents but no acting consul. Accordingly, at the end of November, the Foreign Office telegraphed to Bonny to intercept Consul George Annesley, who at that time happened to be sailing out to take up a new appointment on the Congo;[7] he was instructed to remain in the Oil Rivers instead. Annesley therefore arrived in Old Calabar in December 1889, from where he declared in his first despatch home, 'I have taken charge of this Consulate today'.[8] Thus it was through a series of minor accidents that Annesley arrived in the Oil Rivers to begin what turned out to be his reign of terror.

* * *

George Frederick Nicholas Beresford Annesley was born into an Anglo-Irish aristocratic family in 1852, his great-grandfather being the 2nd Earl Annesley; although his descent through a line of younger sons separated him from the title by some measure, he is nonetheless a distant relation of the present Earl Annesley. His father—also George—served as a lieutenant in the Austrian cavalry[9] before returning to Britain to begin a long career in the Consular Service, rising eventually to consul general for Hamburg and much of northern Germany.[10] For this reason, the younger George was born in Hamburg and took the opportunity to serve in the Prussian army, including during the Franco-Prussian War of 1870–71. His elder brother Henry did the same, and in August 1870 he was killed in action aged just twenty-one, as an ensign in the 2nd Regiment of Foot Guards during the Battle of Gravelotte.[11]

Annesley then followed his father into the Consular Service, where he held various postings, including in Surinam, on the Isthmus of Panama, and in Savannah, Georgia. His appointment as consul to the Independent State of the Congo was gazetted in May 1888,[12] but he managed to secure a lengthy period of sick leave, which is how he came to be travelling out to Africa in late

1889, just when a consul was required for the Oil Rivers. It did not take Consul Annesley long to make his presence felt in the Niger Delta; there were several distinct episodes from his time in charge that illustrate both his character and the daily injustices of the exercise of British imperial power.

The first such incident began early in 1890. Before Annesley's arrival in West Africa, Albert Gillies—one of the British traders whom Hewett had appointed as consular agent—had gone up the Cross River in HMS *Alecto* and met with Abiakari, king of Ikot Ana. Lacking sufficient time on that occasion, Gillies promised to return in the following spring in order to settle, as requested, a longstanding dispute between King Abiakari and the king and people of Akunakuna. Having been briefed on the issue in January, Annesley set out to visit Ikot Ana, which lay approximately 50 miles up the Cross River, in the following month, departing on 8 February.[13] Travelling by canoe with Gillies and Coco Otu Bassey, a senior Efik trader from Old Calabar, Annesley and his small party arrived on the same day at Itu, about 24 miles up the river, where they camped for the night. Annesley then decided that they would spend the following day paying an opportunistic visit to King Andemeno of Enyong, just a few miles up the river, before then continuing on to Ikot Ana on the day after.

Andemeno had for some time been taking advantage of his control over a stretch of the Cross River to levy tolls on the cargoes of palm oil that the Old Calabar middlemen brought down by canoe from the interior; although the British also levied duty on this palm oil trade, Annesley framed the Enyong tolls as 'blackmail' and aimed to stop Andemeno from carrying out a function that was too much like a rival exercise of governmental prerogatives.[14] Accordingly, Annesley and his party left Itu for Enyong on 9 February, for a visit that swiftly descended into farce:

> On our arrival the King ran into his house, barred his door and told his people to tell me he was not there. I then knocked at his door with my walking stick, at the same time telling him to come out, that we were unarmed and that all we wanted was to have a quiet talk with him. However, he refused to come out and told his people to fire upon us, but they only threatened us with their loaded rifles etc. I then again knocked at his door but to no avail. As the crowd around us became more and more aggressive, I gave the King five minutes to come out, at the end of which I fined him one hundred boxes of rods and returned to our canoe followed by an armed mob. We then paddled back to Itu.[15]

From this somewhat ludicrous beginning, however, the Enyong story soon took a rather darker turn. After visiting Ikot Ana as planned, Annesley returned to Old Calabar, noting that he saw watch fires burning all along the river as they passed through Enyong country on the journey home. On his return to the coast, he tried to get the assistance of the gunboat HMS *Peacock* in going back up the river to arrest King Andemeno, but its captain declined to get involved. Accordingly, on 20 February Annesley summoned a meeting with all the British traders and the Efik kings and chiefs, the upshot of which was a decision to prepare for war against Enyong; an Efik force would go upriver to obtain either free passage for palm oil cargoes or the removal of Andemeno. Preparations began immediately.

Having earlier complained about having no police of his own,[16] Annesley hurriedly recruited a makeshift constabulary in early March:

> I have raised a small police force which I have armed with shot-guns and drilled them as well as was possible in such a short time. Their uniform consists of a Fez, dark blue jersey and white loose trowsers with a red stripe on the side.[17]

He also noted their pay and rations, including 'Grog twice a day'.[18] This curious adoption of the longstanding Royal Navy custom may have been a significant factor in the future outrages committed by Annesley and his police; originally intended to make long storage feasible, grog was made by adding rum to brackish water, in order to render it palatable, and had been codified to an issue of fully half a pint of rum per man per day, mixed with water. In order to prevent the occasional bouts of extreme drunkenness that hoarding of this daily ration would allow, the practice was to parade men for the issue of grog twice a day and have them drink it on the spot. Half a pint of rum is equal to about twelve standard measures of spirits, so we can conclude that Annesley's small police force went about their daily work in a state of at least semi-drunkenness. Significantly for his capacity to create fear and disorder, Annesley later expanded his force in January 1891 by recruiting from the Colony of Lagos around twenty men and a sergeant.

Annesley went back up the Cross River on 8 March with his freshly recruited constabulary, preceding the Efik army in the hope of getting King Andemeno to back down.[19] Over the next ten days there followed a complicated series of meetings between Annesley, Andemeno, the Efik leaders and other local chiefs of the Cross River, aimed at resolving the situation. This illustrates the uncertain position of the British consul at that time; he was one of several centres of power making claims to authority and was certainly not yet dominant, especially because he lacked ready access to significant means of compulsion. He was thus allied to the Efik kings and chiefs and leveraged their capacity to exercise force while also attempting to position himself as a supposedly neutral mediator.

In this instance, mediation failed and Andemeno refused to give in to the British and Efik demands. Fighting thus broke out on 18 March, as Annesley described to the Foreign Office:

> On the morning of the 18th as we were leaving Itu for the second island I heard firing and two wounded men were soon afterwards

> brought down. I hastened up to the scene of action and found that the Enyong people had fired upon an Efik canoe, which had ventured a little beyond the second island, and had wounded the two men aforementioned. Both banks of the river were then taken with a rush. Some of the Efik people went along the banks driving the Enyong people before them, others proceeded up the river firing on the villages from their canoes. The King's place, the town of Enyong and all the villages of Enyong proper were burned and the few cows and goats, that the Enyong people had not previously removed, secured. The Efik people had no men killed, but about a dozen were wounded, some very seriously. Several of the Enyong people were killed and about seven or eight were taken prisoners.[20]

This destructive raid up the Cross River had not yet succeeded in removing King Andemeno from power, but, significantly, Annesley celebrated the operation as a valuable demonstration of the capacity of the British–Efik allies to strike into the interior:

> What the immediate result of this expedition will be I cannot as yet say, but one thing is certain, that the tribes living up the river now know that the Efik people are able to go up during the dry season. Up to the last moment Andémeno did not think it possible for the large Efik war canoes to go up to his place. The moral effect on the upper river tribes of three hundred canoes (no tribe on the Cross River ever mustered such a large number of canoes) carrying one or two—some three—small guns (one chief had a Gatling gun) rockets, etc, going up the river at a few days notice has, from what I have seen, been very great. But I fear that as long as King Andémeno is not removed from his position the river will never be thoroughly open for trade.[21]

It was not long before Annesley achieved his aim. Having issued an order in February stopping trade with anyone who recognised Andemeno as king, and then laying waste to Enyong in March, he had made the area virtually uninhabitable. By the middle of May, he was back up the Cross River at Itu to receive the submission of three queens of Enyong, who begged for peace (despite having had their own villages and plantations destroyed in the fighting). They signed the standard treaty of friendship, and Annesley made them sign an additional treaty declaring that they no longer recognised Andemeno as king; he did the same with a new king of Assang. The British consul was delighted with this outcome:

> Only two small villages called Idem Egbo Obo and Atan (which were burnt) are now under the control of Andémeno, Chief of Atan, who has fled to the bush. He is no longer King of Enyong. I have broke up his Kingdom, by making the three aforementioned Queens independent of him, and Assang also a separate kingdom, Andémeno is now powerless and is not likely to do any more mischief. The advantage of having broken up his kingdom is that besides rendering Andémeno powerless, there will be smaller and consequently weaker tribes to deal with in future. The trouble with Enyong may therefore now be considered at an end.[22] [*sic passim*]

This 'divide and rule' strategy was frequently employed by British empire-builders, not least by Annesley himself, even before the Enyong affair. In February, he had settled the dispute between the kings of Ikot Ana and Akunakuna by creating an entirely new king in the border territory of Ukpem, over which they had been arguing, and signing a treaty with him too.[23] It is important to recognise that these tactics were not simply a cunning but inconsequential ruse for moving around kings and queens on a political chessboard. While they seem to have struck people like Annesley merely as clever stratagems, they amounted to wholesale destruction of social structures in these communities.

Clearly, George Annesley was not concerned with these negative impacts as long as British power was advanced. Such attitudes were not limited to professional servants of the Empire; press reporting from the time—surely at least some measure of public feeling—frequently showed a similar lack of empathy. As it happens, the Enyong incident made it into the *Birmingham Daily Post*, in a report that demonstrates less than complete concern for human suffering:

> 'Not at home' is a conventional incantation so useful and in such frequent request among the hosts and hostesses of civilised society, for escaping inopportune or unwelcome visitors, that few people stop to consider the breach of truth and the revelation of personal antipathy which it commonly implies. In West Africa, apparently, they are more fastidious, and for indulging in this polite fiction a short time back, when notified of the approaching visit of a British Consul, King Ndem Eno of Enyong has had his country put to fire and sword ... The result of the fight, which lasted nearly thirty-six hours, was that Ndem Eno's town was almost totally destroyed by fire, and thirty-seven prisoners and thirty-five heads were carried back to Calabar. Ndem Eno then sued for peace to the Consul, which was granted, upon his paying a fine of 1,000 yams, one cow, and one goat. Next time a British consul announces his intention of honouring King Eno with an official visit, his Majesty will probably think twice before saying 'Not at home'.[24] [*sic passim*]

* * *

For the story of the conquest of the Kingdom of Benin, the period in which George Annesley ruled over the Oil Rivers is important largely in its illustration of the nature of British administration in West Africa at the time and of the daily injustices that the imperial system guaranteed. Annesley did, however, visit Benin City, in November 1890.[25] Travelling via the standard Gwato route, Annesley accompanied the palm oil traders Cyril Punch and D. P. Bleasby, both of whom had visited the city before in an effort to establish trade. Although Annesley was the first British consul to visit Benin since Burton in 1862, he failed to meet with the king.[26]

This failure had everything to do with Annesley's own character. The experienced traders explained to him that custom required new visitors to the king to wait for three days before gaining an audience, but Annesley had no patience. As Bleasby later reported to *The Times*, 'Consul Annesley, being rather impetuous, would not wait. He sent repeated messages to the king, threatening to leave'.[27] Finally, with the consul choosing to see the Benin customs merely as prevarication, the party left Benin City without Annesley seeing the king, and without the king's permission to depart.

Oba Adolo had died in 1888 after a lengthy reign of about forty years, and the king whom Annesley failed to meet was his son, Oba Ovonramwen. The oral traditions contain stories of a disputed succession,[28] and Ovonramwen is said to have put several chiefs to death as a result; in general, however, most sources portray him as a peaceable character, even somewhat retiring. In a notably complimentary account of his good nature, notwithstanding the casual racism, Bleasby also gave a description of the new Oba:

> As to the appearance of the king, he is, for a negro, a very pleasant-faced man. His eyes, though rather small, have a laughing expression. He has a short, curly beard, and altogether his face shows a remarkable intelligence. In stature he is about 5ft 6in.[29]

This visit to Benin in 1890 suggests an official British interest in penetrating further into the interior, including into the territory of the Kingdom of Benin, but evidently at this time it was not of sufficient strategic importance for Annesley to overcome his arrogance. The episode therefore provides a glimpse of his defects of character, but his worst and most brutal depravities were still to come.

* * *

Perhaps the most grotesque wrong committed by George Annesley during his rule over the Oil Rivers happened in early 1891, and we know about it only because of witness statements gathered for a subsequent investigation; as will become obvious, it was not something that Annesley himself reported home. The allegations were first raised in a letter written in July 1891 directly to the Marquis of Salisbury by one George Turner, a Sierra Leonean employed as consular clerk in Old Calabar.

Turner wrote that on a night in March 1891 he was being held in the lower storey of the consulate, chained by the neck to an iron pillar for having irritated the consul in some fashion, it being Annesley's regular practice to 'imprison all those who were obnoxious to him'.[30] The ground floor of the building was used as a barracks for the Consular Constabulary, and the soldiers were relaxing outside at about 10.30 p.m. when Annesley came down from his quarters to join them. Speaking through one of their number who understood both Yoruba and English, they discussed Islam and its practices, and Annesley told them about his army experience. The reported conversation sounds very much like the consul getting to know his new recruits, who had been brought from Lagos only a few weeks before. It took place just a few feet from where Turner lay on the ground, pretending to be asleep in order to avoid having to talk to Annesley.

The gathering was suddenly interrupted by the return of one of the soldiers, named Durowoju, who reported that his cap had been taken by a woman who lived at the bottom of the Consulate Hill, evidently in an argument over arrangements with a prostitute. Exclaiming, 'I know the bitch, go and fetch her up!' Annesley despatched Sergeant Edward Davies and some men to bring her to the Consulate, where she was dragged just a few minutes later.[31] Her name was Ekang, and according to her own statement later given to consular officials, she ran a house below the Consulate, where she managed three prostitutes.[32]

Followed by a number of soldiers, Annesley went back upstairs with Ekang and, since she did not understand English, a servant named Punch for translation.[33] In his quarters, while sitting on a sofa, Annesley questioned her and demanded the repayment of the money in question to his soldier, which Ekang refused. In her later statement to Vice Consul Roberts, she reported that Annesley 'seemed to lose his temper and called upon his soldiers to throw her down on the ground and have connection with her'.[34] In other words, this was the British consul—expressly charged with upholding the law—ordering the gang rape of a woman supposedly under his protection. George Turner, still chained downstairs, reported hearing a struggle from the upper story, and then adds some unpleasant details:

> Presently, Edward Davies came down and I heard him say in the Yoruba language, (in which I am proficient) 'The Consul says whoever feels inclined to cohabit with a woman must come upstairs'. So saying he ran up back himself followed by some more soldiers. About an hour afterwards, Davies returned and said (in broken English this time) 'if any Krooboys also wants to do with a woman the Consul invites him upstairs'. None of the Krooboys went.
>
> About half an hour more, I heard the poor girl dragging herself down the stairs, crying bitterly. It was now midnight and the soldiers came down and made it a matter of talk and laughter how Durowoju, Buzac, Atekporlay, and others actually cohabited with Ekang, the Consul himself assisting to hold her down.[35] [*sic passim*]

Sergeant Edward Davies was also interviewed in the later investigation, and his details correspond with Turner's report, except that Davies said only that 'Consul Annesley was present and sat on a sofa looking on while the men were having connection with her', without reporting that he held Ekang down.[36] Importantly, the testimonies from Davies and from Ekang agree on certain telling details, such as the particular sofa on which Annesley had been sitting. Given the consistency of the careful, sworn statements gathered, there can be no serious doubt about the truth of these allegations. Davies said that he could not see how many soldiers raped Ekang, but in her testimony she gave the number as four. Her statement ends with an account of the aftermath of her own violation and of yet another outrage committed by Annesley's men that night:

> she went on her knees to the Consul and asked what she had done, that she should be treated so, but he ordered her to be taken out. Her clothes were off her, and his servant took her clothes after her. She returned to her house which is at the foot of the Consulate Hill. On returning to her house she heard cries and going out saw that the soldiers had caught the girl before mentioned and were holding her on the ground. She saw twelve of the soldiers have connection with her. The Consul was not present at this.[37]

A crucial note here is that this night of outrages by Annesley and his soldiers entered the Foreign Office archives solely because George Turner happened to be imprisoned within earshot of Annesley's quarters and took it upon himself to protest directly to the prime minister. An educated man in British employ, he had the means to write a letter and get it to Lord Salisbury; few witnesses to colonial wrongdoing possessed such advantages. We therefore have no way of knowing how many occasions of a similar kind might have escaped the historical record, under the regime of Consul Annesley and many other officers of the Empire.

* * *

As the brutal violation of Ekang suggests, once Annesley was armed with his expanded military force—from January 1891—he used it to further impose his arbitrary will and to terrify the local people. In the same month in which the Consulate Hill women were brutally assaulted, other cases made it into the historical record: Annesley had his men plunder and burn down houses belonging to a number of the most senior men of Old Calabar. A later investigation recorded numerous sworn testimonies about these events, including from King Archibong himself:

> Yellow King Archibong states:—during my absence to the market on the 28th March, 1891, my house was broken into by Consul Annesley's soldiers and what was not taken away was destroyed—the ceiling stripped off—my wives and female servants whom I left in the house beaten and driven away, and their apartments stripped of everything of value, and my man 'Efure Ufon' who I left to mind my house stabbed with a bayonet by one of the Soldiers from the effects of which he died.[38] [*sic passim*]

In several similar cases, Annesley seems to have targeted wealthy individuals, without supplying any reasons for his actions, for example:

> Edet Ephraim Duke a free born Effik trader of the house of King Duke states when I was absent at my farm in the month of March last I was informed that my house had been plundered broken into and burnt down by orders of Consul Annesley I was unaware that I had in any way offended the Consul.[39] [*sic passim*]

Once again, it is essential to note that these were influential men with the means to ensure that their complaints were heard; we cannot know what abuses Annesley and his soldiers may have carried out against other local people without such capacities. Even though the record is therefore unavoidably selective, the wealth of evidence gathered through these sworn statements leaves no room for doubt about the pattern of behaviour of George Annesley, including his violent nature and indifference to human suffering. This was perhaps most clearly displayed in Annesley's final aggressive episode in the Oil Rivers: his attack on Akwete in June 1891.

Akwete lies some 50 miles inland from Opobo on the Imo River, and by 1891 it was already a significant town. In the British documents it is often rendered as Aquettah, Aquetté, or any number of similar variants. As it was an important centre of the palm oil trade, Alexander Miller, Brother & Co had established a trading station in Akwete in 1888, followed by the African

Association in the spring of 1891.[40] A notable fact from the British side is that the king of Akwete had declined to sign a treaty with Consul Hewett in 1884, so the companies were supposedly operating at their own risk in an uncertain jurisdiction.

The cause of the trouble in June 1891 was a minor argument between a young assistant at the Miller factory, named Watson, and some local men, apparently over several casks of biscuits. Although the matter was of little consequence, Watson (whom Major MacDonald later described as 'an entirely inexperienced youth')[41] seems to have panicked; he fled Akwete for Opobo, where he reported the matter to the head agent for Miller's, Mr Bruce, who informed Consul Annesley. As a consequence, despite the insignificance of the dispute, there was no real prospect of resolving the affair peacefully.

Annesley arrived in Opobo on 15 June, accompanied by his soldiers, and set out for Akwete on 17 June, along with some of the European traders, including Bruce, Watson, a Mr Walker and others. Consular Agent Munro, an employee of the African Association, was despatched to summon all the chiefs of both Opobo and Bonny (who traded at Akwete) to meet the consul upriver. They did as they were bidden, and the way in which Annesley received them is further illustration of his arrogance; the later statement by the chiefs of Bonny also makes clear that the consul was already set on violence:

> We the Chiefs of Bonny met on the 18th and sent a reply to Mr Munro that we shall gladly meet the Consul at Aquetté on Monday the 22nd as we have to get our boys and canoe ready. However we pulled as much as we could and met him at Aquetté on the 21st just at dinner.
>
> The ignominious manner that we were received by the Consul on that evening, was unexpressible. All the other Europeans there as they saw us greeted us warmly; and were glad to see us come; But, he who send for us to come; never lifted his face to look at us. We did not mind all that, but waited till he finished his food. As he gets

> up from the table, he went into his room, so we asked Mr Walker to ask if he has anything to say to us as we are tired, we wish to go into our canoe to get rest: Mr Walker went in to him, as soon as the Consul came without saying a word to us, named five Aquetté chiefs and that he wants them. We said we will go to them in the morning and ask them to come to meeting. Oh! he said, I do not want any meeting, I will burn the town, giving us no more chance to say a word more. We left for our canoes.[42] [*sic passim*]

That Annesley was intent on using force and had no interest in a peaceful settlement is clear from all sources. In the later investigation, the chiefs of Akwete reported similarly, that '[t]he Agents and the Bonny and Opobo Chiefs seeing Consul Annesley was determined to fight begged him not to do so but he however took no notice of their request'.[43] After brief and abortive discussions, Annesley's patience seems to have run out on the evening of 22 June, as reported by the Bonny chiefs:

> We pleaded as much as we could, but in vain. Consul Annesley's determination was for war ... At length in the night of the 22nd June 1891 between 8 & 9 o'clock, the Consul with his warriors marched into Aquetta Town whilst the people were taking their nights rest. Firing right and left the poor unaware natives getting up from their sleep with confusion, tried in vain to take refuge in the bush.—not long, fire was set on one part of the town ...
>
> Truly the Consul has killed as much as he could and burnt Aquetté and did everything there as would please him. Now all our cargos at Aquetté is nearly lost. We are sure that if not properly manage will bring Bankrupcy in our land.[44] [*sic passim*]

Such was the response of Consul Annesley to a dispute over a few barrels of biscuits, in which even Watson himself did not claim to have been hurt in any way. In his subsequent investigation, Major MacDonald found that the casualties in Akwete amounted to 'three women killed and five children burnt'.[45] Annesley himself was wounded by a bullet in the arm,[46] and in a private note at the Foreign Office, Sir Percy Anderson expressed a rare level of dissatisfaction with his performance:

> The original quarrel with the natives was a trivial one ... It is obvious that with ordinary tact and temper such an affair could easily have been assuaged. But Consul Annesley showed neither. He went up with an armed force, hectored, insulted the peaceable Bonny Chiefs and, in spite of the remonstrances of the English traders, began hostilities, shot women and children, with the result that, having fired away 6000 rounds & got a slight wound himself, he had to make an ignominious retreat.[47]

This was George Annesley's last episode of violence in the Oil Rivers. Just a few days after his wholly unwarranted attack on Akwete, he was back in Old Calabar, where, on 6 July, he handed over charge of the Consulate to a newly arrived Captain Synge. On 11 July, Annesley then sailed for Luanda to take up his long-delayed appointment, never to return to the Niger Delta.[48]

* * *

It was not, however, because of the Akwete incident that Annesley left the Oil Rivers. By early 1891, reports of his problematic behaviour had begun to reach the Foreign Office, largely from the British trading companies and, through them, from the kings and chiefs of the region. Major MacDonald had, as we will see in the following chapter, spent 1890 helping to decide the future government of the Niger Districts Protectorate, and in the spring of 1891, he was formally appointed to take charge. When he learnt of the reports of Annesley's actions, he refused even to meet with him for a handover of the affairs of the Consulate. Sir Percy Anderson noted privately that 'Major MacDonald does not want to find Mr Annesley on the Oil Rivers'.[49]

By this time, MacDonald had already been tasked with investigating various charges against Annesley,[50] and on his arrival back in the Oil Rivers he was swiftly confronted with many more. He arrived in Old Calabar on the evening of Saturday, 1 August, and reported that '[t]he whole of Sunday I spent up at the Consulate ... Complaints now commenced pouring in with regard to the behaviour of Consul Annesley and his so called soldiers and police'.[51] On the following day, he held a large meeting of all the kings and chiefs. After lengthy discussion of governmental and commercial matters, MacDonald reported that 'then the King Duke as spokesman said he hoped I would enquire into the doings of Consul Annesley, how that he had oppressed and beaten the people & pillaged & burnt their houses'.[52]

Being a loyal servant of Empire, MacDonald warned the assembled local leaders that they were making grave allegations against the British consul and that if their charges were not fully borne out, they would be punished most severely; he told them that he would, however, enquire into their complaints. As MacDonald then reported to Sir Percy Anderson:

> That afternoon I was occupied for five hours in making a preliminary investigation into some of these charges—and I regret to say that I have little reason to doubt that Consul Annesley seems to have acted in a most unjust, harsh & unwarrantable manner, burning down and sacking the houses of the people—some of the graver charges I had not time to go into, indeed the charges were so numerous that it will take weeks to enquire into them properly. You will recollect that several were sent to me by the Foreign Office before I left London—these I had not time even to enter into. I left the whole matter in the hands of Mr Roberts, Vice Consul, directing him to go carefully into the various charges and have the papers ready for me on my return. From what I have heard of the Consul's goings on in the various rivers he has visited I can only think he must be mad.[53]

From this (and especially from the subsequent investigations), it was clear that Annesley was guilty of serious offences; significantly, however, MacDonald makes no mention of his being arrested and tried, nor even disciplined. Moreover, after just ten weeks in Luanda, Annesley requested sick leave, complaining especially about the 'deadly climate' that he had endured in the Oil Rivers, and suggesting that his condition might be so bad as to require him to leave the service.[54] The reaction of the Foreign Office is a clear demonstration that the priority of officials was the protection of the imperial system; in a note addressed directly to Lord Salisbury, his private secretary Eric Barrington expressed concern about the possible consequences of public knowledge of colonial wrongdoing: 'It will be a good thing if Annesley retires. There are some very nasty stories about his proceedings in the Oil Rivers which are getting about outside.'[55]

Having initialled Barrington's note to confirm that he had read it, Lord Salisbury—who was at this time serving as both foreign secretary and prime minister—appended the brief remark 'very bad indeed'.[56] This proves that the very highest level of the British government knew of the appalling actions of George Annesley in West Africa, but he was allowed to escape all accountability. He submitted his resignation in February 1892, giving as one of his reasons the wound to his arm received in his deadly assault on Akwete.[57] The response proposed by Sir Percy Anderson was that they should 'Accept resignation & recommend for a pension. The charges against him have not yet been proved',[58] blatantly sidestepping the salient fact that they had no intention of holding a trial of any kind. Nowhere in the Foreign Office papers does anyone suggest that Annesley should in fact be prosecuted for his crimes, or punished in any way; the imperial system was incompatible with justice. Annesley was granted a pension[59] and lived in retirement until his death in September 1918.

5

'ALL QUIET IN RIVERS'

MAJOR MACDONALD IN OLD CALABAR

Now that we have put our hands to one of the richest commercial regions on the continent, it is to be hoped we shall persevere in a policy of gradual development.

The Times, 31 July 1891

Before commencing the meeting I informed the chiefs that, when I sent them a message, implicit obedience was what I expected, and what I, as representative of Her Majesty, would have.

Major C. M. MacDonald, 1 September 1891

In the summer of 1891, Major Claude MacDonald finally took charge of the British administration of the Niger Delta. One of the most consequential moments in the history of Nigeria, this marked the replacement of the haphazard dominion of a single consul by a properly organised colonial establishment. Having worked to secure its Niger region claim at the Berlin Conference, and then formally declaring the Protectorate in 1885, it was only now that Britain began to make it a reality on the ground.

Captain Robert Synge was sent out a month in advance with instructions to visit the main rivers of the Delta to announce the imminent arrival of the new consul general, as well as to make a proclamation about the imposition of revised customs duties.[1] Symbolising the official inauguration of the Oil Rivers Protectorate, Major MacDonald then arrived some weeks later; reaching Bonny on 28 July 1891, he telegraphed London: 'Arrived to-day. All quiet in rivers. Proclamation well received.'[2]

After holding a meeting with the Bonny and New Calabar chiefs, as well as with the European traders of both rivers, MacDonald proceeded to his new headquarters at Old Calabar. He later recalled looking upon his official residence 'with a sinking heart', describing it as 'a dilapidated wooden house with a tin roof, surrounded, up to the very front door, with thick jungle, a truly dismal abode.'[3] Having insisted that Consul Annesley depart the Oil Rivers before his own arrival, MacDonald declared the consulate to be in 'a disgraceful state of dirt and disrepair', complaining about windows that were falling in and a leaky roof, perhaps a further judgement upon the character of his predecessor.[4]

Over the next few years, Major MacDonald would transform the house and grounds of the British Consulate in Old Calabar, just as he would transform the nature of the British presence in the Niger region. The professionalisation of administration under his charge marked the transition from informal empire to formal rule, meaning a profound change in relationship between Britain and all the various local polities and power centres. Among other consequences, the arrival of MacDonald in Old Calabar sealed the eventual fate of the Kingdom of Benin; once a properly organised colonial government was under way, the logic of empire required the assertion of control over all the territory it claimed.

* * *

In fulfilment of his duties as HM Commissioner, MacDonald had submitted his final report in January 1890. Besides examining at length the various complaints against the Royal Niger Company, this document also supplied his recommendations on the future of the Oil Rivers, which he couched in expansionary terms:

> There is a large and very rich country, totally unexplored and unworked, to the back of the rivers; at least four rivers, all having deeper and more easily navigated bars than the one at Lagos, exist in the district, and there is excellent lateral communication by creeks or natural canals between all these rivers. Were the Oil River district to be administered as a Colony, the Government would profit by the experience gained in the formation of the other West African Colonies, and I am of opinion that if the administration were carried out in an energetic yet prudent manner, and the attention of the Executive devoted, at any rate at first, to opening up and civilizing the country and establishing it on a firm financial basis, rather than to outward forms, the Colony of the Oil Rivers would in every way be a success.[5]

The phrase 'opening up' was a staple of the colonial lexicon and served (alongside 'civilising') to put a positive gloss on what was in fact, achieved one way or the other, unarguably conquest. Imperial imperatives required Britain to exert control over all the areas it had claimed or risk inviting challenge from other powers; MacDonald was here offering the potential of commercial attractions (and thus tax revenue) that would allow imperial advance in the area to pay for itself. Given the standing horror in London about any added costs for the Treasury, the prospect of financial sufficiency for the local administration would become an ongoing pressure for interior expansion. In summarising his recommendations, MacDonald also raised the possibility of the use of force to achieve this:

> I am of opinion that to put the administration of the Oil River district into the hands of a trading chartered Company would be

> most unadvisable, and that the best form of administering the district, at any rate for some years, would be by a strong Consular Administration, with an Executive to maintain order and assist in opening up the country by means of, when necessary, armed police or constabulary.[6]

This approach to forward movement would become an integral part of the design and execution of the new British establishment in the Niger Delta (even if the traders needed regular encouragement to venture inland).[7] The decision process was, however, lengthy, reflecting imperial bureaucracy and the variety and strength of the different interest groups involved. A hint of this delicate situation can be seen in press reporting from the time:

> With Major MacDonald's report before them, the Government will, no doubt, be able to steer their way through the conflicting statements which have been submitted to them; fair play and the interests of the Empire ought to be the only motives to guide their decision.[8]

In this period, *The Times* was lobbying against the creation of a colony in the region, while the *Liverpool Mercury* was arguing in favour; both were united in opposition to the award of a new royal charter.[9] Throughout 1890, the internal Whitehall discussions and newspaper lobbying continued, all while Consul George Annesley wreaked violence on the Oil Rivers. By December, questions were being asked in Parliament about future plans for the territory, forcing the government to admit that the details had not yet been decided, but that the principle would be continued consular administration with an expanded staff.[10]

Accordingly, in due course MacDonald was appointed as HM Commissioner and consul general in the Oil Rivers Protectorate; although the formal appointment was made only in April 1891, it was officially backdated to 1 January, reflecting the significant preparatory work that he had already undertaken while the government gradually reached a firm decision.[11] A key part of this effort was the recruitment of six vice consuls to serve under him, at Old Calabar and at the planned new vice consulates to be established at Bonny, Forcados, Opobo and Brass and in the lower Benin River.[12]

Another crucial aspect of this preparation was defining the actual borders of his new realm, and MacDonald had therefore been negotiating with both the Colonial Office (respecting the Colony of Lagos) and the Royal Niger Company through the first half of 1891. In May, MacDonald reported an agreement with the Colonial Office in which all 'the Benin Country' would go to the new Oil Rivers Protectorate, while all Yoruba areas would be left to Lagos.[13]

Matters were less straightforward in defining the boundaries with the Royal Niger Company; the *de facto* border between the Company and the Protectorate was lengthy and complicated. The vast areas claimed by George Goldie were largely far to the north, beyond the confluence of the Niger and Benue rivers, but access to this region lay through the main channel of the Niger. Control of this waterway, the lower reach of which was known as the Nun River, was therefore a matter of financial life and death for the Company, and it had always sought to dominate it completely, both commercially and militarily. The boundaries agreed by MacDonald and Goldie therefore had to accommodate this strategic requirement; Royal Niger Company territory would thus include the entire stretch of the main channel of the Niger River all the way to the sea, and to a distance of 10 miles on either side, as well as a wedge of territory between the Forcados River and the mouth of the Nun.[14] This thin strip of territory bisected the Oil Rivers Protectorate, an unfortunate but unavoidable complication.

An important point to note about the formalisation of these British imperial borders in early 1891 is that it marked the final encirclement of the Kingdom of Benin. To the west of the kingdom, all Yoruba areas were now regarded as formally part of the

Colony of Lagos; to the east and north, the Royal Niger Company was expanding aggressively up the great river. To the south, the new administration of the Oil Rivers Protectorate was becoming a reality on the ground, and MacDonald had officially laid claim to Benin territory.

That MacDonald intended eventually to enforce this claim is clear from the preparations that he was making for the relaunched Protectorate. In December 1890 he produced an internal analysis of his staffing requirements and argued for sufficient military force to allow interior penetration. At the time, the British in West Africa had come to view the Hausa people (who dominate what is now northern Nigeria) as something of a 'martial race', to be preferred when enlisting soldiers, much as they viewed the Sikhs in India. Using the contemporary spelling, MacDonald thus proposed recruiting a body of Hausa soldiers to provide the necessary capacity for 'opening up' his claimed territory:

> When I speak of maintaining order, a force of fifty police would be sufficient to maintain order in the European settlements at the mouths of the rivers; but the policy of the future government of the Territories should be to open up the interior, a work which, though undertaken with the utmost patience and forbearance, will require an efficient force to carry it out with any hopes of success.
>
> As a commencement, a force of 100 Houssas with three officers would perhaps be sufficient. I am inclined to think that fairly good fighting material might be obtained from some of the tribes in the rivers. Krooboys are useless as soldiers.[15]

In May 1891, MacDonald therefore sent Ralph Moor—a former officer of the Royal Irish Constabulary whom he had appointed as superintendent of the Protectorate forces—to Lagos to recruit a nucleus of Hausa soldiers.[16] Moor's efforts even made it into the newspapers; on reporting the new arrangements for the Oil Rivers Protectorate in late July, *The Times* (using yet another variant spelling) framed the recruitment of Hausa soldiers very much in terms of interior expansion:

> In a region like that of the Oil Rivers, one cannot expect law and order to be enforced in the same rigid manner as in Europe, or even in the Cape, or an old Crown colony. Much must be left to the Commissioner's tact and discretion. A body of Haussas are now being enlisted for the police service, and in time we may hope that the law will reach well into the interior, and that free traffic will be carried on without the intervention of middlemen ... Now that we have put our hands to one of the richest commercial regions on the continent, it is to be hoped we shall persevere in a policy of gradual development.[17]

Once again, employment of the colonial lexicon should not blind us to the fact that this describes military conquest.

* * *

Once MacDonald had taken up his new post, he swiftly began mounting the displays of power that comprised imperial structural violence. On his arrival in Bonny at the end of July, the expected Royal Navy vessels were not there to meet him ('I found your telegram about the gunboats, but no gunboats');[18] so important was the show of force delivered by the eleven-gun salute that his rank commanded, MacDonald delayed the meeting with the local chiefs by fully two days in the vain hope that the gunboats would appear.

By the time of his arrival in Old Calabar on Saturday 1 August, he had been united with HMS *Swallow* and HMS *Racer*. MacDonald reported home that he spent all day on Sunday at the Consulate, fielding complaints about Consul Annesley (as related in Chapter 4). He then noted:

> The following morning I held a large meeting of the Kings (there are some seven or eight here) besides numberless chiefs & headmen. Captain Finnis fired a salute of eleven guns on my leaving the ship and the same salute on my return. This has done much to impress

> the chiefs with the importance of the business, and small affair as it may seem has helped me considerably.[19]

MacDonald then spent almost all of August touring the principal rivers of the Protectorate, meeting with the kings and chiefs of each river and officially installing his new vice consuls. It is clear from his despatches home that the performative aspects of the imperial structures of violence were not merely harmless ceremonials:

> On arrival at Brass, I was informed that the Chiefs had sent a message to the effect that they had a meeting of their own, and could not come to see me till the next day, owing to the distance they had to travel. On the following day the Chiefs arrived, and, at my request, Captain Finnis, of HMS 'Swallow', landed a party of sixty seamen and marines as a guard of honour for myself.
>
> This guard had a marked effect upon the behaviour of the chiefs, who were inclined at first to be unruly and somewhat truculent in their manner. Before commencing the meeting I informed the chiefs that, when I sent them a message, implicit obedience was what I expected, and what I, as representative of Her Majesty, would have.[20]

The unsettled state of the Brass chiefs would become a significant issue over the next few years, as will be seen. Besides this, during his initial tour of the Protectorate, MacDonald highlighted another matter that would soon turn into a crisis for the British: the great power of Chief Nana of the Itsekiri.

The Itsekiri people (known to the British as Jakri, Jekri or other variants) dominated the Forcados River and the lower Benin River and were highly active as palm oil traders; they were the principal 'middlemen' that the British sought eventually to displace, making conflict almost inevitable once the British set out to penetrate inland. As the greatest of all the Itsekiri traders, Nana Olumo was the most powerful figure in the Forcados and Benin rivers and was able to control access to the interior markets from his headquarters at Brohemie. A sense of both Nana's military capacity and the brewing dispute can be found in MacDonald's description of his visit to the lower Benin River:

> On the 20th August, I proceeded in SS 'Whydah'—accompanied by Her Majesty's Ships 'Swallow' and 'Racer'—through the creeks to Benin, at which place we anchored on the evening of the 21st. The meeting here was the largest and most important of any I had held. Nana came in a war canoe, paddled by upwards of a hundred slaves—with four or five similar canoes in attendance, and with a personal escort of twenty men armed with Winchester repeating rifles. All the other chiefs of any note, escorted by large retinues, were also present.
>
> On this occasion, having two of Her Majesty's Ships with me, I requested Captain Finnis to land as large a guard of honour as possible, and one hundred and twenty seamen and marines paraded on shore. This display has, so I have been informed by all the European traders, had a most excellent effect, such a large number of white men never having been seen in the River before.[21]

Comparing him to King Jaja of Opobo, MacDonald wrote of Nana as a difficulty that would have to be dealt with, noting that while some of the European traders spoke of him as honest and upright, others regarded him as just the opposite. MacDonald's own assessment was that Nana was 'a man possessed of great power, and wealth, astute, energetic and intelligent.'[22]

* * *

The vice consul whom MacDonald installed in the Benin River—and thus the official who would be most directly in contact with Chief Nana—was Captain Henry Gallwey of the East Lancashire Regiment, newly seconded for service in the Protectorate.[23] That extending British reach inland was a priority is shown by the fact that Gallwey had not been in post long before he set out to go up the Benin River as far as it would take him. In October 1891, on the orders of Major MacDonald, he spent several days travelling up the main channel of the river to Sapoba and up the branch known to the British as the Ethiope River.

This latter waterway penetrated deep into the area of the Urhobo people (called 'Sobo' by the British), who were among the principal suppliers of palm oil to Chief Nana and other Itsekiri traders. In meetings with local people in the upper reaches of this river, Gallwey made proclamations of 'free trade', demonstrating that his aim was to help British traders outflank Chief Nana in gaining access to these interior markets; significantly, he was accompanied by Munro of the African Association. Moreover, in his despatch reporting on the journey, Gallwey identified Nana's domination of these markets as the cause of a recent lull in trade on the Benin River and defined him as a problem to be rectified:

> The European traders are responsible in the main for the great power possessed by Nana which power has been for many years unlimited, he has been bowed down to by both the white traders and his countrymen and consequently it is not to be expected that affairs will be altered in a few days, but time must and will bring about the necessary changes.[24]

An important aspect of these plans for the future was the establishment of a fixed British presence in the interior, and part of Gallwey's brief for this trip was the identification of suitable sites for a vice consulate and military posts. Accordingly, he proposed Sapele as an excellent location, lying as it did about 60 miles inland from the mouth of the Benin River, at the strategically useful confluence of the main channel and the Ethiope branch:

> The anchorage here is deep and roomy, and the ground high, though one mass of forest. A most suitable spot to establish factories, especially as all the produce from the Sobo markets passes here on the

> way to the Towns near the mouth of the River. I consider Sapele to be a very good place to establish a Vice Consulate, constabulary Barracks, etc.[25]

Further demonstrating the importance attached to this strategy of forward movement, MacDonald himself soon visited the proposed site, reporting to the Foreign Office that, 'I consider that Sapele would be a very good situation for the establishment of a constabulary station'.[26] Not long afterwards, the vessel *Hindustan* was brought from Bristol and turned into a hulk at Sapele, to operate as a floating base while a site was cleared for construction.[27] In due course, a vice consulate would be established, and Sapele became a significant location for the projection of British power and authority into the interior.[28] Given that this inland move brought British forces significantly closer to Benin City than they had ever been stationed before, it has to be seen as a signal threat to the Kingdom of Benin and its continued independence. As will be seen, Gallwey would prove to have an important role in bringing it to an end.

* * *

In early 1892, Captain Gallwey visited Benin City with the express aim of drawing the kingdom formally into the British treaty system that underpinned their claimed protectorate over the region. Mindful of the failure of Consul Annesley just a year before, he was in contact with Oba Ovonramwen by messenger for some time in advance; as Gallwey reported home, the tone of his own correspondence was stern, bordering on arrogance: 'In these messages I endeavoured to make it plain to him what the object of my visit was, and that should I be unsuccessful, I would on no account make a second attempt'.[29]

Having been satisfied with the assurances received from the Court of Benin, Gallwey set out on 21 March, accompanied by his consular agent Hutton, a trader named Swainson, the

Consulate medic Dr Hanley, and about forty carriers with his luggage. Travelling by launch to Gwato, they stayed one night there, then spent most of the next two days marching through the bush to Benin City, which they reached early in the afternoon of 23 March. On arrival, they were taken to a house that the king had provided for them.

Once settled in his lodgings, Gallwey naturally encountered the customary requirement that new visitors to the city wait three days before gaining a royal audience. Although he complained repeatedly, and even at one point threatened to leave, he was evidently able to contain his impatience more successfully than Annesley and was finally ushered into the king's residence on the afternoon of 26 March:

> After a half-hour's wait I was taken up to a curtain, and after a few minutes waiting, the five chief advisors of the King came forward and gave me the King's 'service' in due form—I returned the compliment—and the King sent me his 'service' a second time and said he would be ready to see me as soon as he was dressed. It appears the King was behind this curtain, as he wished to see me before he decided whether to receive me or not! The process of dressing took nearly 2 hours—and I was conducted to the King. He was surrounded by all his chief men and 'boys'—the latter wearing no clothing of any description. There were about 500 people in all.
>
> The King's dress was composed entirely of coral—with a large coral head-piece and he sat on a throne resembling a big drum with a linen cover on it—his right arm supported by a pedestal—and his left arm by an attendant. I first gave him 'service', and told him that I considered he had treated me very badly—and that the 'whiteman' did not understand such customs. He complained of my having hurried him! The rest of the 'palaver' was most satisfactory—the King and chief men being more than anxious to sign the 'Book', as they called it.[30]

A treaty was accordingly signed right away, in that first meeting.[31] As one of the standard pro forma treaties used in the region (pre-printed, with spaces left for the British official to insert the name of the king or chief in question), this document contains the usual clauses deemed by the British to establish a protectorate: the 'gracious favour and protection' of Queen Victoria, extraterritorial legal privileges for British subjects, the right for missionaries to operate in the kingdom, and so on. Amounting to less than three pages of text, the treaty was executed in triplicate by Gallwey and Oba Ovonramwen (who signed with an X, his name being rendered as 'Ovurami') and witnessed by the three other white men present.

Some of the rights claimed by Britain in the treaty text are sweeping, but all clauses are couched in the legalistic language of international diplomacy, in which degrees of euphemism are both subtle and highly important. An objective observer might feel it unlikely that anyone not versed in the niceties of European statecraft could be expected to recognise that this text was intended by the British to signify that they were taking possession of the kingdom. Most crucially, the practical issue of language interpretation adds an extra layer of improbability to this question of full mutual understanding; referring (in his own spelling) to the Akure dialect of Yoruba, Gallwey himself touches on the challenges of interpretation:

> I found the Interpreter that I took up with me was, owing to his fear of the King, useless, but fortunately, my man Ajaie, proved a most efficient interpreter. He fully explained each Articles [*sic*] of the Treaty, as propounded by me, in the Acure tongue (a country bordering on Benin)—this was passed on to the King's chief adviser, who passed it on to the King.[32]

The conversation between Captain Gallwey and Oba Ovonramwen thus involved three languages and four people, providing a great deal of scope for misinterpretation. Additionally, although the treaty is appended with a statement from the *ad hoc* interpreter, Ajaie, certifying that he has clearly transmitted the meaning of the text, he has signed only with an X, demonstrating that he was not an educated person and perhaps therefore not wholly equipped to convey the intricacies of sovereignty and high diplomacy. Furthermore, given the typical desire of royal subjects to make themselves and their words agreeable to the king, the most positive gloss may have been put on the treaty contents, with the emphasis being placed on the amity being proffered rather than the privileges being demanded. It is thus quite possible that Oba Ovonramwen thought he was signing something akin to a treaty of peace and friendship; this might be supported by the fact that Gallwey noted that the king laid great stress on his desire for the avoidance of war.[33]

Having made this expansionary treaty in a somewhat dubious fashion, Gallwey also begins to develop what became the standing British rationale for exerting power over Benin: the practice of human sacrifice and other local religious customs, bundled together by British officials under the catch-all term 'fetish'. In his report of his journey to Benin City (which he calls by the variant name Ubini), Gallwey made a clear call for suppression of such practices, though the fact that this comes at the end of the despatch might suggest something of its place in the hierarchy of priorities:

> At present the whole Benin Country is, and has been for hundreds of years, steeped in Fetish. The Town of Ubini might well be called 'The City of Skulls'. I saw no less than four crucified victims during my few days there in addition to numerous corpses—some mutilated fearfully—which were strewn about in the most public places. The rule appears to be one of Terror, and one can only hope that this Treaty may be the foundation of a new order of things throughout the vast territory ruled over by the King of Benin.[34]

In forwarding Gallwey's report to the Foreign Office, MacDonald also mentions these local religious customs and—most revealingly—links them directly to issues of trade:

> There is no doubt that the Benin Territory is a very rich and most important one. Minerals, Gum Copal, Gum Arabic, Palm Oil, Kernels etc are to be found in large quantities. Trade, commerce and civilisation however are paralized [*sic*] by the form of Fetish Government which unfortunately prevails throughout the Kingdom.[35]

That MacDonald draws such a direct connection between ending human sacrifice and promoting British commerce must colour the way we evaluate the later claims of British officials (and their supporters in the press) to be working for the good of the human race in demanding intervention in the kingdom. The king of Benin was able to control aspects of trade in certain products through the issue of religious proscriptions (labelled by the British as 'juju'), but this amounted to much the same as the Oil Rivers Protectorate collecting duties on imports and exports and regulating the flow of trade in areas it controlled; the difference was in form, not function. Agitation for an end to human sacrifice and other local religious practices therefore has to be seen largely as a cover for promoting Britain's commercial penetration of what it clearly recognised to be an attractive region; the advancement of trade was, of course, a consistent goal of much longer standing. It is also notable that MacDonald goes on to raise the prospect of using violence to deal with the sacrifices reported by Gallwey:

> I hope before long to be able to put a stop to this state of affairs and I look upon the Treaty, so ably effected by Captain Gallwey, as the first step towards carrying out this much to be desired end. I shall be surprised however if these barbarous practises which have been the Custom of the Country for centuries will be abandoned by the Priesthood without severe struggle, and a display, and probable use, of force on the part of the Government of the Oil Rivers Protectorate which however I should only recommend as a last extremity.[36]

Later in the year, Gallwey returned to this theme in his annual report on his district for 1891–92. Advocating the establishment of military posts in Benin territory, he notes that, 'Owing to the fetish rule several very valuable trade products cannot be touched'.[37] Emphasising the link between local customs and the health of commerce, he holds out hope for change:

> Trade is continually being stopped by order of the King; it generally being impossible to ascertain the why and the wherefore thereof ... The King struck me as being very ready to listen to reason—but he is tied down by fetish customs, and, until the power of the fetish priests is done away with, the trade of the Benin country will continue to be a very doubtful source of profit to any great extent.[38]

Noting that the 'breaking down of this fetish theocracy' would take time, Gallwey—ominously for the future of the Kingdom of Benin—suggested that a 'punitory expedition' might eventually prove necessary.[39] By the beginning of 1893, Major MacDonald had become convinced about the need for violence in the future; when sending Gallwey's annual report to the Foreign Office, rather than speaking of the use of force against Benin as a possibility, he now declared it to be a certain requirement:

> Captain Gallwey's report leaves little for me to add. I am of opinion that there are very great possibilities for this district. Time, and much patience will be required however, before the resources of the district can be even in a measure developed. The great stumbling block to any immediate advance being the fetish 'reign of terror' which exists throughout the kingdom of Benin, and which will require severe measures in the not very distant future, before it can be stopped.[40]

Before MacDonald would be able to extend British rule and commerce into the Kingdom of Benin, however, he found that he had to deal with rival centres of power much closer to the coast. Even above the king of Benin, Gallwey had listed Chief Nana as the principal obstacle to the expansion of trade,[41] and in the Delta rivers there were several other political entities as yet insufficiently cowed. These had to be more fully assimilated into the Protectorate system before British rule could be taken inland.

6

'IN THE END YOU WILL ALL BE DESTROYED'

ENFORCING BRITISH RULE IN THE NIGER DELTA

Should the troops be fired upon or any resistance offered you will at once burn the town down.

Major Sir Claude MacDonald, 20 November 1894

I think the general punishment has probably been ample. We now hear for the first time that hundreds have been killed.

Sir Clement Hill, Foreign Office file note, 10 April 1895

The extension of British imperial rule over the Niger Delta in the 1890s provoked numerous episodes of resistance and reaction, varying in scale according to the size and capacities of the local political entities in question. Ostensibly, the process of expansion happened primarily through the system of treaties which Britain claimed as the basis of its protectorate, but the frequent outbreaks of opposition show this to be a polite fiction: it rested on a foundation of violence, both structural and specific.

From the earliest days of the formalised Oil Rivers Protectorate, MacDonald had been concerned to build the military capacity of his new administration. Significantly, on his arrival in the Delta in July 1891, he was accompanied by Ralph Moor, who had taken charge of creating an armed force and had recently been recruiting in Lagos. Moor would remain as MacDonald's principal aide, and when MacDonald departed for six months of leave in the autumn of 1892, having just been knighted after one year of service in Old Calabar,[1] it was Moor who was appointed as acting consul general. Notably, MacDonald had also appointed several military officers as vice consuls, some of whom were previously known to him professionally, including Captain Robert Synge of the Highland Light Infantry, who had served under MacDonald in the 1882 invasion of Egypt.[2]

The force created by Moor was initially known as the Oil Rivers Irregulars, and he took the title of commandant. In August 1892, he reported that they numbered 165 (including the two white officers) and that arrangements were being made for further recruitment to bring the total complement to 315.[3] The direct connection that Moor made between the size of this force and plans for penetration of the interior is very clear:

> This number will in my opinion be sufficient for present requirements but with increasing trade and the opening up of the country it will no doubt require raising to 500 before very long.[4]

The force was armed with seven 3-barrel Nordenfelt machine guns (with mountings for use on river boats) as well as a 6-pdr artillery gun; Moor expressed a desire to upgrade the rifles from Sniders to Martini Carbines, and to purchase a Maxim gun. In sending his report to the Foreign Office, MacDonald declared that 'very great credit is due to Mr Moor for the energy, tact & zeal he has displayed' in organising the Oil Rivers Irregulars, and that he personally regarded them as 'very excellent fighting material'.[5]

As has already been discussed in earlier chapters, the backing of Royal Navy gunboats was an essential tool for exerting power over the Niger Delta, even if the development of the Protectorate's own armed force made it less necessary. When his period of leave was coming to an end in the spring of 1893, MacDonald wrote from London to request that two gunboats meet him on his arrival back in Bonny in June. Referring to the previous deployment of two Royal Navy vessels to accompany his formal arrival in the territory in August 1891, he was definite about their value to him:

> The presence of these Gunboats was of the very greatest use to me in dealing with the many semi-barbarous tribes with whom I had and have to negotiate, and though the necessity for the presence of any ships of War has almost disappeared, yet I do not hesitate to say that their presence on this occasion will be of the greatest use to me, and contribute very largely to the future peace and quietness of the Protectorate.[6]

We should not let the polite and euphemistic language used by MacDonald obscure the salient fact that he is describing the employment of structural violence in order to terrify local people into submission. Very often, the mere presence of such a war machine would be sufficient to achieve this aim, but sometimes a practical demonstration of their killing capacity was made; writing to the foreign secretary earlier in 1893, MacDonald recalled the reaction of King Abiakari of Ikot Ana as evidence for the effectiveness of displays of naval firepower:

> Abiakari for some years after the visit of HMS 'Alecto' kept quiet, the practise made by this vessel's guns at a target having had a very beneficial effect on him.[7]

Such displays of destructive power typically spoke for themselves, but Consul Annesley—not being much of a diplomat by nature—even once clearly spelt out the threat in a letter to the Chiefs of Opobo, thereby accidentally supplying further evidence of the methods of imperial rule:

> It is not the desire of H.M. Government to harass or trouble anybody without cause and if you continue living in the quiet, orderly

> manner you have done of late, you need have no fear that your town will be shelled.[8]

When back in the Protectorate (now renamed as the Niger Coast Protectorate)[9] after his six months of leave, MacDonald once again reviewed the armed force; with Moor having been promoted to vice consul,[10] the unit was by the summer of 1893 under the command of Captain Price and had grown to 350 soldiers with four English officers.[11] MacDonald reported proudly home that, 'I have no hesitation in saying that this little Force would compare most favourably for drill and discipline with any Native troops either in India or Africa'.[12]

This means of oppression was—in order to maximise its utility—stationed around the Protectorate, with a complement of troops in each vice consulate. Additionally, by August 1893, new vice consular posts had been established in the interior at Degama and Akwete, as well as the post at Sapele already mentioned.[13] This was a clear practical demonstration of intent respecting the policy of forward movement, about which MacDonald and other officials had repeatedly written.

At the same time as these structures of imperial rule were being developed around the Protectorate in 1893, the first serious signs of trouble began to emerge in Brass. As the part of the Protectorate lying nearest to the stations of the Royal Niger Company on the coastal stretch of the main channel of the River Niger, Brass, with its riverine economic system, was especially impacted by the ruthless competition and monopolistic practices favoured by George Goldie. Having taken the role of government over parts of the interior in which Brass traders had long operated, the Company had an obvious competitive advantage. So evident was the resulting problem that MacDonald even expressed a rare measure of sympathy for the local people; writing of Brass in January 1893, he recognised that they were experiencing a genuine injury:

> This district which was at one time one of the most flourishing of the Niger Delta has now, owing to the prohibitive duties imposed by the Niger Company, become the least important from a trade point of view ... The native Chiefs have a grievance against Her Majesty's Government who they allege have allowed the Niger Company to shut them out from the oil markets at which they have traded ever since the abolition of the export slave trade.[14]

Moreover, MacDonald anticipated problems ahead, noting that 'disturbances may always be expected in this district'.[15] His humanitarian concern had limits, though, and by July 1893, he was labelling Fishtown in Brass 'a nest of pirates'[16] after some canoes were seized and other acts of violence reported. Being dissatisfied with the communication he received from King Koko of the Nembe people (the principal local ruler in the Brass River region), MacDonald quashed any inclination to rebellion by hurriedly dispatching to Brass two Royal Navy gunboats (which landed a party of seamen and marines), as well as 200 Protectorate soldiers from Old Calabar. Under this threat of force, the people of Fishtown remained quiet, though this episode was merely a precursor to a more severe outbreak in the future. Before Brass would burst into open revolt, however, Chief Nana Olumo of the Itsekiri became the rival power requiring the most urgent attention.

* * *

The Itsekiri kingdom had grown to prominence on the Forcados River and had expanded its control of trade into the nearby lower Benin River from the early years of the century, because of a sand bar which restricted the entry of larger vessels into its home river. Its capital city, however, remained at Ode-Itsekiri on the Forcados, significantly disadvantaging the king due to his obligation to remain there, while the valuable palm oil trade increasingly fell into the hands of other chiefs. The consequence of this was that, from 1848, the Itsekiri went through a lengthy interregnum, with no member of the royal family being sufficiently wealthy to become king.[17]

In these circumstances, the office of 'governor' of the Benin River had become all the more important. This was a semi-official post dating from the Portuguese period, in which a leading Itsekiri trader was appointed as the principal contact for European traders in the river, and as mediator for disputes between traders who sold to the foreign buyers. Having succeeded Portugal as the dominant European power in the region, Britain had formally anointed the governor in recent decades, including through the award of a staff of office. Conventionally, the post alternated between the royal family and the Olumo family, but when his father died in the role in 1883, Nana succeeded him, a recognition of the realities of his great wealth and trading capacity.[18]

This was the source of the long rivalry between Nana and Chief Dogho Numa (known to the British as 'Dore'), a member of the royal family who expected the position for himself. Chief Nana and his followers were based in Brohemie, which lay hidden on a creek off the main channel, around 10 miles from the sea, while Dogho and his people lived on the other side of the Benin River, a few miles downstream at Batere. Significantly, this settlement lay opposite the British Vice Consulate at New Benin, and Chief Dogho would soon become a prominent ally of the British, a collaborator in the technical sense;[19] as early as 1892, he was hailed by Captain Gallwey as 'a very loyal supporter of Her Majesty's Government'.[20] He would play an important role in bringing down both Chief Nana and the king of Benin.

The first of these episodes came to a head in the summer of 1894. In May, Ralph Moor once again took over as acting consul general while MacDonald went on leave,[21] and in June he visited the lower Benin River to investigate reports of 'the unsettled state of the district'.[22] Finding that trade had been interrupted by disputes in the Urhobo areas of the interior, Moor ordered Chief Nana to withdraw entirely from the Ethiope River—a key source of palm oil—giving him fourteen days to carry this out.[23] During this interval, an experienced British trader named Coxon, agent for the firm of James Pinnock in the lower Benin River, wrote to complain that Nana was 'going the wrong road with the powers that be'.[24] In a highly emotional letter, Coxon insisted that Chief Nana had insulted both Sir Claude and Ralph Moor and that he was dismissive of British pretensions to rule:

> The real fact is, he thinks he is all powerful, and asserts if anyone wants to catch him in Brohemie it will be through Blood, up to the waist! I think the egregious ass will find out shortly what Englishmen are made of, anyhow hence Order No 36 prohibiting the Sale of Arms & Ammunition ... He is a d___d rascal!!! I shant [*sic*] be sorry when his power is completely broken. We will have a much better Trade and more profitable too.[25]

It was in this charged atmosphere that Moor returned to the Benin River on 9 July, bringing with him a reinforcement of soldiers from the Niger Coast Protectorate Force (NCPF) to add to the fifty men already stationed in the district. Discovering that Chief Nana had ignored his orders, Moor gave instructions that the Ethiope River be closed to him, establishing a blockade on the river and seizing any of Nana's canoes that attempted to pass to or from the interior markets.

As the situation continued to worsen, Moor called a meeting of all the Benin River chiefs for 2 August, bringing yet more soldiers from Brass to strengthen his hand. Mindful of the deception through which Consul Johnston had seized and deported King Jaja in 1887, Nana wrote to decline attendance at the meeting, which went ahead without him. Seeking to marginalise Chief Nana, Moor signed a new treaty with all the other Itsekiri chiefs who were present and further declared that neither

Nana nor any of his people were allowed to use any waterway in the district. Should they attempt to do so, all canoes and cargo would be seized, and failure to comply would be met with force.

From this point, the situation deteriorated swiftly; far from submitting to these imperial decrees, Nana was preparing for resistance. Moor's report to the Foreign Office (in which he uses a variant spelling 'Nanna') is here quoted at length as a vivid illustration of the rapid slide into open war between the British Empire and Chief Nana:

> Learning that, in opposition to the orders of the Government, that all the waterways of the district were to be free, a strong barrier had been erected at the mouth of the creek leading to Brohemie Town where Nanna resides I ordered it to be at once removed informing him that neglect of this order might entail serious consequences. On 3rd instant finding that this barrier had not been removed, but appeared to have been further strengthened I requested Lieutenant Commander Heugh of H.M.S. Alecto to blow it up with mines and it will give some idea of the nature of the obstruction when it took ten mines with fifteen charges to remove it.
>
> During this operation four or more shots were fired by Chief Nanna's people at the party engaged on the work and these were replied to by about half a dozen shots and I requested that two rockets might be discharged in the direction of the Town, which lies about a mile and a half back from the river, to deter them from any further interference. After this there was no further sign of active hostility but of course this act materially changes the aspect of affairs, and I have given directions that the blockade of Brohemie Town be most rigidly carried out, nothing being allowed to enter or leave it.
>
> As they grow nothing in or around the Town itself but are dependent for supplies from up river I am in hopes that this course, if, with the forces at command, it can be effectively carried out may eventually bring about submission to the orders of the Government—should it not do so more active steps must be adopted.[26]

The clear intent of this strategy was to starve Nana and the people of Brohemie into capitulation, much as had been done at Opobo in 1889. As in that grisly episode, civilian casualties would be an inevitable result, no doubt weighted largely towards women and children. Moor made arrangements for this blockade of Brohemie and then departed for duties elsewhere in the Protectorate, leaving Lieutenant Commander Heugh of HMS *Alecto* in charge of the operation.

After an abortive attempt by the Royal Navy to test the defences of the town on 25 August (resulting in several casualties), Moor was back outside Brohemie to launch a full attack on 29 August. The combined strength of the NCPF soldiers and Royal Navy bluejackets amounted to over 350 men plus officers, as well as 120 labourers for cutting bush and making roads. They were armed with two Maxim guns, two 7-pdr artillery guns and a rocket tube, with supporting fire from two Royal Navy vessels, the *Alecto* and HMS *Phoebe*. That Chief Nana was able to fend off an assault by this sizeable and professional force says a great deal about his military capacity and the defensive preparations made in Brohemie, which included multiple 8ft stockades made of hardwood logs with artillery emplacements and shelters for the gunners. In the face of these defence works and the difficult, swampy ground riddled with creeks which surrounded Brohemie, the British assault petered out in the afternoon, and a retreat was made. Both of the 7-pdr guns were abandoned in the field.

By the time that this attack was reported home, Moor had put a brave face on the embarrassment and relabelled it as a reconnaissance in force, suggesting that it had successfully demonstrated that Brohemie could not be readily captured:

> The conclusion arrived at from this reconnoitring in force being, that it is at present impossible to take the town by advancing up the creek or through the bush without severe loss of life. It has been determined to shell, blockade, and invest the town, to either force a

> surrender or drive Nanna and his people out of it ... active operations are being carried on in shelling the town, and four armed steam-launches are patrolling to render the blockade effective.[27]

It should be noted that shelling and blockading a civilian population unquestionably meets the criteria for a war crime under Principle VI(b) of the United Nations' Nuremberg Principles. Untroubled by these ethical issues in 1894, Moor expanded his efforts to bombard and starve Brohemie, requesting reinforcements: 'To force surrender quickly by these means the service of two more gunboats required. Captain Powell is cabling Admiralty & Admiral at Cape.'[28]

Two additional vessels—HMS *Philomel* and HMS *Widgeon*—duly arrived, and vigorous shelling of the town continued. By 20 September, it appeared that Nana might be too well dug in, and Moor thus attempted a final diplomatic overture:

> On the 20th ultimo it was deemed advisable to give Chief Nanna a final opportunity to surrender, and I therefore sent messengers into Brohemie Town with letter calling on him to do so. His answer was a verbal one, conveying a distinct refusal, and he cautioned the messengers when leaving not to come again.[29]

The precise text of this verbal answer has sadly gone unrecorded. With this refusal, the British had to find another way to overcome resistance; finally, two days were spent by a large force in cutting a new track through the mangrove swamp to the rear of the town, out of range of the worst of the gunfire from its defenders. This new access route allowed a flanking attack to be mounted, and at dawn on 25 September, the entire force was committed. With Nana's artillery batteries outflanked, their position was untenable, and the defence collapsed. Brohemie was in British hands by nine o'clock that morning, but Chief Nana escaped into the bush. Moor himself entered the town and later reported on the destruction caused by the British bombardment:

> With regard to the condition of the town, it was found that almost the entire portion on the left bank of creek, the side on which we advanced, had been burnt by the shell-fire, and on the right bank nearly all the thatched houses had also been similarly destroyed.[30]

Nowhere does Moor record Itsekiri deaths, whether civilian or combatant; no British casualties were sustained in the final attack, though a Chief Petty Officer Crouch of HMS *Alecto* was injured in the head by a rocket which misfired as it left its tube. On the following day, British forces marched out to Eddu, in the interior behind Brohemie, where another artillery battery was discovered: 'The guns, which were loaded, were destroyed by gun-cotton, and the town, consisting of about sixty or seventy thatched houses, destroyed'.[31] This was the final action in the violent deposition of Chief Nana, and in his despatch home, Moor dedicated significant space to arguing for a campaign medal to be awarded.

Chief Nana himself spent some weeks on the run with a handful of his men, before finally surrendering in the Colony of Lagos at the beginning of November.[32] Displaying his characteristic wit, Nana demanded sanctuary as a subject of Lagos, relying on the fact that the Colony had once claimed all the territory up to the right bank of the Benin River, arguing that he was therefore outside the jurisdiction of the Niger Coast Protectorate. This caused MacDonald, who happened to be passing through Lagos on his return from leave, to urge the formal settlement of these outstanding boundary issues,[33] but he also reported that Nana had abandoned his sanctuary gambit and would travel to Old Calabar with him.[34] In December, MacDonald tried Chief Nana in his consular court, sentencing him to deportation for life (though in the event he returned from exile in 1906).[35]

* * *

While the dispute with Chief Nana was deteriorating into open conflict in the summer of 1894, Sir Claude MacDonald was in

London, using his period of leave to write up a lengthy report on the progress of the Niger Coast Protectorate. Setting out the history of British involvement in the Oil Rivers, he readily availed himself of the colonial lexicon to praise his predecessors: 'The Consuls in the past have done noble service in endeavouring with inadequate means, in a most unhealthy climate, to carry on the work of civilization'.[36] Writing in similar terms about his own staff and their supposed mission, MacDonald summarised the development of his administration in some detail, evidently being concerned to demonstrate the work undertaken to push the British presence inland:

> It will be seen that a firm administrative base has been established along the coastline, and that an advance has been made from thence into the interior at four points ... At Degama and Sapele important military, as well as administrative, stations have been established. These stations will form the centres of civilizing power and authority, and as time goes on further stations will be established in the interior until the whole territory is brought under a settled rule and Government, and slave-raiding, inter-tribal wars, as well as the barbaric cruelties I have already mentioned, are definitely abolished.[37]

It is also noteworthy that MacDonald records that the NCPF, by this time under the command of Captain Alan Boisragon of the Royal Irish Regiment, had been expanded to 450 soldiers, with improved armaments.

As he had promised in his report, on his return to Old Calabar in November 1894, MacDonald swiftly put this additional military capacity to use; now that Chief Nana had been deposed in Benin District, MacDonald could take the opportunity of asserting British claims to rule in Opobo District. Having received intelligence that funerary sacrifices were anticipated at a town in the interior named Ohumbele, MacDonald immediately sent Captain Boisragon with a detachment of 100 men and two other officers for a theatrical display of power:

> The greatest secrecy must be observed so as if possible to take the people of Ohumbele by surprise in which case the show of force will most probably be sufficient to bring about the desired result—viz. a stoppage of the practice of human sacrifice, and the proper establishment of Government authority in the Ohumbele District.
>
> Should the troops be fired upon or any resistance offered you will at once burn the town down and if possible make the king prisoner. Under any circumstances it would be advisable to bring the king as prisoner to this Vice Consulate.[38]

Once again illustrating the performative aspect of structural violence in an imperial setting, the show of force was effective. Roger Casement, the Surveying Department official then serving as acting vice consul in Opobo (and an Irish nationalist later hanged for treason in 1916), reported to MacDonald on the success of the deployment in Ohumbele:

> All has gone well, and the parade of the troops under Captain Boisragon in the town at a meeting held yesterday and again today has produced a visibly salutary effect. The demeanour of the natives has been all that could be desired—they have amply apologised for their past disregard of Government authority, offering to pay any fine I might inflict.[39]

Casement also reported that he planned to retain Captain Boisragon and his detachment in the district for some time in order to march them further inland to Akwete for a similar demonstration of the coercive capacity of the Niger Coast administration.

* * *

It was shortly after the show of force at Ohumbele that the simmering discontent at Brass burst into open rebellion. Having lobbied for years against the seizure of their livelihoods by the Royal Niger Company, by the beginning of 1895 the kings and chiefs of the Brass River had finally had enough. In a remarkably sizeable and carefully planned action at the end of January, they launched an assault on the principal Company station at the mouth of the Nun River; on 2 February, MacDonald telegraphed home: 'Akassa reported destroyed by Natives'.[40] Having noted the unfair treatment of Brass traders as early as his commissioner's report of January 1890,[41] MacDonald was highly aware of their grievances, and throughout the 1895 incident his communications feature a thread of sympathy for the local people. Significantly, within a few days of the destruction of Akassa, he telegraphed home to explain the uprising: 'Reasons for attack deprivation of markets causing great distress and starvation.'[42]

Although the word 'starvation' went unremarked in the Foreign Office files, certainly not prompting investigation or emergency action, we should pause to reflect on its use. This was a very senior official of the British Empire—a consul general and knight of the realm, no less—reporting that people over whom Britain claimed to rule were suffering from deprivation so bad as to cause starvation, because of the commercial sanctions imposed by a British company, backed up by military force both private and imperial. MacDonald was a loyal, indeed aggressive, servant of the Empire, and he would have every reason to depict it in the best possible light; we can be sure that he would not dabble in hyperbole when it came to British wrongdoing. His use of the word 'starvation' thus has to be regarded as an authoritative description of the condition of the people of the Brass River at the time; that we know very little of the detail of their suffering is another result of the epistemological asymmetry resulting from a bureaucratic empire confronting a largely pre-literate polity.

Around 1,500 men from several tribes in the Brass River region, though mainly coming from the dominant Nembe people,[43] took part in the attack on the Akassa station, attesting to the fact that the revolt against the Royal Niger Company was a popular cause.[44] Looking back at a later date, MacDonald even characterised it as 'a national movement',[45] making it one of the earliest episodes of proto-nationalist anticolonial resistance. Seriously concerned at the time about this character of the revolt, following his arrival in Brass on 2 February with fifty NCPF soldiers, MacDonald then hurried off to gather reinforcements, returning to Brass on 12 February. On the following day, he wrote to the kings and chiefs of Brass, urging them to make peace by surrendering their arms. His tone suggests an awareness of the imperial hypocrisy involved in promising destruction to those who had already been badly treated by British commercial interests:

> I implore you, as your friend, to think what you are doing; you know it is impossible to fight against the Queen. It may be a matter of weeks, months, or years, but in the end you will all be destroyed.[46]

Even though the local leaders insisted repeatedly that they had no quarrel with the British government but only with the Royal Niger Company, Royal Navy vessels and further reinforcements of the NCPF continued to gather in the Brass River over the next few days.[47] While MacDonald tried to secure a peaceful surrender, orders came from London for a punitive expedition against the town of Nembe—the capital of the Nembe people and the headquarters of King Koko—which lay some way up the Brass River. At MacDonald's urging, the Foreign Office gave permission for final terms to be offered, comprising the restoration of plunder from Akassa, payment of fines and the surrender of all arms and war canoes.[48] Four days later, MacDonald telegraphed a reply in the negative: 'Brass Chiefs have refused conditions contained in your telegram No 9. Combined attack on Brass towns takes place Wednesday.'[49]

The next communication from Major MacDonald gives a short but vivid description of imperial violence in action. Reporting on the attack on Nembe (generally spelt 'Nimbe' by the British at the time) and the neighbouring town of Bassambri, he illustrates both the profound inequality in military force and the willingness of Empire officials to adopt brutal measures of collective punishment:

> No 17. My Telegram No 16. Advanced Wednesday, same evening seized Sacrifice Island after destroying powerful obstruction in creek. From Sacrifice Island sent ultimatum, terms refused. Natives turned out in war canoes, opened fire, fire returned, three canoes sank, no casualties our side. Friday dawn Navy Marines Protectorate troops advanced through creek, after a sharp fight lasting till afternoon Nimbe entirely destroyed, Bassambri severely shelled. Regret to report Lieutenant Taylor Navy two men killed five wounded. Ultimatum has been sent Fishtown & Twon [*sic*]. If refused towns will be burnt tomorrow.[50]

Two days later, MacDonald cabled to report that Fishtown had also been shelled and burnt, urging that 'punishment for Akassa outrage now sufficient'.[51] In the wreckage of the town of Nembe and other towns, over thirty cannon had been found; the number of Brass dead went unrecorded but must have been significant given the scale of destruction. It should be noted that this violence was inflicted on the local people even despite MacDonald himself admitting that the Nembe people had 'thundering good reasons' for their act of resistance.[52] Even this punishment, however, was insufficient for London, who insisted that the Brass peoples surrender their personal firearms; in a private letter to Sir Clement Hill, MacDonald expressed the challenge this represented in somewhat jocular terms:

> P.S.—Just got the Foreign Office telegram saying that I must make the Brassmen disgorge their rifles—more joy! I start to-morrow with that intention; how it will all 'pan out' will be hard to say; a native of this part of the world would sooner part—a great deal sooner—with the wife of his buzzum than with his 'bundork'. Consequently the burden that you have put upon me is greater than some of you wot of.[53] [*sic passim*]

While MacDonald pursued talks with the Brass leadership, he continued to urge London to accept the Nembe surrender without insisting that they give up their remaining weapons; additionally he argued that an enquiry into the grievances against the Royal Niger Company should be promised. When the Foreign Office suggested making the holding of an enquiry conditional on the surrender of rifles[54] and then raised the prospect of further military operations against the Nembe,[55] MacDonald responded in extraordinary terms; in a telegram containing most unusual language for a senior official, he sounds like someone who has reached the limits of his patience:

> No 26. Your telegram No 15—Brass people thoroughly understand that reparation has been and is being made for past offences; canoes, cannon, prisoners, and plunder surrendered; those chiefs who committed atrocities, fined; trade almost ruined; towns destroyed; hundreds killed; women and children starving in bush; smallpox rife; rainy season commencing. I have visited towns destroyed, and seen all this. In name of humanity, strongly deprecate further punishment, and request settlement of question. Senior Naval Officer entirely concurs.[56]

Even in the face of such emotive language from one of their own, the response of the Foreign Office was laconic: 'I think the general punishment has probably been ample. We now hear for the first time that hundreds have been killed'.[57] Though apparently unruffled by this report of mass civilian casualties, the British government did at least agree to regard the crisis as settled, and in due course Sir John Kirk was appointed to investigate complaints against the Royal Niger Company. His report of March 1896 effectively led to both the deposition of King Koko[58] and the winding up of the royal charter of the Company (though not the corporation itself) in 1899. The uprising at Brass thus had significant consequences for the structures of rule in the

Niger Delta region, allowing the British to further reshape the political landscape to their own designs.

* * *

With Chief Nana deposed and the Nembe people of Brass brutally subdued, the British had, by the summer of 1895, largely completed their work of bringing the coastal regions of the Niger Delta firmly into the imperial system. In the territory claimed by the Niger Coast Protectorate, there remained only one significant alternative centre of power: the Kingdom of Benin. Although Captain Gallwey had returned with a treaty in 1892, Benin remained inadequately assimilated into British administrative and—most importantly—economic structures, and the logic of empire required that this anomaly be dealt with. With littoral dominance secured, the Kingdom of Benin was to be the next target.

In September 1895, Ralph Moor, who was once again standing in for MacDonald as acting consul general, reported on a failed attempt by Vice Consul Crawford to visit Benin City in the previous month. Employing the familiar colonial lexicon, Moor makes clear the priorities that lay behind the effort:

> The object of the expedition was to open up that country for trade, which is now practically at a standstill in that portion of the Benin district, though flourishing most satisfactorily in other parts, and further to proceed beyond the territories of the King of Benin to explore and open up the country ...
>
> From all information available the country is thickly populated and highly productive, but the tyranny and oppression of its rulers prevent any civilising influences extending into it, and render life and property so insecure as to prevent nearly all trade.[59]

On 6 August, Vice Consul Crawford had gone up the creek to Gilli Gilli in the steam yacht *Daisy*, accompanied by a detachment of the NCPF from Sapele, comprising Captain Maling, thirty men and a Maxim gun.[60] At Gilli Gilli, they were met by a messenger from Oba Ovonramwen, who said that the king was most anxious about the approach of the expedition, fearing deposition in the manner of Chief Nana, and that he therefore refused a meeting. Over several days, numerous messages were exchanged with the king, but even after Crawford sent away the bulk of the NCPF force with the Maxim, his suspicions were not allayed, and he would not grant permission to visit him. Finally, the local carriers refused to travel to Benin City out of fear of the king, and then disappeared overnight. Crawford had no option but to get back into the *Daisy* and depart; he did, however, take the opportunity of gathering some military intelligence:

> Notes have been made as to Gwato town, its approaches and capabilities for the housing of troops in case of any future trouble; the same has been done with respect to [Gilli Gilli], about three-quarters of a mile from Gwato on the same bank ... Captain Maling has taken a rough sketch plan of Gwato Town and its approaches.[61]

In response to this failed mission by Crawford, Moor was quick to suggest the use of force to integrate the Kingdom of Benin more properly into the British sphere:

> I respectfully submit that on the first opportunity steps should be taken for opening up this country, if necessary, by force ... I am sure that any expenditure incurred would be fully compensated by the large increase that would result in the sale of British manufactured goods in the country opened up.[62]

Suggesting the months of January to March as climatically the best time of year for military purposes (thus avoiding the rainy season), Moor advocated mounting an expedition within a few months, demonstrating the typical impatience of an ambitious imperial servant. His expansionary aims were shown in a rather more informal fashion in a private letter to Sir Claude MacDonald in October; referring to Soapey Sponge, the notorious freeloader from R. S. Surtees' novels who was known for outstaying his welcome on country house visits, Moor made it clear that he was seeking to engineer a permanent advance into Benin:

> At Warri, Crawford is pegging in and informs me the King of Benin has sent messages to Chief Dore to make amends for his late disgraceful conduct—I have sent Crawford careful instructions how to carry on in the matter with a view to obtaining an invitation from the King to visit his country. Should we succeed in getting an invite, will take full advantage of it and act like Soapy [*sic*] Sponge—Once we get in he'll find it hard to get rid of us again.[63]

MacDonald, however, suggested to the Foreign Office that more time should be devoted to obtaining a peaceful integration of the Kingdom of Benin into the Niger Coast Protectorate. Notably, by putting off military intervention for one year, this advice effectively determined the timing of the end of the independent Kingdom of Benin:

> With regard to the steps that Mr Moor suggests should be taken to open up the Benin country, I am of opinion that this dry season, December to March, should be utilized in patient and persistent efforts to open up communication with the King and his people and to ascertain if any means, short of force, could bring about a peaceable solution of affairs; if this is found to be impossible an expedition, similar to the one sent by the Colony of Lagos against the King of Jebu, should be organised ... Failing all peaceable means of arriving at a solution an expedition of this kind should be sent in the dry season of 1896–97.[64]

XVII2

7

'THERE WOULDN'T BE A SINGLE SHOT FIRED'

CONSUL PHILLIPS GETS HIMSELF KILLED

> *I am certain that there is only one remedy, that is to depose the King of Benin from his Stool … I therefore ask His Lordship's permission to visit Benin City in February next, to depose and remove the King of Benin.*
>
> Acting Consul General Phillips to Foreign Office, 16 November 1896

> *King's message to Consul-General—That he is making his 'father', and cannot possibly see us under a month, and on no account to go to him. Dore says it will be certain death to go. Consul-General says he will go.*
>
> Diary of District Commissioner Burrows, 2 January 1897

At the beginning of 1896, Major Sir Claude MacDonald was appointed as HM Minister to China and Korea;[1] he would later go on to become the first British ambassador to Japan. Although he is better known for this Asian chapter of his career, his legacy in West Africa is significant: under MacDonald, the haphazard informal British rule over the Niger Delta had been transformed into a properly organised, aggressive imperial administration, and the coastal regions were largely subdued. In establishing the Niger Coast Protectorate, he thus became one of the key figures in the creation of what is now Nigeria, though it was left to his successor to extend British rule deep into the interior.

After deputising for MacDonald over several years, Ralph Moor was the obvious candidate for promotion, and he duly took over as consul general in February.[2] Having always shown a marked appetite for interior penetration in his previous despatches, Moor now had a free hand and wasted no time; in the same month, he sent Vice Consul Crawford to investigate the construction of a road between Warri and Sapele[3] and began making extensive plans for moving inland. London was also exerting pressure for forward movement; in March, the Foreign Office informed Moor that the Marquis of Salisbury had directed that:

> attention should now be paid to further development of trade with the interior, which will best be effected by gaining the confidence of the natives. His Lordship would be glad to learn what steps are being taken in this direction.[4]

In response, Moor furnished a detailed account of his proposed strategies for expanding inland. He planned to send 'small expeditions of a peaceable nature in all directions' to meet with local people and gather information on the available economic products and undeveloped resources.[5] Surveys would be taken for roads into the interior, and ultimately a reliable map made. Waterways would continue to be patrolled by Protectorate forces, and prompt police action would be taken where necessary to suppress those who lived by 'land piracy'.[6] He proposed to establish 'permanent posts further in the interior from time to time to act as bases for further development'[7] and to secure the planned road routes. Moor therefore had extensive pacific ideas for forward movement, but he was clearly not going to rely upon them alone: 'In the event of the foregoing peaceable means proving of no avail it then becomes necessary to resort to force in specific cases'.[8]

As the principal unconquered polity in the area claimed by the Niger Coast Protectorate, the Kingdom of Benin was of course one of these 'specific cases'. Setting out a catalogue of complaints about the 'attitude' of the king of Benin and his control of trade, Moor also linked the lack of British access to the territory to the 'evil practices' of local custom.[9] Notably, he followed MacDonald's recommendation of October 1895 in proposing the use of military force to remove the king in the coming dry season of 1896–97:

> I consider that if the efforts now being made continue unsuccessful until next dry season an expeditionary force should be sent about January or February to remove the King and his JuJu men for the sufferings of the people under their rule are terrible. This would of course necessitate the establishment of a post in that country which would serve as a good base for further development.[10]

At the Foreign Office in London, Sir Clement Hill welcomed Moor's summary as 'a record of work pointing in the right direction'.[11] Moreover, while agreeing broadly with Moor's sentiments regarding Oba Ovonramwen of Benin, he emphasised the need for patience and for choosing the right time:

> The great thing is that our men should keep their heads & not burst into 'punitive expeditions' on every pretext. The King of Benin may have to be dealt with but it should be set about with care & with a sufficient force, & at our own time.[12]

This suggests that Hill was very alive to the tendency of imperial officials on the ground to interpret their instructions in the most expansive way possible, and sometimes to let their ambitions run ahead of good sense. The profound irony here is that at the time when Hill wrote this note, the Foreign Office had just appointed as deputy commissioner & consul for the Niger Coast Protectorate the very man who would wildly exceed his instructions and cause a crisis over Benin: James R. Phillips.

* * *

Given that Phillips played—as we shall see—the central role in precipitating the fiasco that led directly to the end of the Kingdom of Benin, it is worth considering the man, his background and his capacities.

James Robert Phillips was born on 11 September 1863 in Carlisle,[13] where his father was archdeacon at the local Church of England diocese. He attended Uppingham School, joining the lower school in 1876 and the upper school in 1878.[14] Leaving Uppingham in July 1882, he matriculated at Trinity College, Cambridge in October of the same year and completed his BA degree in 1885. Following a few years as a solicitor in Carlisle, Phillips sought a new career in colonial service, and in 1891 he was appointed as sheriff and overseer of prisons in the Gold Coast. In June 1896, while home on leave in Barrow-in-Furness, he was appointed as deputy commissioner and consul of the Niger Coast Protectorate.[15] This new role was intended to streamline the administration of the Protectorate by providing a deputy who stood ready to take over for the consul general during his temporary absences or periods of leave.

These bare facts tell us that Phillips had a background of some privilege, including boarding school, Cambridge University and a family of significant social standing. The archives further reveal something of his character and intellectual merit. After his death in Africa (which we will come to shortly), the Uppingham School magazine took the rare step of immediately publishing an obituary, given the newsworthy nature of his demise. Naturally striving to be as positive as possible about an Old Uppinghamian who had just died on the imperial frontline, this biography is quite startling for its revealingly slight praise:

> He was not head and shoulders above the rest of us in anything, except, perhaps, that priceless thing which we called 'keenness'. He was not a first rank scholar ... He was not a first rank athlete ... He never wrote anything brilliant for this magazine.[16]

Celebrating Phillips for reading his Bible regularly and for the 'genial indignation' with which he 'hunted out evil', the unnamed obituary writer seems unable to find anything positive to say about his intelligence. His highest available praise is that Phillips was 'a sportsman'. Moreover, an edition of the same school magazine later in 1897 carried an article that was similarly damning through faint praise:

> There was nothing so remarkable about him as a young man at school or college, or at Carlisle, to make him eminently noticeable ... except that he was a high-spirited young man, full of life and energy, he probably did not impress his contemporaries.'[17]

This same writer records that Phillips was brusque in manner but possessed 'transparent honesty' and was 'a man of conspicuous sincerity of purpose'. The overall tone of the piece is emotionally patriotic, using purple prose to commemorate Phillips as a champion of Empire who sacrificed himself in the work of spreading civilisation to the unenlightened.

These sources all give us, therefore, a picture of Phillips as the archetype of the English public schoolboy, prizing brawn, enthusiasm and unthinking patriotism over matters intellectual. He embodied—indeed, strove to embody—the Muscular Christianity of *Tom Brown's School Days*,[18] and evidently his background and education gave him a degree of confidence and certainty of action unrelated to his level of intelligence. Ultimately, these qualities would lead to disaster.

* * *

Although Phillips received his commission in June 1896, his departure for the Niger Coast Protectorate was delayed, in part so that he could consult Consul General Moor in London on his next leave, as well as owing to slight illness—Phillips complained to the Foreign Office that, 'I have had a touch of liver & fever since I have been in England'.[19] As a consequence, Phillips remained at home until the autumn; in the meantime, talk of forward movement in the Protectorate continued in official circles, and the men on the ground went on pushing the boundaries of their instructions.

In July, Ralph Moor reported to the Foreign Office on the work of Assistant District Commissioner Lecky in Benin District: he had pushed inland to the east of Sapele, signing treaties with village chiefs and making a sketch map. Moor was clear about the ultimate goal of this expedition:

> The general object was make to friends with the Chiefs and peoples in the country around the territory of the King of Benin, with a view to the opening up of his country by peaceable means if possible ... the King of Benin, in spite of Treaty and remonstrance, still carries on his evil practices.[20]

In the same month, the Foreign Office retroactively gave its formal approval of the actions taken by Vice Consul Crawford in mounting a punitive expedition in Warri District a few weeks before.[21] In the context of the decisions made by Phillips later in the year, this routine approval of violent methods takes on a new significance. Firstly, the aggressive intent of the mission was explicit and not obscured by euphemism; in his despatch to Moor, Vice Consul Crawford could hardly have been more direct:

> Sir, I have the honor [*sic*] to report that on the 16th inst. I proceeded to Merrie together with Mr Locke District Commissioner, Mr Holt Assistant District Commissioner and twelve armed men and destroyed a portion of that Town.[22]

Secondly, the Foreign Office approved this action even while noting that they had said that no expeditions were to be mounted without permission, owing to Moor's forthcoming period of leave.[23] Their approval of forward movement in this instance may well have later been an influence on Phillips and his decision-making at the crucial moment that came at the end of the year.

Moor went on leave in August 1896, and with Phillips not yet in post, Vice Consul Gallwey stepped in as acting consul general, continuing the momentum of interior penetration. On 1 September, he wrote to London requesting fully 200 treaty forms,[24] implying significant plans for village diplomacy, and in October he sent home ten new treaties signed in the Opobo District.[25] In the same month, Gallwey also joined the calls for aggressive action against the king of Benin:

> The only way to satisfactorily bring the King to his senses and open trade permanently is by means of a demonstration in force to Ado Benin [*sic*]. There would probably be no resistance—if any, it would be of a very mild kind.[26]

* * *

When James Phillips reached the Niger Coast Protectorate, he was therefore plunged into an atmosphere of forward movement, with much active discussion of a military advance into Benin, and several fellow officials lobbying for it. He arrived at Forcados on 24 October, where he was met by Captain Gallwey in the steam yacht *Ivy*, and formally took over his duties on the following day.[27]

Displaying his characteristic energy, Phillips then immediately set out on a tour of the principal stations of the Protectorate, visiting Warri, Sapele, the Benin River, Brass, Bonny, New Calabar and Opobo, finally arriving at headquarters in Old Calabar only on 12 November. He was pleased to report a positive impression of the Protectorate administration, noting that he was 'much struck with the excellence of the organisation, and the zeal shown by almost every officer whose work I inspected'.[28] In summarising these first impressions, Phillips also revealed something of his high (arguably excessive) degree of confidence in himself and in his own level of knowledge:

> I find that from my Colonial experience I am able to speak with authority on the subject and I have no hesitation in saying that the

general organisation of the executive as far as it has gone leaves nothing to be desired.[29]

It was doubtless with this sense of supreme confidence that Phillips sat down on the following morning, having been in charge of the Protectorate for just three weeks and one day, to write a despatch requesting permission to launch an invasion of the Kingdom of Benin with the aim of deposing Oba Ovonramwen. Mentioning his recent visit to the lower Benin River, Phillips reported that he had held a long conversation with the Itsekiri chiefs and the British traders based there, from whom he claimed to have obtained a very clear idea of the state of affairs in the kingdom. After expanding at length on the poor state of trade and the evils of the king, Phillips made a direct bid for leave to use military force:

> To sum up, the situation is this:—The King of Benin, whose country is within a British Protectorate, and whose city lies within fifty miles of a Protectorate Customs Station and who has signed a Treaty with Her Majesty's Representative, has deliberately stopped all trade and effectually blocked the way to all progress in that part of the Protectorate ... I am certain that there is only one remedy, that is to depose the King of Benin from his Stool ... I therefore ask His Lordship's permission to visit Benin City in February next, to depose and remove the King of Benin.[30]

Though he had not yet himself attempted to visit Benin City, Phillips insisted that 'pacific measures are now quite useless', and that he did not anticipate 'any serious resistance from the people of the country'.[31] He proposed nonetheless to take a force of 250 NCPF soldiers, two 7-pdr artillery guns, one Maxim gun and one rocket apparatus, reinforced by 150 Hausas from Lagos, if the Colonial Office could be induced to assist. Fully aware that the Foreign Office would be highly sensitive to the expense of any imperial adventure of this kind, Phillips added a postscript assuring London that he expected to reimburse the cost of invasion through the ivory to be found in the palace in Benin City.

Phillips reinforced his request for permission with a private letter to Sir Clement Hill, which was sent on the same mail steamer and was therefore received at the Foreign Office on the same day. This text demonstrates that one of the advantages that Phillips possessed in making his case was a willingness to ignore nuance; being satisfied with only a slight understanding of the issue, he was able to convey a sense of authority in making his recommendation:

> I hope Lord Salisbury will allow me to tackle the Benin City business. I am very clear in my mind that there is no other way of doing it except by deposing the King—that we are bound to open up this country is I think not to be denied and I think that now is the time to do it—we have waited quite long enough and trade is at a standstill.[32]

As he had done in his official despatch, Phillips once again underestimated the other side, a mistake that would soon prove disastrous:

> I don't think there will be any occasion for any fighting but we will go prepared for it ... Captain Gallwey who knows the country and people says that there wouldn't be a single shot fired.[33]

While the crucial despatch and letter were on board ship in the Gulf of Guinea, steaming slowly towards England, Ralph Moor was on leave in London. Having occasion to write to the Foreign Office on other matters, he took the opportunity to advocate once again for a violent approach to the Kingdom of Benin:

> Strenuous efforts have for the last eighteen months been made to open up the Benin country by peaceable means and to compel the King to adhere to the terms of the Treaty made in 1892—to give up human sacrifice and other evil practices; but with very little result. I

> fear that this country will never be effectually opened to civilisation and trade except by force of arms.[34]

Responding to Moor's urging in an internal Foreign Office note, Sir Clement Hill—even before the arrival of the communications from Phillips—recognised the pressure from the Protectorate officials, but suggested patience: 'The Niger Coast people are very anxious to have a go at Benin but I think they should not be in a hurry'.[35]

The despatch and letter from Phillips arrived at the Foreign Office on 21 December. Although we have no way of knowing whether Sir Clement rolled his eyes at yet more intemperate missives from energetic officials of the Protectorate, we do know that he sent on the despatch to Ralph Moor, the Intelligence Division of the War Office and the Colonial Office to solicit their views. Remaining open in principle to an invasion of Benin, Hill urged a swift reply because 'time is short if the good season is to be utilized'.[36]

Moor's letter in response, dated 26 December, is highly revealing about his longstanding appetite to engineer a military solution to what was now being called 'the Benin question'.[37] Notably, Moor reports that as long ago as November 1894 he had begun preparations to march on Benin City, using the force already assembled in the Benin River for deposing Chief Nana; MacDonald had, however, arrived back in Old Calabar in the following month and decided upon continued peaceful efforts. Referring to his subsequent recommendation in September 1895 that force should be employed in opening up Benin,[38] Moor offered his strong support to the strategy proposed by Phillips, agreeing that 'further pacific measures are quite useless and only likely to damage the prestige of the Government with all the surrounding Native tribes'.[39]

A remarkable admission is quietly made by Moor in this letter, revealing an important fact not elsewhere highlighted in communications with the Foreign Office—secret preparations for an invasion of Benin had been ongoing since the summer of 1895:

> I may here state that for the past eighteen months an 'Intelligence' officer has been continuously at work preparing all necessary information for the carrying out of offensive operations and the approaches to Benin City and the country around are now fairly well known as also the opposition likely to be encountered.[40]

Moor ends his letter with firm support for the use of military force to integrate the Kingdom of Benin into the British Empire:

> The king should be deposed and removed from the country and the ring of Ju Ju men broken up. It will then of course be necessary to establish a military post at Benin City. The operations must be undertaken in February or March at latest in order that a post may be effectually established before the wet season sets in early in June. I do not anticipate any very serious opposition but I should recommend that in addition to the force suggested by Mr Phillips, Her Majesty's Navy render assistance by sending a gunboat with a small force of Marines and a Maxim gun.[41]

This recommendation by Moor arrived at the Foreign Office on 29 December; six days later, the Colonial Office also responded, with the news that no soldiers could be spared from the Colony of Lagos.[42] With no additional troops available, and faced with the prospect of requiring assistance from the Royal Navy (meaning an undesirable financial outlay), the Foreign Office decided against the proposal. On 9 January 1897, it informed Phillips that 'Her Majesty's Government have decided that the expedition should not take place this year'.[43]

* * *

Unknown to the Foreign Office officials as they drafted this despatch, however, Phillips was already dead, along with almost all of his expedition party. He had set off for Benin City six days earlier without waiting for permission from London, and his contingent had been destroyed. We will come to a consideration of his reasons shortly, but first, the basic facts.

On 29 December, Phillips wrote to the Foreign Office (in his final despatch from Old Calabar) to report that he was setting out in the *Ivy* to visit Brass and the Benin River.[44] Significantly, he omitted to mention that he planned to visit Benin City with a large party of colleagues and carriers. Not having had an answer to his request for sanction to mount an invasion, Phillips had organised an unarmed expedition instead, comprising a total of nine British men, the Consulate interpreter Herbert Clarke (a Sierra Leonean), a number of clerks and manservants, approximately 250 carriers (comprising both Kroomen and Itsekiris) and the drum and fife band of the Niger Coast Protectorate Force. Besides Phillips, the British members of the party included Major Crawford (vice consul of the Benin & Warri District), Ralph Locke (district commissioner at Warri), Captain Alan Boisragon (commandant of the NCPF), Captain Maling of the NCPF, Kenneth Campbell (district commissioner at Sapele) and Dr Elliot, the medical officer for the district.[45] These officials were joined by Thomas Gordon of the African Association and Harry Powis from the firm of Alexander Miller, Brother & Co. Of these British members of the party, the only survivors were Locke and Captain Boisragon, who would later publish his own account of the events.

Having disembarked a force of the NCPF at Brass, Phillips proceeded to Sapele, where much of the expedition assembled. The mission party then set out from this station early in the morning of 2 January, travelling downstream along the Benin River in the *Primrose* and the *Daisy*, heading towards the entrance of Gwato Creek.[46] At this early stage, the expedition was accompanied by District Commissioner Burrows, whose official diary provides a terse but vivid account of the beginning of the journey, and of the efforts of local chiefs and advisors to persuade Phillips to abandon his plan. Just after nine o'clock, while still in the main stream of the Benin River, Phillips and his company met Chief Dogho in his canoe, and Burrows records that they stopped for fully half an hour while the chief attempted to convince Phillips not to proceed.[47] Using the British rendering 'Dore' for the name Dogho, Boisragon later recalled the meeting, revealing something of the attitude that would bring disaster:

> Chief Dore before he left us told us the Benin men meant to stop our getting to Benin City, and tried to persuade Phillips not to go on ... all the Jakris fear the Benin City men so much that we thought nothing of his advice or warning.[48]

Phillips was, however, persuaded to send back the drum and fife band—while they were armed only with ceremonial swords, their uniforms suggested to onlookers that this was a military expedition and might thus prompt an immediate violent response.[49] The band therefore transferred to Chief Dogho's canoe, and he returned them to Sapele.

In the meantime, the main party entered Gwato Creek, and after travelling about 4 miles reached the home of Chief Dudu, another of the leading Itsekiri chiefs who worked with the British. As Burrows records, at this place a clear message was received from Oba Ovonramwen that his ritual obligations prevented him from receiving Phillips at that time:

> January 2nd, 1897, 12.10pm—Anchored at Dudu's town. King's message to Consul-General—That he is making his 'father', and cannot possibly see us under a month, and on no account to go to him. Dore says it will be certain death to go. Consul-General says he will go.[50]

Evidently, Phillips was unmoved by this urging, sending the messengers back to the king to say that he was continuing in his plans to visit. Over the next few hours, further messengers arrived from Oba Ovonramwen to say that the king was concerned about being seized by the British, and that if Phillips were to come to Benin City, he was to do so alone, accompanied only by one of the Itsekiri chiefs.[51] Ignoring this pacific overture, Phillips and the entire mission continued onward, arriving at about four o'clock at Gilli Gilli, where they stayed overnight.

During the stop at Gilli Gilli, the British officers sent for Dudu Jerri, the headman of a large Itsekiri village that lay near Gwato, in order to gather intelligence:

> Dudu Jerri turned up soon after, and he was also full of warnings and forebodings, all of which we laughed at at the time. He declared that Gwatto [*sic*] was full of Benin soldiers, who wouldn't let us land there, and would fire on us if we attempted to do so.[52]

Even in the face of these warnings, Phillips would not change his mind; on the following morning, 3 January, the party advanced to Gwato, after Dudu Jerri had gone ahead to inform the town chief of their imminent arrival. Evidently, the Benin soldiery had diplomatically decamped from the town, and the British mission landed in the late afternoon, spending the night in a large house provided for them by the chief. Further efforts to persuade Phillips to turn back were to no effect; as Burrows recorded in his official diary when at Gwato: 'Consul-General determined to go on'.[53]

On the morning of 4 January, therefore, the full mission party assembled at Gwato and marched off for Benin City at 7.30 a.m.; Burrows saw off the expedition and then returned to Sapele in the *Primrose*.[54] Captain Boisragon recalled that the path through the bush was broader than usual for the area, but still only suitable for marching in single file, meaning that the party of over 250 men formed a lengthy and vulnerable column.[55] He also records the order of march (as decided by Phillips), noting that the line was led by an Edo guide named Basilli and an orderly called Jumbo, who was wearing a blue police uniform and carrying the consul general's flag; next came the interpreter Herbert Clarke, then Phillips, Major Crawford, Boisragon himself, Captain Maling (who was making a road survey), Locke and Dr Elliot. Powis, Gordon and Kenneth Campbell were further down the line, engaged in supervising the carriers.[56]

Another order issued by Phillips was to have important implications for the chances of survival of this exposed marching column: officers were allowed to carry their pistols, but they were instructed to keep them strictly out of sight, for fear of alarming the local people. Given the heat and humidity, and the consequent need to march in shirtsleeves, all members of the party had locked away their bulky service revolvers in their travelling chests, which were in the charge of the long line of carriers.[57]

After marching all morning, the expedition stopped for lunch at the third village on the path. During this interlude, more messengers from Benin City were received, then had to depart without having persuaded Phillips to delay. Continuing in their march, the column had travelled approximately 14 miles inland from Gwato when disaster struck. Captain Boisragon later described the ambush:

> It was then about 3 p.m., and we were walking in much the same order as when we started, except that Locke had stopped behind to tie up his bootlace, when suddenly a shot rang out a few yards behind us, to be followed immediately by a fusilade [*sic*], that seemed to go back almost to the last village we had passed ...
>
> At the first shot we couldn't believe that the firing was in earnest, and thought, as someone suggested, that it was only a salute in our honour. However, that idea was soon exploded by the cries from our wretched carriers, and yells from the Benin men. As soon as we were certain what it was, I sang out that I was going back to get my revolver, and Crawford said he would do the same, but poor old Phillips, for some reason of his own, said, 'No revolvers, gentlemen'.[58]

Despite this order from Phillips, some of the officers ran down the line to try to recover their pistols, but without success—the carriers had been attacked first, and many had fled into the bush. Phillips himself was killed early on, as well as Campbell and Gordon, who being with the carriers had fallen in the initial assault. Very little was to be seen of the Edo soldiers—they had deployed all along the line of march in a parallel track cut for the purpose, ready for the ambush, and were able to shoot down the expedition party from within the bush.

With the path now littered with dead bodies and the expedition party in chaos, the remaining Brits were unable to find the baggage with their pistols. They tried to make their way back down the path to Gwato, but the going was slow, and they were under intermittent fire from the shadowy Edo in the bush. Elliot was bleeding badly from a wound in the head, and then Crawford took a full charge of shot in the groin, forcing the others to try to carry him. Soon, Powis was killed, despite his efforts to use the Edo language that he had learnt in trade. In short order, Maling, Crawford and Elliot were hit again, and died. Boisragon and Locke had both been wounded but were still alive.

Abandoning the path, the two remaining British survivors struck out into the bush to its north, on the opposite side from which the ambush came, and struggled through the dense vegetation. As recounted in Boisragon's highly coloured book *The Benin Massacre*, they managed to stay alive through a desperate six-day wander through the jungle, living on plantain and dew water. Eventually, they found a creek and some friendly Itsekiri, who brought them down to Chief Dudu's town on Gwato Creek, where they chanced upon a Protectorate launch.

In the meantime, the first news of the attack on Phillips and his expedition only reached officials early in the morning of 7 January, when District Commissioner Burrows was awoken at the Sapele Consulate by a messenger from Chief Dogho:

> January 7th, 1897, 3 a.m.—Received letter from Chief Dore, stating expedition had been fired on, and white men killed.[59]

With the nearest telegraph station being at Brass, it took some days to get word to London. Finally, at noon on 10 January, the Foreign Office received a telegram: 'White expedition to Benin captured and reported killed by natives.'[60]

* * *

Given these basic facts, what can we conclude about Phillips and his strategic reasoning? Why did he set out for Benin City without waiting for official approval, and moreover, why did he continue his expedition in the face of dire warnings against it?

In the letter appointing him as consul and deputy commissioner of the Niger Coast Protectorate, the Foreign Office instructed Phillips—as was standard practice—to refer to the archives of the Consulate in Old Calabar for guidance in his duties.[61] Notably, in his despatch of November advocating the violent deposition of Oba Ovonramwen,[62] Phillips duly referenced three documents in support of his proposal: MacDonald's despatch of May 1892 (suggesting that use of force against Benin would likely be necessary),[63] and two from Moor, in which he directly advocated an armed expedition to Benin (September 1895),[64] and described aggressive movements aimed at 'opening up' the kingdom (July 1896).[65]

With this documentary record of British officials advocating over several years for the use of force against the Kingdom of Benin, combined with the atmosphere of forward movement among Protectorate officials in the summer and autumn of 1896, Phillips would have been in no doubt that the deposition of Oba Ovonramwen would be welcomed by his colleagues. As to the timing, he would have been very aware that MacDonald had effectively set the date for an invasion of Benin when restraining Moor in his ambitions in the autumn of 1895.[66] The identification of the coming dry season of 1896–97 as the best time for military action therefore had almost a scriptural authority for the officials on the ground, given MacDonald's high reputation as the father of the Protectorate. Important in this respect may be a degree of coordination between Phillips and Moor during their discussions in England before Phillips travelled out to the Niger Coast; as Phillips noted in his November proposal, Moor was 'fully cognizant of all matters dealt with in this despatch',[67] and it is evident that Moor was very keen to settle the Benin issue as soon as possible.

Why then did Phillips set out without waiting for permission from London? He had not yet received approval for an armed expedition, and accordingly he planned an unarmed mission as what seemed to be a way around this lack of official blessing (the side arms carried by the officers being of no material importance). This explains his willingness to send home the drum and fife band, and his strict instructions to keep revolvers out of sight. A significant factor in this plan was doubtless that Phillips was aware of several occasions in 1896 in which the Foreign Office had retroactively approved forward movement—even military action—despite their formal instruction not to mount expeditions without permission; besides the punitive expedition mounted by Crawford in Warri District as mentioned above, Gallwey had in October sent Boisragon to Qua Ibo with an NCPF detachment to punish a village named Mpok;[68] retrospective approval from the Foreign Office duly followed, without demur.[69] Thus Phillips had every reason to expect that his actions would be approved after the fact.

Even if his absolution was assured, why did Phillips insist on continuing with his expedition in the face of mounting evidence that it would fail? The king of Benin had made it abundantly clear, via numerous messages, that he did not wish to receive him at that time, and he had even offered the compromise solution of meeting Phillips alone. Why would the acting consul general press on with his large party, knowing this? Although we can never really know what was in his mind, all the evidence suggests that a failed mission was precisely what Phillips wanted: being turned away would provide just the rationale that he needed for an invasion and would force London to approve his bold proposal to depose the king. As Boisragon noted in his subsequent book, he personally expected that they would be turned back by Benin soldiers, and that 'if we had been stopped, it would have meant that, when sanctioned by the Foreign Office, the next expedition to Benin City would be an armed one'.[70] This was not hindsight bluffing from Boisragon; as reported in the *Morning Post* when his escape was confirmed in January, he had written to his wife on 25 November, well before setting off for Benin City, and said that they would 'in all probability be stopped and sent back'.[71]

That this was Phillips' intention appears to be confirmed by his colleague Henry Gallwey. Out of contact while conducting a survey inland in Opobo country, Gallwey only learned of the ambush on 15 January; with Phillips dead, he once again took over as acting consul general and swiftly reported to London what information he could gather. In explaining the motive for the expedition, Gallwey effectively notes that Phillips was ticking a box to demonstrate that force would be required: 'Mr Phillips' opinion was that every pacific means towards approaching the King of Benin would not be complete until he, as Acting Consul General, paid a visit to the King'.[72] Phillips had, in his November despatch, untruthfully reported that all peaceful means had at that time already been exhausted; putting this claim right while attempting to force London's hand therefore appears to have been his aim. It may be that he had in mind the example of the 1892 British invasion of Ijebu in the Yoruba country bordering the Colony of Lagos, which was launched because of the 'insult' of the Ijebu declining to discuss trade with Acting Governor Denton of Lagos during his visit in 1891.[73]

Phillips' catastrophic error lay, of course, in his underestimation of the Edo response to his unauthorised incursion and in his failing to take seriously local advisors and their urgent warnings. Having been in the Protectorate for only three weeks before proposing an invasion of Benin, Phillips had very little understanding of the kingdom and the likely actions of its officials. He was in no position to judge the situation from experience and so should have listened to the advice from Chief Dogho and other local men, who clearly spelt out the danger the expedition faced. Racism was of course a crucial factor in the dismissive attitude of the British officials to such warnings; for example, Boisragon wrote about the emissaries from Oba Ovonramwen at Gwato in an astoundingly offensive way, even when he seems to think that he is paying them a compliment: 'These three gentlemen were then introduced to us, and, though very like monkeys in personal appearance, they looked quite a superior class of animal to the Gwatto [*sic*] people'.[74]

This racist arrogance united with Phillips' overconfidence and limited intelligence to make a fatal combination. Prizing action above thought, and clearly convinced that an officer of the Empire could do as he pleased, Phillips led his expedition to disaster. He alone bears the responsibility.

* * *

On receiving news of the destruction of the Phillips expedition direct from the telegraph station at Brass, Rear Admiral Harry Rawson, who had been in charge of the Cape Squadron of the Royal Navy since May 1895,[75] immediately despatched three gunboats to the Niger Coast.[76] He also reported to London that he was ready to proceed there in his flagship HMS *St George* if required. This swift but unruffled response demonstrates the routine nature of this kind of emergency for the commander-in-chief at the Cape of Good Hope; his squadron stood ready as a kind of imperial fire brigade, ready to deploy around Africa wherever British interests required violent assistance. Having served in the Royal Navy since 1857 (when he was just thirteen years old), Harry Rawson was himself highly experienced in the exercise of imperial force. His credentials included commanding British forces in the shortest war in history, namely the Anglo-Zanzibar War of 27 August 1896; from declaration of war to unconditional surrender, this conflict (comprising essentially a naval bombardment of the sultan's palace) lasted just 37 minutes, but in this time the Admiral nonetheless managed to cause around 500 Zanzibari casualties.[77]

With Rawson's gunboats already steaming for the Benin River, the death of Phillips reached the British public in the newspapers on 12 January, when *The Times* reported the 'Massacre of a British Expedition in West Africa'.[78] By the next day, the press was already reporting a punitive expedition as a likely response, with the *Morning Post* labelling Oba Ovonramwen a 'savage monarch' and a 'monster of cruelty';[79] meanwhile, the *Manchester Guardian* noted that an expedition was expected and called Benin City the 'City of Blood'.[80] Newspapers around the country followed this lead (not least because of syndicated copy); even if the authorities in London had been minded to react to events in the Niger Coast Protectorate with circumspection, public opinion would have demanded swift satisfaction, such was the immediate outcry.

In the event, there was no real discussion in Whitehall about whether an expedition would be mounted against Benin; under the brutal logic of empire, a military response in such circumstances was automatic and unavoidable. Neither was there much consideration of the precise aims of any operation—this being a routine affair for the British Empire machine, the standard operating procedure was well understood by all concerned.

The only material discussion was over the level of resources that would be required to guarantee success, and over who would command the campaign. As swiftly as 11 January—the day after receiving news of the ambush—the Foreign Office wrote to the Admiralty to enquire about available naval forces; they also asked for 'one or more gunboats' to be sent to the Benin River, even before a strategy had been discussed.[81] As mentioned above, Rawson had already taken the initiative to send HMS *Widgeon*, HMS *Alecto* and HMS *Phoebe* to the region. In addition, HMS *Theseus* and HMS *Forte* were lent from the Mediterranean squadron for temporary service in West Africa.[82]

Ralph Moor cut short his leave and by 12 January was in the Foreign Office for urgent discussions; the War Office appointed Lieutenant-Colonel Bruce Hamilton to assist him by taking charge of land forces for the duration of the campaign, and both men hurried to Liverpool with their staffs to take ship for Africa.[83] On 13 January, Rear Admiral Rawson was ordered to proceed from South Africa to the Brass River 'using convenient despatch'.[84] With the concentration of naval forces, it was soon decided that the operation would be led by the Royal Navy and commanded by Rawson; on 15 January, he was telegraphed accordingly:

> The expedition against Benin City will be organized under your direction as a Naval Expedition ... You will satisfy yourself as to the sufficiency of the force you propose to land.[85]

Although it cost him his life, Phillips had therefore succeeded in forcing the hand of the British government. He had finally delivered the outcome sought by numerous officials over the years: the forces of the Empire were mobilising, and the Benin Punitive Expedition was under way.

8

'OVERWHELMING FORCE'

THE BENIN PUNITIVE EXPEDITION

Having satisfied yourself as to the sufficiency of the force you propose to land, you will make the necessary arrangements for the successful conduct of the expedition, the objects of which are, to rescue any possibly surviving members of the party attacked by the King of Benin; to take the City of Benin; and if possible to capture the King.

Admiralty to Rear Admiral Harry Rawson, 23 January 1897

I am landing seven hundred fighting men against Benin as Consul General concurs with me that future moral effect throughout Protectorate renders large force desirable.

Rear Admiral Harry Rawson to Admiralty, 16 February 1897

With James Phillips having blundered his way to an accidental martyrdom, the future of the Kingdom of Benin had essentially been decided. The forces of the British Empire were gathering to exact vengeance and to seize territory, and the final outcome would never be in doubt: given the vast imbalance in raw power and modern technology, the military campaign ahead would be largely a matter of logistics.

Having already telegraphed Rear Admiral Harry Rawson to put him in command of the expedition, London followed up on 23 January with detailed, formal orders. Declaring that Phillips and his party had been 'murdered', the Admiralty officially informed Rawson that 'it has been decided by her Majesty's Government that an expedition shall be despatched for the punishment of the King for this outrage, and that the force to be employed shall be furnished from the Squadron under your orders'.[1] Including his flagship HMS *St George*, Rawson would have fully nine Royal Navy warships in the theatre of operations, and in addition the hired transport *Malacca* (fitted out as a hospital ship) was setting off for the Niger Coast with extra forces and supplies. This vessel carried a further eighty-two Royal Navy personnel, as well as 120 Royal Marines plus three officers, and a full complement of medical staff.

With the bulk of the Niger Coast Protectorate Force also at his disposal, Rawson would therefore have significant resources on which to draw. Notably, while sending this large contingent, the Admiralty at the same time urged restraint upon him, being concerned about the costs involved:

> My Lords have provided you with what should be an ample reserve of force, and your experience of African warfare will lead you to consider the question of numbers very closely, bearing in mind that it is undesirable to employ a larger force than is necessary for the attainment of the object of the Expedition.[2]

Given the routine nature of this kind of 'punitive expedition' in the British Empire context, there had been very little discussion in London of its specific goals; all the officers and officials involved understood the standard operational template and needed little guidance. The Admiralty was, however, obliged to include formal instructions in its official orders, and it set them out briefly:

> Having satisfied yourself as to the sufficiency of the force you propose to land, you will make the necessary arrangements for the successful conduct of the expedition, the objects of which are, to rescue any possibly surviving members of the party attacked by the King of Benin; to take the City of Benin; and if possible to capture the King.
>
> This done, the occupation of the town and district of Benin is to be left to the Protectorate forces, and the work of re-embarkation to be commenced with as little delay as possible.[3]

Notably, the British government already knew very well that there was no prospect of finding survivors of the Phillips expedition,[4] so the inclusion of this as a goal must be interpreted as a desperate hope, or—more likely—as a diplomatic rationale for the punitive expedition's true aim: the occupation of the territory of Benin. This primary goal was elsewhere emphasised; in communication with the War Office, the Foreign Office briefly summarised the object of the operation to be 'permanently occupying the town and district of Benin by a force of the Protectorate constabulary'.[5]

Also notable was the natural willingness of the officials on the ground to interpret the standard operational procedure in the most aggressive way possible. Captain Gallwey—still acting consul general until Ralph Moor arrived back in the Protectorate on 3 February on board HMS *Theseus*[6]—went significantly further than London in outlining his understanding of the aims of the expedition:

> I would add that the destruction of Benin City, the removal and punishment of the King, the punishment of the fetish priests, the opening up of the country, etc. will prove a wonderful impetus to trade in this part of the Protectorate, and at the same time do away with a reign of terror and all its accompanying horrors.[7]

His working assumption that the wholesale destruction of the city would be the aim of the operation certainly represents a further step than London would put into writing, but it was in accord with numerous other punitive expeditions in the Niger Coast Protectorate and elsewhere in the British Empire. Gallwey—who always displayed much more than the average level of casual racism typical of British imperial documents—also offered his view that the Edo 'is not a fighting man and a great coward into the bargain', and that as a consequence, 'I do not think the King will offer much resistance as far as actual fighting goes'.[8] Combining his racism with some gathered intelligence from his own journey to Benin and from the recent ambush (and using the British term 'Bini' for the Edo), Gallwey was clear that the Kingdom of Benin did not amount to a significant military opponent:

> Captain Boisragon and Mr Locke both noticed that the enemy were armed almost entirely with flint lock guns (long Danes) and did not notice any rifles.
>
> The enemy are probably very badly armed—and are a very timid race. When I was in Benin City in 1892, I saw a few old cannons lying about unmounted—chiefly of Portuguese make. The Binis not being watermen, the stations at Sapele and at the mouth of the river are perfectly safe from any offensive movement.[9]

This lack of Benin military capacity gave a freedom of action to the British invaders that allowed the men on the ground to plan for more expansive goals than were captured in the official instructions from London. Using a calculus more political than military, they sought to mount a display of British power that would redound around the region as an example to others. Once back in the Niger Coast Protectorate, Consul General Moor mentioned this strategic aim in a telegram on 7 February: 'As overwhelming force is available it will be landed for the purpose of creating an impression throughout Protectorate and neighbouring territory.'[10] On the following day, he expanded on this theme:

> I fully concur in the line of policy adopted, that of landing an overwhelming force as it is available on the spot, and the impression created thereby in the Protectorate and adjoining territories for probably hundreds of miles will, no doubt, be of great service in the future in rendering the lives of European officers much safer, and their work of opening up country easier.[11]

The fact that Moor also took time to emphasise that the expenses involved were 'incurred with a view to creating an impression throughout British territories in West Africa'[12] may suggest that his aim was to ensure that his own administration escaped the financial responsibility for the expedition. He was supported in this view by Rawson himself, who reported to London that, 'I am landing seven hundred fighting men against Benin as Consul General concurs with me that future moral effect throughout Protectorate renders large force desirable.'[13]

* * *

As can be clearly seen in the newspapers of the time, there was significant popular support for the Benin expedition; extensive press coverage, including daily updates of progress, reflected great public interest, and no opposition was expressed in the mainstream papers. Most covered the subject in a surprising degree of detail, down to the nuts and bolts of supply logistics and daily movements of Royal Navy vessels. Patriotic displays were also mounted in support of departing soldiers; when the *Malacca* sailed from the Royal Albert Docks in London on Saturday, 23 January, the *Morning Post* reported that it was seen off by the band of the Grenadier Guards, accompanied by cheering crowds:

> The scene was most impressive, and as the men filed up the gangway the band struck up the Marine's regimental march, 'A Life on the Ocean Wave', 'Rule Britannia', and the National Anthem. This was the signal for round after round of enthusiastic cheering, renewed

> again and again as the great steamer gradually made its way out of the dock. As she entered the Thames and proceeded away under half steam the cheers were renewed and responded to by the men, the air being filled by cries of 'God-speed' and 'Safe return' ... All along the river the men were loudly cheered by the seamen on board the various steamships, and at Woolwich a number of soldiers assembled and gave the men a parting cheer.[14]

Such rallying to the flag was not seen only at home. The same edition of the newspaper also reported that Ralph Moor and Lieutenant-Colonel Hamilton, heading for the Protectorate on the steamer *Bathurst*, had called in at the Canary Islands, where they were entertained to a lunch by patriotic well-wishers; they could not, however, also attend a 'grand banquet' arranged in their honour, being anxious to depart for the theatre of operations.[15] Crowds were seen in Sierra Leone, too, cheering off a detachment of the West Indian Regiment as it left for the Niger Delta.[16]

Being keen to furnish its readers with as much information as possible about this popular cause—the most exciting story in the news that month, and one attracting undivided opinion—the *Morning Post* reported on the stores being loaded for transport to Africa. In the hands of this reliably imperialist paper, even the despatch of supplies became a celebration of colonial violence:

> The employees at the Royal Arsenal, Woolwich, and the Royal Victualling Yard, Deptford, were working up to midnight yesterday in getting war stores ready for the Benin Expedition. Two hundred tons of food and other supplies have been despatched from Deptford Victualling Yard and Woolwich Dockyard. No guns, shot, shell or ammunition have been sent from Woolwich, the war vessels engaged in the Expedition being well supplied with these. One hundred boxes of war rockets and supplies of the electric search-light have been sent from Woolwich Arsenal, the latter for discovering the operations of the enemy at night and inspiring awe into the semi-savages to be

> attacked, and the former for driving the enemy from the bush and setting fire to any towns or villages where the British forces may be opposed or which the enemy is likely to fall back upon.[17]

Along with 500 Royal Marines and bluejackets, the *Malacca* had already taken out significant stores of food and equipment, and the supply list provides a curious insight into military life of the late Victorian period, the high watermark of the British Empire. For the Benin campaign, the *Malacca* carried 2,200 tins of condensed milk, 300lbs of Cocoatina, 200 tins of Bovril and forty-eight boxes of 'Soup Solidified'.[18] There was 'essence' of mutton, beef and chicken, along with mutton broth, chicken broth and calves' foot jelly, as well as 120 tins of Liebig's Extract of Meat. Twelve dozen bottles of Stower's lime juice cordial would provide Vitamin C, and there was plentiful alcohol: thirty dozen pints of St Marceaux Champagne (vintage 1890), 600 bottles of old tawny port (vintage 1878), numerous bottles of both Scotch whisky and Irish whiskey, and 600 bottles of Australian wine (both red and white).

Besides these victuals, the *Malacca* carried a lengthy list of camp equipment and hospital materiel, including 320 tents, 435 axes, 400 bill hooks, 200 yards of mosquito netting, eight zinc urinals, sixteen chamber pots and 160 enamelled soup plates. Although most of the military stores would be supplied by the Royal Navy vessels present in the theatre of operations, the *Malacca* nonetheless took out some munitions, including ten Maxim gun tripods supplied by the Maxim Nordenfelt Company,[19] 100 belts of Maxim ammunition, 300 naval swords (Mk II, 27"), and 201 war rockets with fixtures and fittings.

* * *

Within just a few days of the death of Phillips and his party, therefore, the Royal Navy was converging on the Niger Delta from several stations around Africa, and the *Malacca* was steaming out with the necessary reinforcements and supplies; though the British Empire could often be cumbersome in its decision-making thanks to its great size and the absence of a unified grand strategy, on occasion it could spring rapidly into action. Rear Admiral Rawson experienced no serious obstacle in assembling the necessary force for the expedition under his command, with only relatively minor matters complicating otherwise smooth logistics (for example, some difficulty in sourcing the 800 pith helmets required to protect landed marines and sailors from the harsh African sun).[20]

In fact, the principal challenge that Rawson faced was the somewhat surprising problem that nobody knew exactly where Benin City actually was; since only a tiny number of British officials had previously visited the city, no astronomical observations had ever been taken to allow its precise location to be fixed, and its position on British maps of the period was thus based essentially on guesswork. The Benin Punitive Expedition had therefore set out to invade the kingdom without having an accurate idea of where their end goal was. As Rawson reported to London at the end of January:

> My chief difficulty up to the present has been the want of information about Benin, more especially its position—charts No 1302 and 594 placing it in very different positions, so that until I can ascertain the distance the expedition will have to march I cannot settle the time it will take or make final arrangements.[21]

Having become aware of this knowledge deficit immediately upon being put in charge of the operation, Rawson had cabled to the Niger Delta to arrange for as much intelligence about the Kingdom of Benin to be gathered as possible:

> I telegraphed both to the Commissioner and Senior Naval Officer at Brass to ascertain from them on record, every particular they could give as to the enemy's force, arms, and method of attack,

> roads, creeks and routes to Benin, how the town is situated, whether stockaded or not, and how approached; also any other information procurable.[22]

Following receipt of these instructions from Rawson, on 18 January Captain Thomas MacGill of the cruiser HMS *Phoebe* (briefly the senior naval officer in the theatre of operations) sent HMS *Widgeon* to take Captain Gallwey up the Benin River to Sapele, in the hope that he could gather some intelligence:

> The 'Widgeon' has taken the Acting Consul General, Captain Gallway [*sic*] up to Sapele, and on her return, I hope to get a great deal of useful information about Benin City, the roads to it etc etc from Captain Gallway [*sic*], who is one of the few white men who have been to the town.[23]

On his arrival at Brass on 20 January, Captain Michael O'Callaghan of the cruiser HMS *Philomel* took over as the senior naval officer and reported on 27 January that the *Widgeon* had returned from Sapele, 'bringing a good deal of information'.[24] Lieutenant and Commander Edward Hunt, captain of the *Widgeon*, was swift to report his impressions from the Benin River:

> The City is not stockaded, according to the latest information, and the natives are only armed with 'long Danes' (flint-locks) and are not believed to have any breech-loading rifles ... As he has no 'army', it is impossible to form any idea of the forces at the command of the King of Benin ... His method of attack is also unknown, as he has had no previous experience ... On account of the enemy having probably massed in Benin City, the Jakris (the waterside tribe) are chary of approaching it, after having lost so many carriers, and it is very difficult to obtain any reliable information.[25]

On the following day, Captain Gallwey set out his recommendations to Rear Admiral Rawson, focusing on the best route of advance on Benin City. Amidst the general atmosphere of uncertainty regarding enemy forces, Gallwey's official position and brief experience of the Kingdom of Benin made him the closest thing to an expert on the subject available to British forces, and his views therefore carried authority. For Gallwey, the key factor was the availability of water on the route of march, and this determined his eventual recommendation to Rear Admiral Rawson:

> You may have already decided on what lines you intend to act, but I give you my opinion in case it may be of use to you when you are drawing up your plan of attack ... Undoubtedly the City should be approached by two or three separate columns on different routes but unfortunately the fact of having to carry water puts a very serious obstacle in your way. The three available routes are from Ikuru, about 16 miles from Benin City; Gwato, 25 miles; and Ologbo, said to be 9 miles.
>
> I know the Gwato route, having visited the City in 1892, and can vouch for the fact that for the first twenty miles or more of the road there is no water. Nothing is known for certain of the water supply on the Ikuru and Ologbo routes. The few whitemen who have visited the City have invariably gone by the Gwato route. Further, I fear that the narrow and snaggy nature of the Ikuru creek puts that route out of the question ... There is good water at Ologbo, and that place is reached from Warrigi (on the right bank of Benin River). The march from Warrigi to Ciri is about 6 miles, and Ologbo is about a mile further upstream on the opposite bank of the Ologbo creek ... Taking the above facts into consideration, I consider that the best route of attack is by way of Ologbo.[26]

As will be seen, these arguments were decisive in the plans drawn up by Rawson over the following two days. Gallwey also noted that he had sent orders for a road to be cleared from Warrigi to Ciri and for a large clearing to be prepared at the latter for a camping ground. He further reported that, 'Mr District Commissioner Burrows is gaining all information he can about the movements of the enemy and is procuring the services of the most reliable guides obtainable'.[27] Continuing in his relaxed view of the opposition, Gallwey reminded Rawson of his opinion of the fighting qualities of the Kingdom of Benin and of Oba Ovonramwen himself: 'Knowing the Bini as I do, I cannot conceive that he would take any offensive action.'[28]

Captain O'Callaghan supported the proposed Ologbo line of attack, not least because the Edo defenders would likely anticipate that the invasion would come via the standard Gwato route, known as the 'King's road':

> From what I can gather, the natives (Benin) are all deserting their smaller towns and concentrating on Benin; they are supposed to have a few rifles, and a lot of flint-lock guns. At Benin city there are a few smooth bore guns ... I should think that they will expect us to come by what is called the King's road, and prepare accordingly; they are said to be very clever at making pitfalls, with sharp stakes sticking up, and almost impossible to see; also small spikes stuck in the ground, sometimes poisoned.[29]

O'Callaghan also forwarded a curious note from Private Adeshina, a Yoruba soldier of the NCPF and a former slave of Chief Nana who had some experience of Benin City; full details of his career path are not recorded, but it is quite possible that he joined the NCPF in the aftermath of the defeat and deposition of Chief Nana in 1894. A rare African voice in the British documents from the Benin expedition, Private Adeshina did not place much faith in the Edo soldiery:

> I am a Yoruba, and was caught and sold as a slave to Nana about 9 years ago. I passed through Benin city. I do not know much about it as I was only there two days, but afterwards while a slave of Nana I used to trade with Benin people travelling half way to the city ... The King of Benin has between 40 and 50 small towns who will fight for him. I do not know how many men altogether he has but they

> depend more on Jujus and will not fight strong, they will probably run away to the bush when they see us coming.[30]

* * *

On 30 January, on his flagship HMS *St George*, Rear Admiral Rawson arrived at Brass, from where he reported to the Lords of the Admiralty on the preparations made during the journey from Cape Town:

> During the passage, stores, provisions etc for the whole force were prepared and packed on board the flagship and I drew up such detailed orders for the expedition as the information then in my possession permitted ... A copy of such orders as I have already been able to prepare are enclosed; from which their Lordships will gather that I have organised the expedition on the largest scale, so as to be ready; but should the intelligence I receive at Brass lead me to decide that so large a force is not required, I can easily reduce it.[31]

Evidently, the information deficit respecting the Kingdom of Benin and its regional geography required a degree of contingency planning. As will be seen, in the event some important adaptations were forced upon the expedition as a result of unforeseen eventualities, but the conduct of the invasion was largely as anticipated by Rawson on 30 January. The General Orders that he issued on that day comprise a detailed set of instructions for the conduct of the campaign ahead: Rawson had decided to create a main base at Warrigi, land his force there and advance on Benin City via the Ologbo route recommended by Captain Gallwey. The fact that the orders were based directly on the template prepared by Sir Garnet Wolseley for the Ashanti campaign of 1873–74 suggests a high degree of continuity in British military involvement in West Africa.[32]

Among numerous points of interest in the General Orders, a striking fact is that the first (and lengthy) section is on the health and hygiene of the troops, suggesting that British commanders saw the dangers of sunstroke, malaria and dysentery as a greater threat than enemy forces. One of the directions for the conduct of the men while ashore was that the invasion force must not burn villages without permission:

> No village or camp is to be set on fire, except by orders of the Commander-in-Chief. Officers and men are reminded of the danger and delay which occur if a village is set on fire before all the ammunition and baggage have made their way through it.[33]

Given the fate that lay ahead for the Benin Bronzes, there is a certain irony in the orders issued by Rawson that, 'All plundering and unnecessary destruction of property are to be strictly repressed'.[34] This instruction was followed by an order to urge men to be kind to 'the friendly natives' for very practical reasons: 'If the carriers run away, the men will be without food'.[35]

Having recorded his debt to Wolseley's earlier set of orders, Rawson notably chose to add the concluding words of his predecessor to his own General Orders:

> Sir Garnet Wolseley finished his orders with the following remark, which the Commander-in-Chief wishes to impress on every officer and man:
>
> It must never be forgotten that providence has implanted in the heart of every native in Africa, a superstitious awe and dread of the white man, that prevents the negro from daring to meet us face to face. A steady advance or a charge, no matter how partial, if made with determination, always means the retreat of the enemy. Although, when at a distance, and even when under a heavy fire, the enemy may seem brave enough,—from their practice of yelling, singing and beating drums, in order to frighten the enemies of their own colour, with whom they are accustomed to make war,—they will not stand against the advance of the white man. So, if surrounded by howling enemies, the men must rely upon their own British courage and discipline, and upon the courage of their comrades.[36]

With these sentiments Wolseley conveniently ignored the technological chasm between the two sides, instead attributing British success to a vague racial superiority, providentially granted. That such racist attitudes should be formally incorporated into official orders as a matter of routine helps to explain the development and continuation of structural racism as a legacy of the British Empire period. Rawson added his own note of prejudice: 'In short,—the rule for fighting will be rapid fire by volleys, and rapid advance without losing touch. The blacks can never stand a charge'.[37]

Rear Admiral Rawson ended his General Orders with a summary of the plans for disembarkation, with the Benin Punitive Expedition planned to reach Warrigi on 10 February. The invasion force to be landed amounted to a total of 1,262 men, comprising 708 fighting men plus officers, staff, medics and carriers. They carried sixteen Maxim guns, six artillery pieces and 198,240 rounds of rifle ammunition.

* * *

A few days later, with Consul General Moor by now back in the Protectorate, Rawson telegraphed London to report that all required vessels had arrived except the *Malacca* and HMS *Magpie*, and that he had hired four steamers in Lagos for troop transport duty.[38] On the same day, he went up to Sapele with Moor in the *Ivy* for a reconnaissance. Accompanying them was Commander Reginald Bacon, the chief of the Intelligence Department for the Expedition, who noted that at the site of the main base at Warrigi, 'signs of activity were apparent; provisions were being landed, a pier built, and a large portion of the bush cleared to build storehouses'.[39]

Rawson sent HMS *Philomel* up the Benin River to cover this forward movement, along with the *Phoebe*, *Barrosa*, *Widgeon* and *Alecto*, while the *St George*, *Theseus* and *Forte* anchored off the

Forcados River to await the *Malacca* and her reinforcements. Regarding the NCPF force, Rawson later reported:

> The Niger Coast Protectorate troops were, in the meantime, moved up to Warrigi, with a party of native road-makers, to complete the road to Ceri [*sic*], and to form a camp there for the whole force; thus enabling the bluejackets and marines to march to Ceri [*sic*] the same day they were to land at Warrigi.[40]

Moor recorded that Lieutenant-Colonel Hamilton advanced to Ciri with his men on 6 February, and on the following day he telegraphed to London that their arrangements for the expedition were now complete as far as was possible.[41] Moor and Rawson then returned to Brass on the Protectorate yacht *Ivy*, to send final telegrams and to await the arrival of the *Malacca*.[42]

The steamer reached Forcados on 8 February, and with the road-building and camp construction at Ciri already complete, the Benin Punitive Expedition was ready to start. Rear Admiral Rawson sent his invasion force into the Benin River on the following day:

> On the 9th instant, the landing parties from H.M. ships 'St George', 'Theseus', and 'Forte', and the Royal Marines from the transport 'Malacca', were conveyed in the four hired steamers, viâ Forcados and Nana Creek, to Warrigi, where they arrived the next afternoon.[43]

* * *

The attack on Benin City would be carried out by the main column on this southern route via Ologbo, but Rawson had also planned on distracting the enemy with two additional detachments, covering both of his flanks. Aware that the Benin forces would likely anticipate that the principal British assault would come from Gwato, Rawson told the Admiralty on 4 February that he was despatching a force under Captain O'Callaghan of HMS *Philomel*, comprised also of men from the *Barrosa*, *Alecto* and *Widgeon*, to 'attack and destroy Gwato causing a diversion in that direction'.[44] To protect his eastern flank, 'Another force from "Phoebe" and "Alecto" will hold Sapoba', a town lying up the Benin River tributary that was known to the British as the Jamieson River.[45] Moor described the planned destruction of Gwato as a 'feint attack' and saw both detachments as serving to help prevent the escape of Benin forces outside the theatre of operations once the main attack on the city was begun.[46]

Accordingly, Captain O'Callaghan departed from the base at Warrigi on 8 February and anchored off Gwato Creek, taking his small boats up the slim waterway for a reconnaissance on the following day. Since this creek was unnavigable for all the Royal Navy vessels except for the third-class cruiser HMS *Barrosa*, the force was transferred into ship's boats and six Itsekiri war canoes for the landing. The straightforward language that O'Callaghan used in reporting this operation should not blind us to the fact that he is describing scorched-earth tactics in what was unarguably a civilian area:

> On the 10th having reconnoitred Gilli Gilli in the morning, I left the ship in the boats of HMS 'Philomel', 'Barrosa' and 'Widgeon' about 11.30am and occupied Gilli Gilli, no opposition, burnt all the huts and cut down banana trees and left the place again at about 3pm. Proceeded up the creek to Gwato landing place. Having searched the bush with volleys and fired about six rounds from the 3 Pr Q.F. Gun in the direction of the town, landed 80 men, 40 seamen and 40 marines, and marched up the path which ends in a defile to Gwato Town ... On our arrival there the place was apparently deserted. Searched all the bush with volleys and marched to the further end of the town and commenced marching back.[47]

At this point in the operation came the first engagement with the Benin armed forces of the entire war; unseen enemy were reported in the bush, and further blind volleys were fired in their general direction. For the first time, this British fire was returned, and a pitched battle developed:

> Considerable bodies of the enemy tried to get round to our rear by our right flank, but exposing themselves to the marines they suffered considerably, many men being seen to fall and to be dragged away. For about an hour the enemy kept up a pretty hot fire but then having made no impression on our force the firing and cheering ceased. I then advanced the men well to the front, set fire to the remaining huts, and blew up two large houses with guncotton. Having burnt all the houses and all firing from the natives having ceased, I marched the men back to the boats unmolested. We got to the boats about 6.30pm. Our casualties were three severely and three slightly wounded. I then returned to HMS 'Barrosa'.[48]

On the following day, the eastern flank diversionary contingent also advanced, and it similarly encountered resistance:

> On the 11th instant, the other force, under Captain MacGill (with men drawn from the 'Phoebe', 'Alecto' and 'Magpie'), which had proceeded up the Jamieson River to Sapoba, built a stockade four miles to the northward of that place, where the main road from Benin branches in two directions.
>
> Here the party employed in building the stockade were attacked from the neighbouring forest, and a sharp engagement took place before the enemy were driven away.[49]

Having thus taken up their positions to the west and the south-east of the main area of operations, the detachments under Captains O'Callaghan and MacGill would remain in place until the fighting was over some days later.

* * *

With the principal force of the Expedition having arrived off Warrigi on 10 February, preparation was complete. Admiral Rawson and his staff joined them on the following day, and the invasion of Benin was duly launched: 'On the 11th instant the main attacking column landed at Warrigi, and the 1st division proceeded with Head-Quarters Staff to Ciri'.[50] The road constructed by the NCPF allowed a swift march, and the whole force rapidly covered the 6 miles to 'an excellent camp'[51] at Ciri, which they occupied overnight.

Since Ologbo lay on the other side of the Ologi Creek (and 2 miles upstream), Rawson had planned to throw a bridge over the waterway; in the event, however, this proved 'impracticable owing to swamps',[52] and most of the force had to be transported there from Ciri by water. Commander Bacon later described the approach to Ologbo:

> Early on the morning of the 12th February the advance began. Colonel Hamilton, with sixty-two N.C.P. men, twenty-nine of A Company 1st Division, with one Maxim, under Lieutenant Fyler, R.N., and another under Captain Burrows, N.C.P.F., were embarked in the *Primrose* and two surf-boats to make the first landing. One Maxim was in addition mounted on the *Primrose* to search the bush and cover the disembarkation.[53]

Lieutenant-Colonel Hamilton—personally in charge of this advance guard—reported on the capture of the town:

> We steamed slowly towards Ologbo beach, firing the Maxims as we advanced to clear the bush ... Arriving at the beach at 8.10am, the troops landed and advanced about 200 yards to a large clearing, where they were formed in a hollow square. The enemy at once opened fire from the edge of the bush, and we heard numbers of them shouting. As we returned fire they retired, but repeated these attacks from time to time.
>
> At about 9.30am Captain Koe, Lieutenant Daniels, and one man Niger Coast Protectorate force were hit, and the launch having just returned from Ciri with the second detachment, I pushed on along the bush path to the village for 500 yards with one company Houssas and one Maxim, supported by half a company Naval Brigade. This position was maintained until 12 noon, when, on the arrival of the third detachment at Ologbo beach, I advanced on the village with three companies Niger Coast Protectorate force, one company Naval

> Brigade, one rocket-tube, and two 7-prs. The enemy retired after a slight resistance, and we were established in village (1,100 yards from the beach) by 2 p.m.[54]

The advance into Ologbo represented the first intrusion of the main column into what was unarguably territory of the Kingdom of Benin, explaining the determined resistance that it encountered. Even despite this opposition, the British force took Ologbo with zero casualties, Captain Koe and Lieutenant Daniels (incidentally the sole African officer of the NCPF) only being wounded, along with three NCPF soldiers who received slight wounds.[55] The Edo defenders, on the other hand, seem to have paid heavily. No definite figures are available, but Commander Bacon (who, as intelligence officer, was charged with recording information) noted something of the enemy death toll on entering Ologbo:

> The dead, with the exception of six bodies, had been removed. Subsequently, one heap of thirty-eight was found about half a mile away, so their loss must have been considerable. This first touch of the enemy showed that the Beni were not to be discounted in the easy and off-hand manner which experts had imagined, since they had kept up a sustained attack for two hours against Maxims and volleys, and probably lost a large number of killed, besides wounded who had got away.[56]

It is notable that in this account (which is taken from the book he published immediately after the Expedition), Bacon adopts the usual colonial formula of indirectly complimenting the British soldiery through talking up the fighting qualities of the enemy; if the opposition were truly wretched, no honour would accrue to those outmatching them. The telling fact is the stark contrast to the vicious, hyperactive racism that Bacon elsewhere displays, which is greatly in excess of the casual prejudice typically found in British colonial documents of the period; none is quoted here because it is truly grotesque, but it can readily be found in his published work. As will be seen, these attitudes coloured Bacon's perception of the Kingdom of Benin during and after the Expedition.

In his racist way, Bacon records that the two parts of Ologbo (the main village and the riverine beach) were to be established as a major base:

> Both camps were soon scenes of busy preparation, especially that on the beach, which was designed to become a large depôt. Shelters had to be built for the men, covered with green leaves to protect them from the sun and dew; boilers were set up for boiling the river water before drinking; the low bush fringing the camp had to be cleared, and storehouses erected for the provisions and water. The carriers were assigned a separate camp, defended by the main one; this is quite necessary, as their constant jabbering all through the night is one of their many evil points.[57]

On the following day, the invasion force regrouped; as Lieutenant-Colonel Hamilton noted, the '13th instant was spent in Ologbo village getting up water and supplies'.[58] Provisions and stores were transported from Warrigi and large volumes of water boiled, ready for carrying up the line. Admiral Rawson and his staff advanced to Ologbo beach, and arrangements were made for Hamilton and his vanguard to continue the advance early the next morning.

* * *

During the night came the first of what would be many alarms over the next few days, when at three o'clock in the morning a messenger from the beach camp reported to the main camp at Ologbo that the enemy were in the bush all around.[59] The British force stood to their arms and manned the perimeter, but no attack came; eventually, at half past four, the bugler blew reveille, and campfires were lit for the regulation breakfast of cocoa and biscuit. Shortly afterwards, the invasion force began its march into the interior of the kingdom; as Lieutenant-Colonel Hamilton later reported:

> 14th instant advanced along Benin road at 6.45 a.m. ... At about 10 a.m. the scouts reported the enemy in front ... From this point there was a running fight, firing volleys and advancing along the two paths. The enemy replied well to our volleys, and stood wherever there was sufficient cover.[60]

Commander Reginald Bacon gave a vivid, if somewhat excitable, account of the beginning of this extended engagement with Benin forces:

> Steadily and slowly we marched, occasionally hearing signal guns fired by the Beni, till at last at 10 a.m. the scouts reported the enemy in force ahead. As the scouts had none too much ammunition, and were only raw levies, Colonel Hamilton opened them out, and took the leading company of Houssas, Maxim, and rocket-tube, through them, and having found the ambush path advanced a second company along it. We then passed from the monotony of the march to the excitement of a running fight. Firing sectional volleys and then advancing; the enemy yelling and firing, then retiring and again advancing with a yell.[61]

Elsewhere, Bacon recorded the remarkable fact that in several days of fighting, he almost never actually laid eyes on the opposing forces. In offering rare praise for the bush fighting skills of the Edo soldiery, he is also unintentionally revealing about the degree to which the defending army was outmatched technologically and logistically, and that it was little able to counter Maxim guns and artillery shells:

> Personally though the whole of the advance I was with the leading company I only twice saw a native although numbers were within 20 yards of the path—they either climbed trees or lay down behind them, within a few yards of the path & deliberately picked off indi-

> viduals, retiring to reload ... The enemy on no occasion attempted to rush the column, although they at times approached the head of the column shouting, and the attacks on the centre appear to have been by more or less isolated individuals. The leading company seemed to sweep them on before them.[62]

The target destination for 14 February was a point on the route to Benin City (about 4 miles north of Ologbo) at which another path branched off, reportedly to a village; the British force accordingly named the location 'Cross Roads'. In describing the advance to capture this place, Commander Bacon shows something about the mentality of the colonial officer:

> This running fight continued till 11.30, when we ran right into a clearing, which proved to be the enemy's camp at Cross Roads. Sentries were posted, and the bush cut to further clear the camp, and a general rest was ordered till half-past one. This day happened to be the birthday of Captain Carter of the Protectorate Force. Before starting he had wished for a good brush with the enemy as a birthday present, and as he was the one who led the company on the ambush path, his wish was gratified. So we all drank his health and happy returns of the day with a wineglassful of stout, a bottle of which had been brought with us from the headquarter mess.[63]

Secure in the knowledge of British technological supremacy over the ill-equipped local fighters, and blithely confident in his ideas of his own racial superiority, Bacon is able to treat colonial warfare as a big adventure, something to be wished for as one might hope for a good day of grouse shooting. The celebratory atmosphere that he records suggests that these officers felt themselves to be at little risk, despite their later claims about the fighting prowess of their enemy.

After this planned period of rest (and impromptu birthday party), a large detachment of the advance guard set out to locate the reported village, which Hamilton had been 'ordered to destroy',[64] but no evidence of any settlement could be found after several hours of marching, and the column returned to camp. This minor failure further demonstrates the difficulties of campaigning in the absence of full knowledge of local geography. It is also notable that Hamilton had been ordered to raze a civilian settlement when there can have been no intelligence indicating that it was any kind of military target.

The information deficit faced by the invading force is also reflected in the way that Bacon—though the senior intelligence officer for the entire Expedition—was able to make only the haziest estimations of the numbers of enemy soldiers facing them:

> The enemy's camp at Cross Roads had evidently been a large one; at least twenty camp-fires were burning, and a very large number of yams cooking, either in the clearing itself or the paths leading from it, so we could count on having a considerable force of the enemy on ahead waiting for us next day.[65]

On the following day, 15 February, the advance guard departed from Cross Roads in the direction of Benin City.[66] Bacon noted that they 'had a good lie in'[67] first, as they were due to await the arrival of Captain Campbell and the rest of the 1st Division before pushing on to Agagi, where they expected to find a ready source of urgently needed water. Hamilton recorded that the advance turned into another running battle:

> Advanced at 12 noon from cross roads, troops in the same order as on the 14th. At 1.25 p.m. we were fired into from both flanks, and, pushing forward along the path, the attack gradually extended along the whole of the line. This continued at intervals as we advanced until 3 p.m., when two rockets over their camp clearing, where we heard them assembled in front of us, appeared to put them to flight. Shortly after this, Agagi village was reached ... Casualties: one private Niger Coast Protectorate force killed, one scout and one carrier wounded.[68]

According to Commander Bacon, 'Attack after attack was made by the enemy on the head of the column during the afternoon, but the volleys kept them at a respectable distance'.[69] He noted that they arrived at Agagi at about four o'clock. While Hamilton advanced his detachment, the remaining elements of 1st Division occupied the camp at Cross Roads, along with Rear Admiral Rawson and his headquarters staff.[70] With the advance guard having reached Agagi, the Benin Punitive Expedition was over halfway to its goal.

* * *

Admiral Rawson had chosen the Ologbo route to Benin City largely on the basis of the water requirements of his sizeable column. It was therefore highly problematic when Lieutenant Turner arrived at Cross Roads at two o'clock in the morning on 16 February bearing a message from Agagi that there was no water to be found.[71] Rawson later noted that, 'It had been anticipated that there would be water at Agagi, suitable, at any rate, for the carriers',[72] but in reality, 'There were three large wells—but no water—completely dried up'.[73]

This posed a 'very serious'[74] question for the Expedition, since there was no water available between Ologbo and Agagi, and no intelligence of any supply between Agagi and Benin City. The transport of sufficient volumes of water for the entire column as planned would have required significant delay, which Rawson was urgently keen to avoid (not least because of the increased risk of malaria and dysentery affecting his men). He reported that, 'I therefore decided to push on at once by forced marches to Benin, with a flying column'.[75] The force would be reorganised, and the 2nd Division would move up only as far as Cross Roads.[76] The headquarters staff moved swiftly into action, and new orders were issued before daylight:

> In consequence of the reports from the front that no water is to be found and that it is absolutely necessary to give carriers a quart a day, a flying column only will be sent on at present ... Men are to carry

> blankets and flannels only. 5 days provisions only are to be taken, and water for 3 days at 2 quarts for whites.[77]

The absence of water at Agagi was the single biggest challenge of the entire Benin Punitive Expedition, and it forced a significant change in the order of battle by reducing the force planned to march on Benin, as well as necessitating that other elements of the column be repurposed. Once again, this highlights the challenge of conducting operations with limited knowledge of the locality, and it suggests that Rawson had had to plan on the basis of general knowledge of Agagi and its characteristics rather than specific and recent reports. Reginald Bacon summarised the reorganisation of the force, also giving some accidental insight into the living standards that an officer would ordinarily expect on a march through the jungle:

> Every man not absolutely necessary, or in the fighting line, was left behind, and all extra baggage. No officer was allowed more than one carrier,—practically the whole of the extra food, wine, and spirits, belonging to the headquarter and other messes, was left behind, and officers and men, from the Admiral downwards, limited to two quarts of water per diem, to include cooking ...
>
> The 2nd Division was given the task of erecting water-tanks at Cross Roads, and of guarding the line of communication and collecting stores at Agagi, and, if time permitted, at Awoko.
>
> Of course all the water had to come from Ologbo beach and be boiled, so there was plenty to occupy the time of those left behind.[78]

By the rapid rearrangement of the column, the unexpected obstacle was readily surmounted, and thenceforward there was no serious problem. Lieutenant-Colonel Landin of the Army Service Corps even overcame the standard army–navy rivalry to later record that, 'The arrangements for water supply from CROSSROADS to Benin City were made by the Royal Navy and on the whole worked well.'[79]

16 February was spent reorganising the force and bringing up the rest of the flying column from Cross Roads to Agagi; the advance on Benin City would be made by 240 NCPF soldiers, 120 marines and sixty bluejackets from HMS *Theseus*, along with scouts, four Maxim guns, two artillery pieces, a rocket and demolition party, medics and officers.[80] In the middle of the afternoon, Rawson arrived at Agagi with Captain Campbell and the remainder of the 1st Division, meaning that everything was in place; as Commander Bacon recorded: 'We had now with us all the men who were going to form the column for the push to Benin'.[81]

* * *

On the following day, the flying column set out on what was planned as the penultimate day of the advance on Benin City, heading 5 miles to Awoko. In Hamilton's account:

> February 17.—The advanced force left Agagi under my command at 6.30 a.m ... The enemy cleared out in front of us as we proceeded. At one village, which we reached about 11.00 a.m., we were fired on, and one carrier wounded.[82]

Ralph Moor reported that, 'On the march three camps of the enemy and one village were taken, a running fight being kept up the entire journey',[83] while Commander Bacon declared that, 'From Agagi to Awoko the attacks were feeble'.[84] Awoko was occupied at about two o'clock,[85] and it was found to be 'a small village of no great pretensions, with only two cocoanut-trees [*sic*]'.[86] Although the settlement was modest, it lay just 7 miles from Benin City and thus within a day of marching; the scant resistance that the forces of the Kingdom of Benin were able to offer even at this proximity to their capital city demonstrates the profound military imbalance between the two sides. As Bacon later wrote:

> After about an hour in camp, a shot in the bush announced the vigilance of the enemy, and one poor carrier came staggering, badly injured, out of the bush where he had been collecting wood (he died the same night). The same shot hit the sentry of the water tins just below the eye, but luckily the distance off of the gun prevented his being seriously hurt.[87]

The sum total of the casualties of the British force for the advance to Awoko on 17 February was therefore one local carrier killed (name not recorded) and one bluejacket slightly injured (Robert Dye, an able seaman from HMS *St George*), as well as a local scout severely wounded (name not recorded).[88] It seems remarkable that an invading force could advance to just a few miles outside the capital and suffer so few casualties, a development that illustrates the deep technological gap separating the Benin forces from the British interlopers.

Reginald Bacon further describes how a display of this asymmetry was exploited that evening for some psychological warfare; after dark, four signal rockets were fired, 'just to give our friends in the bush something to think about'.[89] He also recorded going to bed with a seemingly childlike excitement about the day ahead:

> we were not further troubled that night, but fell asleep thinking of what marvels that wondrous city we had come so many thousand miles to see would disclose to us on the morrow.[90]

* * *

On 18 February, the leading elements of the Benin Punitive Expedition left Awoko at daylight for the final march on Benin City.[91] As Commander Reginald Bacon later remembered it: 'Up at 4.30, and issued cocoa to all hands, as usual each man taking an allowance of biscuit in his haversack. Started at 6 a.m., and the advance-guard was fired on at once'.[92] From Awoko to the target destination, the British force came under the usual fire from the ghostly Edo soldiers in the bush:

'During the whole of this day, the head and both flanks of the column were constantly attacked'.[93]

As they advanced along the narrow pathway, firing regular volleys at the unseen enemy in the jungle, the British column came upon increasing evidence that they were nearing Benin City. Ralph Moor, who in his despatches over the years had typically expressed particular concern over the practice of human sacrifice in Benin, noted a grisly discovery:

> About 1½ miles from the city, two fresh human sacrifices were met with in the path, the unfortunate beings having had their arms tied behind their backs and been gagged with pieces of stick. They had been cut from the chest down and across the stomach and their entrails were hanging out. This no doubt was Ju Ju sacrifice to prevent the white man entering the town.[94]

Bacon recorded the same corpses in his book in more emotive language, noting that one was a young woman who had been 'horribly mutilated';[95] he would later go on to revel in the evidence of human sacrifice found in the city—a valuable *post hoc* rationale for the invasion. Shortly after this gruesome finding, the advance guard came upon the only defensive position protecting Benin City, though as noted by Lieutenant-Colonel Hamilton, it did not long detain them:

> At 1 p.m. a stockade was reported in front. It was built across a causeway which led over a deep dry dyke about 30 yards wide, and it was defended by several old pieces, which were fired before we arrived close enough for them to hurt us. The stockade was blown up by Commander Bacon, R.N.[96]

That these basic fortifications caused very little delay in the advance is clear from the timings recorded by the officers with the vanguard. Bacon described pushing on from the ruined stockade, which had been destroyed using guncotton by a demolition party under his command, and then occupying a nearby settlement:

> The scent was now getting hot; it was 1 p.m., and we knew we were near Benin. Three hundred yards brought us to a clearing, which proved to be the little village Igba, a mile from Benin. Here we halted and brought up the guns and rocket-tube to fire towards the city (whose rough direction only we knew), and served out a little water to the men, who wanted it badly.[97]

Rawson himself recorded that 'the 7-prs. and rockets were fired with extreme elevation over the supposed strongest position of the enemy, and where Benin City was thought to be',[98] once again revealing the British invaders' lack of knowledge of the local geography. Despite the vague targeting, Moor noted that this fire 'was subsequently found to have been well directed for the rockets and effects of shell were found in the city'.[99]

Following a halt of approximately half an hour, the advance was resumed; since the leading company of NCPF soldiers had run out of ammunition, a company of bluejackets from HMS *St George* was called up to replace them for the final advance on the city.[100] After they had continued along the path for around one mile, a clear area was detected ahead, and Rawson reported that, 'the enemy were, for the first time, actually seen—a body of them attempting to charge the head of our column as we advanced out of the narrow bush path'.[101] This proved to be the edge of Benin City, where the jungle path emerged into a broad street running east–west, which adjoined the main thoroughfare of the city. At this point, the resistance of the Benin forces became desperate, and the resulting halt of the column brought Lieutenant-Colonel Hamilton up to the head of his vanguard. He reported the advance into Benin City that followed:

> Going forward I found Captain Barrow's [*sic*] Maxim in action, under a heavy fire, at a point where the bush-path debouched into a broad ride running at right angles to it. A big gun had been firing down the path at close quarters here. The bluejackets formed line on either side of the end of the path, and as more men came up the whole were

> formed into a hollow square, covering the point of exit. The chief fire came from the direction of the King's house to our left, where many men were seen, and a number of old cannon were firing. When the 7-pr guns and rocket-tubes had been brought into action for a short time, an advance up the ride towards the King's house was commenced. During this advance we were continually fired into from all sides, and fired volleys in reply ... At about 300 yards from the King's house a big gun was fired, after which there were a few dropping shots, and the resistance seemed to collapse.[102]

According to Ralph Moor, 'The troops with a cheer charged the last 200 yards into the city, which was actually taken at about 2 o'clock'.[103]

* * *

Admiral Rawson cabled to London that Benin City had been captured after 'sharp fighting',[104] noting that since the king and all inhabitants had fled, he had been unable to seize Oba Ovonramwen as the Admiralty had wished.[105] Ralph Moor reported to the Foreign Office by telegram, 'City now deserted. Neither King nor Juju men captured', and also claimed 'considerable resistance taking city'.[106] Although British accounts of this kind emphasised the tough odds that they had faced in overcoming determined defenders, it should be noted that casualties among the British force during the final assault on Benin City amounted to just four killed and twenty-six injured, including carriers.[107] As was usual, the invading force did not record the number of Edo dead and wounded.

The British first impressions of the city were overwhelmingly dominated by the horrifying evidence of human sacrifice and by the accompanying foul odours. In his initial telegram home, Rawson reported that the place 'stinks of human blood: sacrifices and corpses everywhere'.[108] Noting that 'Benin is an irregular straggling town formed by groups of houses separated from each other by patches of bush',[109] Commander Bacon described an open area of common land to the west of the palace as being 'simply strewn with bodies in every stage of decomposition, skulls and bones'.[110] Unsurprisingly, given his previous concerns about the practice, Ralph Moor wrote somewhat emotively of the sacrificial remains:

> The city presented the most appalling sight, particularly around the King's quarters, from which four large main roads lead to the compounds of the bigger Chiefs, the city being very scattered.
>
> Sacrificial trees in the open spaces still held the corpses of the latest victims—seven in all were counted—and on every path a freshly-sacrificed corpse was found lying, apparently placed there to prevent pursuit. One large open space, 200 to 300 yards in length, was strewn with human bones and bodies in all stages of decomposition.
>
> Within the walls the sight was, if possible, even more terrible.[111]

Charged with preparing an official report on the sanitary condition of the city, Dr Robert Allman, the principal medical officer of the Niger Coast Protectorate, took detailed notes:

> On the principal 'sacrifice tree' facing the main gate of the King's compound there were two sacrifices (crucifixions), & lying around the foot of the tree there were 17 newly decapitated bodies (including 3 Europeans,) and 43 decapitated bodies in various stages of decomposition.
>
> On the 'sacrifice tree' to the west of the main entrance a woman was crucified, and at the foot of the tree four decapitated and eviscerated bodies were found. On going westwards towards the plain leading to the Gwato Road a sickening sight was met with. One hundred and seventy-six (176) human sacrifices and decomposing bodies were found, the stench from which was so intolerable that the sanitary gang under my supervision had on more than one occasion to beat a hasty retreat.[112]

The dreadful odour was remarked on by all the British occupiers, with Bacon remembering it as 'indescribably sickening'[113] and declaring that it was something that 'no white man's internal economy could stand'.[114] Indeed, the air quality was so bad that on the day of arrival, several cases of fainting and sickness occurred,[115] and the medical officer reported an even more serious effect:

> The day after our arrival here nearly all the European officers, and a great number of the Native Troops and carriers, suffered acutely from a form of epidemic Diarrhoea, caused by inhaling the putrid atmosphere.[116]

It was through investigating what they called the 'Juju places'[117] or 'sacrifice compounds'[118] that the British forces first came upon the great artworks for which the Kingdom of Benin is especially known in the present era:

> These spaces were about a hundred and fifty yards long, and about sixty broad, surrounded by a high wall, and covered with a short brown grass. At one end was a long shed running the whole breadth of the enclosure, and under this was the altar. The altar was made by three steps running the whole length under the shelter of the shed; slightly raised for some distance in the centre, on which raised portion were handsomely-carved ivory tusks placed on the top of very antique bronze heads. Near these tusks were carved clubs, undoubtedly for use upon the victims of the sacrifice. The altar was deluged in blood, the smell of which was too overpowering for many of us. This same awful smell seemed to pervade the whole compound, as if the grass had been watered with blood.[119]

Their first sight of the Benin Bronzes provoked varied reactions in the British officers. Ralph Moor firmly connected the artworks with the human sacrificial practices, declaring the brass heads of the altars to be 'hideously-constructed'.[120] In contrast, Reginald Bacon was highly complimentary, despite his enthusiastic racism and determined efforts to emphasise the gory details of human sacrifice. Giving an account of the exploration of the palace complex, he recorded the discovery of the famous plaques:

> The storehouses contained chiefly cheap rubbish, such as glass walking sticks, old uniforms, absurd umbrellas, and the usual cheap finery that traders use to tickle the fancy of the natives. But buried in the dirt of ages, in one house, were several hundred unique bronze plaques, suggestive of almost Egyptian design, but of really superb casting. Castings of wonderful delicacy of detail, and some magnificently carved tusks were collected ... Of other ivory work, some bracelets suggestive of Chinese work and two magnificent leopards were the chief articles of note; bronze groups of idols, and two large and beautifully-worked stools were also found, and must have been of very old manufacture.[121]

Despite these differing aesthetic judgements, all the artworks that could be found were swiftly packed up, ready for transporting all the way to London for sale. James Phillips had promised large stores of ivory in Benin City, which could be sold to defray the cost of invasion; these castings and carvings would do just as well.

* * *

Given the need to keep costs down and Rawson's ongoing concerns about exposing the men to additional risk of malaria, he and his staff had drawn up plans based on the Expedition remaining in Benin City only until 20 February. In the event, the NCPF was running short of ammunition and stores, so the main force remained until the twenty-second in order to ensure that the occupying troops were in a defensible position.[122] However, the most pressing concern on taking the city was the shortage of water; at daylight on 19 February, two-thirds of the entire force, with all the carriers, were therefore sent out as a water party, returning around three hours later having found a good source about 2 miles to the north.[123] Much time over the following days was spent getting water ready for the return march to Warrigi.

Some considerable time was also expended demolishing various parts of the city. Rawson reported that on the afternoon of 19 February, 'a strong force was marched out, and destroyed Chief Ijuma's compound', and that on the following days two parties 'were sent out to destroy the Queen-Mother's and Chief Ichudi's compounds. Also the sacrificial and crucifixion trees, and the whole of the Ju Ju houses'.[124] The razing of captured settlements was standard practice for the British Empire in punitive expeditions in Africa, and in Benin City it was combined with a righteous display of the destruction of the places of worship of the local religion. These acts would assist in bolstering claims that the entire expedition was prompted by a desire to end the practice of human sacrifice.

In the event, the British force razed the entire city to the ground, though the final destruction was caused by accident:

> At 4 p.m. on the 21st instant, a fire, started by the carriers, spread in a few minutes over the whole town; and by the promptitude of Captain Campbell, of H.M.S. 'Theseus,' the wounded were got out while the temporary hospital was actually on fire.
>
> Some arms, ammunition, and most of our provisions, were burnt. Fortunately, however, the 'Forte's' company, under Lieutenant F. R. Harrold, arrived within an hour with a fresh supply.[125]

This conflagration destroyed the palace and the surrounding quarters of the town, meaning that, following the earlier deliberate demolitions, there was almost nothing left but open ground. Ralph Moor declared that the fire was 'unfortunate only in that we were unprepared for it' and welcomed its 'cleansing effects' despite the loss of baggage and provisions.[126] While it would have been wholly in keeping with British practice to burn down the palace, we can be sure that it was an accident on this occasion, for Lieutenant-Colonel Hamilton had all his belongings destroyed in the blaze, as we know from his claim for reimbursement;[127] his list of destroyed kit also tells us that he had travelled to Benin City with a camp bed, an umbrella, two pairs of pyjamas, a cummerbund and two pairs of silk-and-wool drawers. Additionally, Moor noted that, 'The effects of the late Mr Phillips and his party were found in the King's palaver-house almost intact, but unfortunately they were subsequently destroyed by fire'.[128]

With the city razed to the ground on the late afternoon of 21 February, and with the fortunate arrival of a supply column that same evening, departure on the morning of the twenty-second was very timely. Having gathered sufficient water for the return march south and prepared the defensive works for the NCPF detail that would stay as an occupying force, the Expedition prepared to set off for home. Rawson noted his final arrangements:

> I left, for the use of the Protectorate force, two Maxims and one rocket tube, with the necessary ammunition; also the Martini-Henry rifles which had been issued to the scouts. I also transferred to them two of the four days' provisions brought up by the 'Forte's' company.[129]

With that, and with the ruins of Benin City still smouldering, Admiral Rawson and the Benin Punitive Expedition departed in the early morning of 22 February 1897. Oba Ovonramwen was a refugee king, his city and palace had been destroyed, and the entire Edo cultural inheritance was packed up and heading for London. The Kingdom of Benin was no more.

9

THE AFTERMATH

Now this is the whiteman's country. There is only one king in the country and that is the whiteman … Ovonramwen is no longer king of this country.

Consul General Sir Ralph Moor, 7 September 1897

To CURATORS of Museums, Antiquarians, Curio Collectors, &c.—COLLECTION of curiously and Elaborately-carved IVORY TUSKS, captured at the fall of Benin City, supposed to be of great age, to be SOLD, by AUCTION, by HALE and SON, on the 18th AUGUST, 1897, at two o'clock precisely, at 10, Fenchurch-avenue, E.C., where they are now on view.

Classified advertisement, *Morning Post*, 13 August 1897

The Benin Punitive Expedition headed homewards on a return march that was 'uneventful, but slow on account of the wounded', bivouacking one night at Awoko, then at Cross Roads, before arriving at Warrigi on 24 February.[1] The force at Sapoba under Captain MacGill received orders on the same day, and accordingly they burnt their stockade and returned to Warrigi on the twenty-fifth.[2] Having been ordered to remain at Gwato until relieved by NCPF troops, Captain O'Callaghan withdrew his force on 27 February,[3] and on the same day the main contingent departed Warrigi: 'The whole of the force were re-embarked by the evening of the 27th instant'.[4] Agreeing with Moor that he would order HMS *Barrosa* to visit Forcados once a week in case naval assistance was required,[5] Admiral Rawson sailed out of the Benin River and thence back to Cape Town, having destroyed Benin City a mere five weeks after first receiving his orders.

Rawson also informed London of the final casualty figures for the Expedition. Those killed in action amounted to two officers and eight men (which he helpfully subdivided into '5 whites, 3 blacks'), with six officers and forty-four men ('22 whites, 22 blacks') wounded in action.[6] There were five deaths 'from the effects of climate' (all white) and two deaths by accident. The Edo death toll was never authoritatively recorded, but given the reports of body counts from sources such as Commander Bacon—as well as the lethal effectiveness of Maxim guns, 7-pdrs and Martini-Henry rifles—it must assuredly have been in the hundreds, and quite possibly in the thousands when displaced persons and disruptions to local food supply chains are taken into account.

An important factor in this respect is that the departure of the naval forces did not mean a complete end to the fighting; the NCPF had to establish itself as an occupying army, as well as locate and arrest Oba Ovonramwen, which meant sending out columns into the bush. Ralph Moor described his new establishment in what was left of the captured city:

> The entire naval brigade left under Admiral Rawson on morning of the 22nd instant, and the native troops, under Lieutenant-Colonel Hamilton, moved into the camp selected and partially prepared. There are 270 troops in all, with a complement of 350 carriers; but with escorts and a small flying column out opening roads, there will only be about 200 in camp as a rule.[7]

As was typical for Moor, he expressed the scorched-earth tactics of the invaders in terms of his moral outrage over the practice of human sacrifice; even after the fire that had razed virtually all that remained of the city after the initial planned demolitions, he was determined to complete the punishment:

> All buildings on this site, saturated as it is with the blood of human victims, will be levelled to the ground, and no building of any description will ever again be allowed to be erected thereon. If a town is again built it must be nearer the water, which is now 3 miles distant.[8]

This redevelopment of what eventually became a new Benin City began with the construction of defensive positions for the NCPF camp, including lodgings for the new 'political resident' who would be left to rule over the former kingdom. Once the naval force was withdrawn from Warrigi, the main base for travelling to Benin once again became Gwato,[9] and Moor was quick to despatch Captain Gallwey with a detachment to secure the road there and to relieve the naval column.[10] While occupying Gwato, Captain O'Callaghan had taken the opportunity to prepare defensive positions, as well as to build a pier and a new road to connect the main town to the river.[11] Additionally, Rawson had left 30 miles of telegraph wire with all the necessary batteries and equipment to allow Moor to put Benin City into direct communications with Gwato.[12] The British wasted little time in laying down the infrastructure required for effective occupation of the valuable new territory.

* * *

On the same day that the main column marched away from Benin City, messengers arrived from Oba Ovonramwen asking if he could come in for a palaver; Moor would make no promises as to safe conduct, but said he would suspend hostilities until 26 February so that the king could come in if he desired.[13] Discussions continued through these messengers for some days beyond this deadline (while the NCPF force completed their new camp and fortifications), until Moor telegraphed London on 5 March to announce that his patience was at an end: 'Defensive position completing. Negociations [*sic*] for surrender protracted to failure. Direction King and chiefs ascertained. Start pursuit tomorrow.'[14]

Accordingly, Moor set out from Benin City on 6 March with a flying column, comprised of Lieutenant-Colonel Hamilton, sixty men, one Maxim gun and a rocket tube. After five days of fruitless searching and further burning of villages, they returned to Benin City on 11 March. Telegraphing home, Moor sought to put a positive gloss on the attempt:

> Pursuit carried through seven villages in northerly direction, about 30 miles; no attempt resistance. Found very extensive bush town building, probably two to three thousand: King's people all fled easterly direction. Burnt town. Consider action will have excellent effect.[15]

Moor later reported that during the entire journey, 'no opposition was experienced, and no shot fired by the enemy', and that since he was by that time 'fairly satisfied that there is no fight left in the Binis', he would bring forward his preparations for the establishment of the permanent post and the withdrawal of all surplus troops and carriers.[16] Leaving District Commissioner Alfred Turner as the new political resident, supported by 120 NCPF soldiers and their officers, Moor departed Benin City on 15 March with Hamilton and the remainder of the force. He noted to London that he intended to complete the unfinished business: 'I propose returning to the Benin district and visiting Benin City before the end of April, by which time it will I trust be arranged that the King and Chiefs come in to palaver'.[17]

* * *

In the event, it was not until early August that Oba Ovonramwen—whose support and supplies had been dwindling over several months of royal vagabondage—surrendered himself to the British occupiers. The king had sought refuge in the territory of the Royal Niger Company in June, but after a stiff engagement with Company forces (in which a Lieutenant Fitzgerald was killed), he returned to his former kingdom. Following further weeks of pursuit, he entered the ruined Benin City on 5 August, 'preceded by a messenger with a white flag, and accompanied by 800 unarmed men, with ten chiefs, 20 of his wives, and a reed band'.[18] Captain Roupell, who was then acting political resident following the death of Alfred Turner, forced Oba Ovonramwen to make a public submission to the British on 7 August, when the king prostrated himself and touched his forehead to the ground in front of his gathered chiefs and people. He was then held prisoner, along with a number of his chiefs, while awaiting trial for the attack on James Phillips and his party.

Given its symbolic importance, the consul general (who had by this time been knighted as Sir Ralph for his services in the invasion)[19] decided to conduct the trial himself. Moor thus travelled from Old Calabar with sixty NCPF soldiers and on 1 September began proceedings. Remarkably—given that he had, after all, been deposed—Oba Ovonramwen was acquitted of the charge of ordering the attack on the British mission in January; instead, the court found six chiefs guilty of involvement. Moor judged that the order to ambush the Phillips party was given by the Ologbosere, a powerful chief who was second in command of the Benin army, and found that the king had merely instructed his men to monitor the foreigners. Two of the chiefs in question were executed by firing squad, two committed suicide in custody, and one died before trial;[20] the Ologbosere, however, was not in British hands and continued an anticolonial guerrilla war for two years, until he was finally caught and executed in June 1899.

The acquittal of the king did not, of course, mean the reversal of the British invasion of his kingdom. During the proceedings in his consular court on 7 September, Moor made this very clear by making an emphatic public announcement:

> Now this is the whiteman's country. There is only one king in the country and that is the whiteman ... Ovonramwen is no longer king of this country; the whiteman is the only man who is king in this country and to him only service is due.[21]

Ovonramwen was stripped of his powers and almost all of his tributary income, and was denied the attendance of most of his retinue. There is reason to think that Moor was considering retaining the king in Benin City as a puppet ruler, but in the end (following an attempt by the king to escape from the Protectorate yacht *Ivy* on 9 September), it was decided to sentence him to exile for life, despite his acquittal. Before the end of September, Oba Ovonramwen was thus taken to Old Calabar, where he would live quietly until his death in 1914.

* * *

News of the victory reached London while Rawson and his column were still marching south, back to their vessels. Unofficial word had been telegraphed home, and on 22 February the intelligence was confirmed in Parliament by George Goschen, the First Lord of the Admiralty.[22] He declared that Benin City had been captured 'with very little loss of life',[23] to cheers from the House of Commons.[24]

Having followed the campaign with eager interest all the way through, the press seized on the story, especially relishing the lurid details of human sacrifices found in the ruined city. This gruesome element both added sales-worthy drama and bolstered the frequent claims of British moral supremacy over a barbarous enemy: 'The Admiral confirms the statements which have been published of the horrible state of the place, owing to the human sacrifices carried out by the orders of the King and the fanatical Ju-Ju priests'.[25] Extensive coverage across a wide range of newspapers sought to ensure that this episode of imperial conquest was fixed in the public mind as a triumph for civilisation, and the gory subject of sacrifices made excellent copy for the popular illustrated papers of the time. The *Illustrated London News* even had a special correspondent, Henry Seppings Wright, in Benin City in the wake of the conquest,[26] and while smaller rival *The Graphic* had no eyewitness pictures, it made the most of the dramatic subject nonetheless:

> So another Reign of Terror in West Africa is ended. Benin City is in British hands, and fetish and Ju-Ju will go the way of their fellows in Ashanti. Not that the success was lightly won, for the Benin natives proved tough fighters indeed ... At last the force came out into the open close to Benin City, and charged in splendid style down the broad avenue leading to the town ... British dash and discipline soon told; the natives gave way, and Admiral Rawson and his men entered the King's compound as masters of the town.[27]

Celebrations were not limited merely to the printed realm; just the day after announcing the seizure of the Kingdom of Benin in the House of Commons, George Goschen was once again talking of the expedition, this time as the guest of the City Carlton Club. Surrounded by a great many aristocratic panjandrums and financial dignitaries, the First Lord gave a speech that was calculated to stoke the vanity of his imperially minded audience, and that was widely reported at length in the newspapers:

> Let me for one moment dwell with some pleasurable pride, in which you may share, on the fact that in the last few years on four or five occasions British endurance, British coolness, British organisation have lead [*sic*] expeditions undertaken in the midst of tremendous difficulties to a most satisfactory and successful issue. (Cheers) Honours are shared by men of various races serving under the stimulating influence of British officers (Hear, hear).[28]

Referencing recent and ongoing British military actions on the North-West Frontier of India, in Egypt, and elsewhere in West Africa, Goschen placed the Benin invasion firmly in the context of a long series of expansionary colonial wars:

> And last, but not least, turn to the punitive expedition under Admiral Rawson—(cheers)—sent out to avenge the cruel murder of certain white men—an expedition thoroughly well organised, that has met with the most complete success, and has occupied the City of Benin. (Loud cheers.)[29]

It was not just senior members of government and the financial world who joined in the festivities; many among the general public felt moved to celebrate too. When Ralph Locke, one of the only two British survivors of the Phillips mission, arrived home to Kent at the beginning of March, the local residents mounted a remarkable welcome:

> Mr Locke was accorded an enthusiastic reception when he arrived with his brother at Newington Station, near Sittingbourne, on Saturday night. The station yard and its approach were covered with flags and bunting, and a large crowd had assembled, some of whom carried torches. Coloured fires were also lighted. Mr Locke was presented with a short address, congratulating him upon his escape after the terrible sufferings he had undergone, and wishing him a speedy restoration to health. The horses were taken out of the carriage, and Mr Locke and his brother and sister were drawn through the village, accompanied by a torchlight procession. At Hartlip the church bells were wrung.[30]

Similarly, when the Royal Marines arrived at Portsmouth on the *Malacca* later that month, they were greeted by a supportive public:

> After the invalids, except Captain Byrne, had been removed in launches to Haslar Hospital the rest of the troops landed and were despatched to their various barracks. Many of the streets were decorated with flags, and as the men marched through the streets with

> the bands playing 'Home, sweet Home', the crowds which lined the route cheered them to the echo.[31]

This kind of exuberant welcome is, of course, in part a wholly understandable display of relief at the safe return of sons and husbands from an uncertain and distant venture involving a degree of peril. Given the triumphant nature of such events, and the imperial form that they unavoidably took, however, there is scope for asking whether these members of the British general public were in fact celebrating what they thought they were. Would such crowds have assembled if they had known the reality of colonial violence? Would dozens of private citizens flock to honour an Empire official if they knew how many African villages he had burnt down? These questions are of continuing relevance in the twenty-first century, since unexamined (and often surprisingly fond) notions of the Empire remain in the British popular consciousness, frequently creating fundamental misunderstanding of the real nature of Britain's imperial history.

We can see that, in some respects, this was a direct result of the biased coverage offered by the newspapers of the era, and of the willingness of the leaders of the nation to employ imperial rhetoric (including regular claims of British exceptionalism) for their own political purposes. One of the most strident voices of this kind was Joseph Chamberlain, the colonial secretary at the time of the conquest of Benin, who stood second to none in his efforts to promote the Empire and imperial ideology in the late Victorian age. Eager reporting of his remarks throughout the press would ensure a regular injection of misrepresented facts into the popular discourse; take, for example, the speech that Chamberlain made to the annual dinner of the Royal Colonial Institute in the wake of the capture of Benin City, as reported in the *Morning Post*:

> We feel now that our rule over these territories can only be justified if we show that it tends to the happiness and prosperity of the peo-

ple—(cheers)—and I maintain that our rule it is which has brought security and peace and comparative prosperity to countries that never knew it before. (Cheers.) In carrying out this work of civilisation we are fulfilling what I believe to be our national mission, and we are finding scope for the exercise of those faculties and qualities which have made of us a great governing race. (Cheers.)[32]

Such claims are quite clearly at variance with the facts, but a senior member of government was nonetheless willing to make them in front of 300 members of the society, to be repeated via the newspapers to hundreds of thousands of readers around the country. Chamberlain went on to rhapsodise about *Pax Britannica* and then mocked those few 'philanthropists' who would sometimes complain about colonial violence:

You cannot have omelettes without breaking eggs. (Loud cheers.) You cannot destroy the practises of barbarism, of slavery, and of superstition, which for centuries have desolated the interior of Africa, without the use of force—(cheers)—and if you will fairly contrast the gain to humanity against the cost which we have to pay for it, I think you may well rejoice at the success of expeditions such as those which have recently been conducted.[33]

On this occasion, the formal reply to the guest speaker was given by the Earl of Onslow, himself a colonial official of long standing and at the time the under-secretary of state for India. His words, and the gleeful response of the audience, thoroughly undermine Chamberlain's claims about spreading civilisation and reveal the hypocrisy behind the British Empire project:

It now remained for Englishmen to see that the traditions which had founded that great Empire were maintained. We had possessed ourselves of the fairest portion of the world—(laughter)—and the only problem that remained was that we should keep it. (Prolonged cheering.)[34]

Since the Irish nationalists were among the very few opponents of imperialism in the British Isles at the time, it fell to

John Dillon, MP for Mayo East in Ireland, to point out the disingenuous nature of the claims made by Chamberlain and others. *The Times* reported on Dillon's intervention in a House of Commons debate on Africa on 2 April:

> It had been assumed by various speakers as an admitted fact that the chief object of the European Powers who interfered in African affairs was to carry to those remote regions the blessings of Christianity and civilization ... He contended that the expedition to Benin was in the interest of commerce and not of humanity.[35]

* * *

Dillon's was a rare instance of opposition to the invasion of Benin. Besides a vocally supportive public, the British official sphere was also in a celebratory mood, all the way to the very top of the social hierarchy. Having earlier telegraphed to praise the troops on their advance,[36] even before news was received that the city had been taken, Queen Victoria again commanded that her congratulations be sent once the victory was known:

> The Queen desires to express to Adml. Rawson her great admiration of the conduct of the brave men under his command who must all have gone through such a terrible trying time on their march to Benin which was so successfully captured.[37]

Ralph Moor had written to London only a few days after the city fell in order to 'strenuously urge' that a campaign medal be issued.[38] The Queen formally approved the award in July, and it was decided that all men present in ships and at base would receive the decoration, not only the men on the march to Benin City itself.[39] Before this, a small flood of rewards was given. The Royal Navy promoted twelve officers 'for services in connection with the Benin Expedition',[40] and numerous honours for expedition members were formally gazetted in May.[41] For their part in commanding the Gwato and Sapoba columns, Captain O'Callaghan and Captain MacGill both became Companions of the Bath, as did

Captain Egerton, Rawson's chief of staff. Commander Bacon was awarded a Distinguished Service Order, along with four other officers. Lieutenant-Colonel Hamilton was promoted to colonel, and Captain Gallwey became a major. Most notably of all, perhaps, Rear Admiral Rawson was knighted as a Knight Commander of the Order of the Bath, and as before mentioned, Ralph Moor became Sir Ralph Moor KCMG in July. There were thus generous social and professional rewards to be had from participating in the Benin Punitive Expedition.

Besides these celebrations and public honours, the Benin invasion was kept in the national consciousness in a number of other ways. Captain Boisragon swiftly wrote a book about his experience with the Phillips mission, publishing *The Benin Massacre* in September.[42] Commander Bacon followed in November with his own book, *Benin: The City of Blood*,[43] in which he focused especially on the evidence of human sacrifice found by the invaders. The expedition also made it into the *Boy's Own Annual* published for Christmas 1897, with the prolific novelist George A. Henty 'guiding us to the "Fetish Hole" in West African swamps, suggestive of the bloody policy of Kumasi and Benin'.[44] William Gordon Stables, another productive juvenile novelist of imperialist bent, similarly brought out *The Naval Cadet* in time for Christmas, in which young Creggan 'sees service on the west coast of Africa, and is in at the storm of the bloodstained city of Benin'.[45]

Memorial funds were launched for some of the British dead. Friends and colleagues of James Phillips established the Phillips Memorial Committee[46] and placed a plaque in his memory in the chapel at Uppingham School. Major Crawford was commemorated with a stained-glass window (showing St Alban and St Martin, both holding swords) in Christ Church, Barnet, which was unveiled by the Earl of Strafford in November.[47] Perhaps the strangest ritual of remembrance was, however, the 'Capture of Benin City' display at the annual Royal Tournament, held in May 1898 at the Royal Agricultural Hall in Islington.[48]

Mounted as a mock battle to show off the skills and technology of the armed forces, this climactic performance was judged by *The Times* to be the 'most successful "combined display" of recent years';[49] the same reviewer described the scene of the recreated Benin City in the arena, full of British soldiers pretending to be Edo warriors:

> There is great beating of tom-toms and shrieking of savage music, as the King, preceded by his Court, comes out into the open walking under his great umbrella. He is a fine if barbaric figure, every inch a savage monarch, although in truth he is a quiet gentleman in the Army Service Corps.[50]

Captives were shown being dragged to the king's compound, and a great sword was made ready for execution. Then, with a flourish, the British forces arrived:

> Hausas dash forward first and are almost repulsed. The Bluejackets and Marines reinforce them ... there is such banging of a seven-pounder and a rocket tube, such crashing from a Maxim carried on the tripod that was actually used at Benin, such rattling of musketry, and shouting, and promiscuous slaughter as never was seen ... A fine British cheer from the sailors and much waving of the Union Jack from the captured city end the performance and, most emphatically, bring the house down.[51]

* * *

Of all the things that kept the invasion of Benin in public awareness, however, preeminent above all was the great body of cultural treasures seized from the defeated kingdom. The surprising discovery of intricate cast metal pieces and delicately carved ivory offered splendid opportunities to the British officers and men to plunder some trophies of war. This was also the official reaction; once back in Old Calabar in the wake of the fall of Benin, Ralph Moor wrote to the Foreign Office to report that he was despatching a memento for presentation to Queen Victoria:

> I have selected two carved ivory tusks and two leopard figures made from ivory which I am sending home in charge of Major Landon ... The ivories would require polishing and putting in good order as they were unfortunately slightly damaged by fire though first rate specimens.[52]

For his part, Admiral Rawson sent a 'magnificently-carved'[53] ivory tusk to the Admiralty.[54] The officials in Whitehall replied with a clipped expression of gratitude for the 'interesting trophy' and promptly sent it to the Royal United Services Institution, following which it was soon placed on public display.[55]

Immediately after the expedition, as news emerged of curious artistic discoveries, the major museums of the world began to take an interest. Having seen newspaper reports of antique ivory and bronze pieces being brought out of Benin, Charles Hercules Read, keeper of the Department of British and Mediaeval Antiquities and Ethnography at the British Museum, swiftly wrote to his superior to request that the Foreign Office be approached:

> I think it would be desirable to ascertain from the proper quarter whether these articles, and perhaps many other similar things that have been discovered by our officers in Benin, could not be secured for the British Museum. So far as my department of the Museum is concerned, I should be quite prepared to recommend the Trustees to pay a fair price for any such objects.[56]

A vigorous lobbying campaign by Read eventually paid off, and the official booty from Benin City, seized by Ralph Moor to help pay the cost of the invasion, was in due course sent to the British Museum.[57] Importantly, however, the cache of treasures impounded by Moor (comprising especially the c. 300 brass plaques that are now iconic of Benin artistry) formed only a fraction of the total number of looted artworks. The Austrian doctor and anthropologist Felix von Luschan, who was on the staff of the Königliches Museum für Völkerkunde in Berlin at the time, later counted c. 2,400 pieces taken from Benin City in the wake of the invasion, though this total includes some strictly utilitarian items.[58]

Trade in plundered Benin works began as soon as officers of the expedition force returned to the coast in West Africa; indeed, it was a newspaper report from Lagos that alerted Read to the existence of Benin treasures.[59] Private sales of looted pieces swiftly became a regular feature of the art world in London, and the main newspapers over the following few years were peppered with classified advertisements announcing them, such as this typical example from 1898:

> Mr. J. C. STEVENS will SELL by AUCTION, at his great Rooms, 38, King-street, Covent-garden, as follows, at half-past 12 precisely each day:—THIS DAY (Monday).—A most interesting and valuable collection of Curios from Benin City, by order of an officer in the recent Expedition; also Relics, Antiquities, Arms and Armour, Native Weapons, China, Paintings, Bronzes, Carvings, Ancient Implements, &c.
>
> Tues.—Poultry, Pigeons, Canaries, Ducks, Geese, &c...[60]

Through such means, many of the Benin treasures changed hands rapidly. As early as April 1897, Richard Quick at the Horniman Free Museum in south London had acquired enough pieces to mount an exhibition,[61] photographs of which appeared that month in the *Illustrated London News*.[62] Some months later, Charles Read was finally able to mount the first Benin exhibition at the British Museum, when all the plaques went on display in September in a temporary home in the Assyrian basement.[63]

The press reaction was dominated by an uncertain mixture of admiration at the evident artistry and incredulity that such work could have come from the 'City of Blood'. In a lengthy review, *The Standard* hailed the 'remarkable specimens', proclaiming that 'in design and execution they are unequalled by anything hitherto attributed to the negro races' and wondering whether they were in fact of 'native workmanship'.[64] *The Times* offered some slightly grudging praise:

> Two long screens in the middle of the room are covered with bronzes or brass plaques, about 300 in number, with figures in high relief, cast and slightly finished by tooling, which, both by the novelty of the subjects and the technical perfection of the work, are surprising evidence of the skill of the Benin native in the casting of metal ...
>
> That the Benin workmen were very expert in this method is fully shown by the perfection of the castings they produced. Those who cannot be enthusiastic about their art value or their importance from an ethnological standpoint will still admit that as castings they leave but little to desire.[65]

Following this exhibition, around 200 of the plaques were formally given to the British Museum by the Foreign Office, and the rest were sold in a series of auctions in late 1897;[66] the British authorities had, of course, always intended to monetise whatever booty could be found in Benin City, in order to defray the costs of the invasion. At the same time, therefore, seventy to eighty Benin ivory tusks were sold in the City of London at £80 each,[67] raising revenue for the Niger Coast Protectorate equivalent to around £500,000 at the time of this publication.[68]

The disposal of the plaques by the Foreign Office and especially the active private market in Benin pieces allowed museums and collectors around the world to move rapidly to assemble collections of this desirable new category of artefact. General Augustus Pitt-Rivers purchased a large number of Benin works using his inherited fortune, which derived in part from the West Indies slave trade; his private museum shortly thereafter became the basis for the Pitt Rivers Museum at Oxford University. Given its hometown's West African connections, the Liverpool Museum also acquired a Benin collection, along with numerous European museums, such as the Museum für Völkerkunde in

Vienna and the Museum für Völkerkunde in Dresden. Above all the others, however, Felix von Luschan was the most acquisitive, and he eventually amassed well over 500 Benin works for the Museum für Völkerkunde in Berlin, now the Ethnologisches Museum in the Humboldt Forum.

Not everyone was happy with this international interest in the Benin treasures. In his own book on Benin art, the British curator and anthropologist Henry Ling Roth wrote bitterly of the loss to the British Museum caused by the Foreign Office sale:

> Not only was the national institution thus deprived of its lawful acquisitions, but at the same time another government department sold for a few hundred pounds a large number of castings which had cost thousands to obtain, as well as much blood of our fellow countrymen.[69]

Without a hint of irony, Roth complained that the Benin artworks had been removed from the country:

> From what I can ascertain, the bulk of these bronzes has been secured by the Germans, and it is especially annoying to Englishmen to think that such articles, which for every reason should be retained in this country, have been allowed to go abroad.[70]

EPILOGUE

In his *History of Nigeria*, Sir Alan Burns, who was deputy chief secretary to the government of Nigeria in the 1930s, declared that 'the settlement of the Benin country' was the final important act of the Niger Coast Protectorate.[1] Marking the effective end of the conquest phase in the region, the invasion of Benin eliminated the last remaining local power of any consequence, and the borders of British territory were thus defined. Much brutal 'pacification' was yet to come in several areas, but more developed structures of colonial rule could soon be established. The Niger Coast Protectorate evolved into the Protectorate of Southern Nigeria at the beginning of 1900, with Sir Ralph Moor as the first high commissioner;[2] with the winding up of the royal charter at the same time, the territory of the Royal Niger Company became the Protectorate of Northern Nigeria. In 1914, the two protectorates (by then also including the Colony of Lagos) were combined into a single Colony of Nigeria, with essentially the borders of the country we know today.

As this book has sought to show, the 1897 attack on the Kingdom of Benin must be seen in this context of British expansion in the wider Niger region; the death of James Phillips and party had nothing substantive to do with the ultimate fate of Benin except in determining the timing of the final military occupation. Once a British claim over the area had been made in the 1880s, the remorseless logic of empire required that it be enforced, lest a rival European power step in. The fact that the British advance into the African interior was defensive—reflecting relative decline amid growing competition from France, Germany and other countries—made it no less aggressive or less costly for local people in their lives and liberties. The increasingly shrill patriotic speechifying of Chamberlain and other imperial cheerleaders of the time betrays a rising insecurity about *Pax Britannica* and an anxiety that British supremacy was in doubt.

The narratives spun and the grand claims made spurred further colonial excesses at the time, and their impact continues into the twenty-first century. Propagandistic assertions that Britain was spreading democracy and liberty around the world were flatly contradicted by the colonial reality of coercion both military and legalistic,[3] but nonetheless they still influence our ideas about the Empire today. We have seen in these pages something of the way the British press covered the assault on Benin, and the triumphalist celebrations it prompted; such forms of discourse have a lasting effect. In other media too, the positive gloss was maintained, presenting the Empire project in a profoundly misleading light. Going to the movie theatre in 1935, British audiences could see such things as *Sanders of the River*,[4] in which District Commissioner Sanders was portrayed as a benevolent ruler of his district, deeply loved and respected by the dutiful local natives. Even thirty years later, when decolonisation was well under way, cinemagoers were presented with films like *Zulu*,[5] in which plucky Brits in Africa fought courageously and honourably against all the odds. Above all, the story of the Empire has become strangely conflated with the memory of World War Two to produce a seamless narrative of Britain as a defender of 'freedom', in ignorance of the brute reality of imperialism.[6]

I can attest to the insidious power of these narratives—and to our collective failure to address our imperial past properly—from my personal experience. At university I acquired two degrees in history, including a master's in British Empire history, and nonetheless I graduated with a relatively neutral position on imperialism. I even remember, much to my current shame and embarrassment, telling a friend in the late 1990s that while British colonialism couldn't really be justified, 'at least we weren't as bad as the French', thinking of the exceptionally brutal wars that France fought in an effort to hang on to Vietnam and Algeria in the 1950s and 1960s. My university should not bear the blame; it was a pretty good one, and my graduate supervisor was assuredly the finest imperial historian of his generation. The problem is a much bigger, systemic issue in British culture and society. For the past century or so, we in Britain have allowed ourselves a free pass, at least in our ways of doing history for public consumption. We haven't really been forced into a reckoning with our imperial legacy, and we have largely overlooked our brutal history of colonialism around the world because it is more convenient and financially advantageous quietly to ignore it.

For myself, learning about the events of the 1897 invasion of Benin was critical in furthering my understanding of colonial violence, and thus my understanding of the world that we live in today. Researching and writing this book has been an important part of the process of turning me from a somewhat neutral observer into a militant anticolonial, and I am now committed to doing what I can to tackle this national knowledge deficit and the imperial nostalgia that warps our thinking about the place of Britain in the world today.

I began the prologue of this book by quoting the title of Audre Lorde's conference paper from 1979, which is in itself a statement of great power: 'The Master's Tools Will Never Dismantle the Master's House'.[7] Reading this landmark piece for the first time was something of a personal milestone for me; I felt that I finally understood something of the postcolonial reality of the modern world, and how imperial hangovers continue to shape the lives of millions, almost always negatively. Lorde is writing of a slightly different but very related context (the racist patriarchy in the United States of the 1970s), and her analysis is directly relevant to the legacy of empire. If we continue to think of and discuss the British Empire in the same terms as before—the terms that suit the legacy power structures—we cannot even begin to address the inequalities and injustices that date from the imperial period and are still manifest in the present day. We must obtain a better understanding of the history of European colonialism and how it continues to shape societies around the world.

The reason why structural injustice tends always to exist was powerfully described by Thucydides over 2,000 years ago. In the famous Melian Dialogue, the aggressively imperialist Athenians arrive during the Peloponnesian War on the island of Melos with the intention of taking over; when the principled-but-defenceless Melians politely object, Thucydides has the Athenian representatives make a blunt statement of realpolitik:

> when these matters are discussed by practical people, the standard of justice depends on the equality of power to compel and that in fact the strong do what they have the power to do and the weak accept what they have to accept.[8]

When I doggedly read the *History of the Peloponnesian War* some years ago (it isn't a racy read), this quotation struck me powerfully, as it explains so much about the nature of empire. In fact, so important did it become to me that I had the key extract from this sentence tattooed on my arm. Awareness of the statement's salient fact is, I think, morally imperative for us all. Unequal power creates unequal assurance of justice, meaning injustice.

This inequality of power is demonstrated by the fact that the Benin Bronzes (and thousands of other items seized abroad during the colonial era) remain in the possession of those who looted them and those who happily bought stolen property from the plunderers. That the Bronzes have not yet been returned is a gross continuation of the invasion, amounting to ongoing Empire; until the Benin Bronzes are returned to the Edo people, the conquest of the Kingdom of Benin is not entirely over. More broadly, without reparations and without return of stolen treasures, the exploitation of Africa by Britain and the West continues, both symbolically and materially.

Leading barrister Geoffrey Robertson QC is extremely clear that the invasion of Benin was a war crime, according to the legal standards of both 1897 and the present day.[9] To date, the senior leadership of the British Museum has been unmoved by such inconvenient facts. In *A History of the World in 100 Objects*,[10] Neil MacGregor (who was director of the British Museum when he wrote the book) shamefully attempts to hide behind a dubious claim that the details of the events leading up to the attack on Benin are 'vigorously disputed'. He labels the stolen artefacts 'booty' and recognises that the British action was violent, but he glaringly fails even to consider the question of repatriation of the Bronzes. This position is logically untenable and morally unacceptable, but it is perhaps unsurprising from one who is professionally obliged to make the case for retaining possession of stolen property; no doubt MacGregor feared the implications for the wider collection under his charge at the time. If we consider the history behind many of its items, we may in fact reach the unavoidable conclusion that, besides being culturally the richest spot on the planet, the British Museum also stands ready to serve as the evidence room for the biggest war crimes tribunal of all time.

The complete and comprehensive return of all the pieces plundered from Benin is a moral requirement (the mooted idea of 'lending' some pieces to Nigeria being a grotesque insult). On the face of it, it is generally assumed that returning the Bronzes would leave Britain (and other countries in the possession of stolen goods) worse off: a priceless collection of cultural treasures would no longer be on British soil. However, I would argue that Britain would in fact be vastly better off, if the return of the artefacts were undertaken as part of a final process of decolonisation, that of decolonising our minds.

We urgently need to overcome, once and for all, our Empire legacy and the imperial nostalgia that still ruins our thinking about our place in the world. Had the political process of decolonisation, from the 1940s onwards, been accompanied by a genuine cultural shift in which we had sought to deal properly with the social and legal consequences of colonialism, Britain would be more at peace with itself in the modern world. Numerous injustices would already have been reversed, rather than lingering for decades. Our future would be much brighter; for one thing, the destructive absurdity of Brexit would have been impossible if Britain had freed itself from lingering imperial delusions and reconciled with the past. The Benin Bronzes must be returned as a moral necessity; everyone would gain from an injustice being put right.

NOTES

PROLOGUE

1. Audre Lorde, 'The Master's Tools Will Never Dismantle the Master's House', title of conference paper presented in New York on 29 September 1979, published in Audre Lorde, *Sister Outsider: Essays and Speeches*, Trumansburg, NY: The Crossing Press, 1984.

1. THE KINGDOM OF BENIN

1. Iro Eweka, *Dawn to Dusk: Folk Tales from Benin*, London: Frank Cass, 1998.
2. D. M. Bondarenko & P. M. Roese, 'Benin Prehistory: The Origin and Settling Down of the Edo', *Anthropos*, Vol. 94, No. 4/6, 1999.
3. John Iliffe, *Africans: The History of a Continent*, Cambridge: Cambridge University Press, 2007 (2nd edition).
4. R. A. Sargent, 'From A Redistribution To An Imperial Social Formation: Benin c1293–1536', *Canadian Journal of African Studies*, Vol. 20, No. 3, 1986.
5. *Ibid.*
6. Graham Connah, 'New Light on the Benin City Walls', *Journal of the Historical Society of Nigeria*, Vol. 3, No. 4, June 1967.
7. Robert S. Smith, *Warfare & Diplomacy in Pre-Colonial West Africa*, London: James Currey, 1989 (2nd edition).
8. *Ibid.*
9. A. F. C. Ryder, *Benin and the Europeans 1485–1897*, London: Longmans, 1969.
10. O. B. Osadolor & L. E. Otoide, 'The Benin Kingdom in British Imperial Historiography', *History in Africa*, Vol. 35, No. 1, 2008.
11. J. D. Graham, 'The Slave Trade, Depopulation and Human Sacrifice in Benin History', *Cahiers d'études africaines*, Vol. 5, No. 18, 1965.
12. Paula Girshick Ben-Amos, *Art, Innovation and Politics in Eighteenth-Century Benin*, Bloomington & Indianapolis: Indiana University Press, 1999.

13. Robin Law, 'Human Sacrifice in Pre-Colonial West Africa', *African Affairs*, Vol. 84, No. 334, January 1985.
14. Joseph Nevadomsky, 'The Benin Kingdom: Rituals of Kingship and their Social Meanings', *African Study Monographs*, Vol. 14, No. 2, 1993.
15. Girshick Ben-Amos, *Art, Innovation and Politics in Eighteenth-Century Benin.*
16. *Ibid.*
17. J. U. Egharevba, *A Short History of Benin*, Ibadan: Ibadan University Press, 1968 (4th edition).
18. Frank Willett, *African Art*, London: Thames & Hudson, 2002 (new edition).
19. Girshick Ben-Amos, *Art, Innovation and Politics in Eighteenth-Century Benin.*
20. Smith, *Warfare & Diplomacy in Pre-Colonial West Africa.*
21. Asutosh Satpathy, 'State Formation in Nigeria: A Historical Background', *World Affairs: The Journal of International Issues*, Vol. 1, No. 1, June 1992.
22. Olaudah Equiano, *The Interesting Narrative of the Life of Olaudah Equiano*, London: Penguin, 2003 [1789].
23. *Ibid.*
24. Girshick Ben-Amos, *Art, Innovation and Politics in Eighteenth-Century Benin.*
25. *Ibid.*
26. Obaro Ikime, 'Colonial Conquest and Resistance in Southern Nigeria', *Journal of the Historical Society of Nigeria*, Vol. 6, No. 3, December 1972.
27. *Ibid.*
28. Charles H. Read & Ormonde M. Dalton, *Antiquities from the City of Benin and from Other Parts of West Africa in the British Museum*, London: The British Museum Press, 1899.

2. WEST AFRICA AND THE BRITISH INTRUSION

1. Published by the Emory Center for Digital Scholarship at Emory University in Atlanta, Georgia, and freely available at www.slavevoyages.org.
2. David Cameron, speech at the Britannia Naval College, 12 October 2012, text published by the Cabinet Office, 17 October 2012.
3. Eric Williams, *Capitalism & Slavery*, Chapel Hill: University of North Carolina Press, 1944.
4. Kehinde Andrews, *Back to Black: Black Radicalism for the 21st Century*, London: Zed Books, 2018.
5. John W. Sweet, 'The Subject of the Slave Trade: Recent Currents in the Histories of the Atlantic, Great Britain, and Western Africa', *Early American Studies*, Vol. 7, No. 1, Spring 2009.
6. Walter Rodney, *How Europe Underdeveloped Africa*, London: Bogle-L'Ouverture Publications, 1972.

7. Martin Lynn, *Commerce and Economic Change in West Africa: The Palm Oil Trade in the Nineteenth Century*, Cambridge: Cambridge University Press, 1997.
8. Adiele E. Afigbo, 'Africa and the Abolition of the Slave Trade', *The William and Mary Quarterly*, Third Series, Vol. 66, No. 4 (Abolishing the Slave Trades: Ironies and Reverberations), October 2009.
9. John Gallagher & Ronald Robinson, 'The Imperialism of Free Trade', *The Economic History Review*, Second Series, Vol. VI, No. 1, 1953.
10. *Ibid.*, p. 3.
11. Richard Burton to Foreign Office, 22 May 1862, National Archives, FO 84/1176.
12. *Ibid.*
13. *Ibid.*
14. *Ibid.*
15. *Ibid.*
16. Richard Burton to Foreign Office, 26 August 1862, National Archives, FO 84/1176.
17. *Ibid.*
18. *Ibid.*
19. *Ibid.*
20. Charles Adderley MP, House of Commons, 21 February 1865, *Hansard*, Vol. 177, c. 535.
21. Scott R. Pearson, 'The Economic Imperialism of the Royal Niger Company', *Food Research Institute Studies*, Vol. 10, No. 1, 1971.
22. A. W. L. Hemming, 'Memorandum on Proposed Extension of British Authority in the River Niger and the Neighbourhood', 3 May 1883, African No. 259 Confidential, National Archives, CO 879/20.
23. *Ibid.*
24. A. W. L. Hemming, 'Minutes on Foreign Office Letter of 8th March 1882', 19 March 1882, African No. 259 Confidential, National Archives, CO 879/20.
25. Lord Kimberley, 6 April 1882, African No. 259 Confidential, National Archives, CO 879/20.

3. 'THE RUSH FOR AFRICA HAS BROKEN UP THE LITTLE FAMILY PARTY': THE SCRAMBLE OF THE 1880s

1. A. W. L. Hemming, 'Minutes on Foreign Office Letter of 12th March 1883', 24 March 1883, African No. 259 Confidential, National Archives, CO 879/20.
2. *Ibid.*
3. Sir Robert Meade, 28 March 1883, African No. 259 Confidential, National Archives, CO 879/20.
4. *Ibid.*

5. *The Times*, 25 October 1883.
6. *Ibid.*
7. *The Times*, 11 March 1884.
8. Martin Lynn, *Commerce and Economic Change in West Africa: The Palm Oil Trade in the Nineteenth Century*, Cambridge: Cambridge University Press, 1997.
9. *Ibid.*
10. Manchester Chamber of Commerce to Lord Granville, 4 April 1884, National Archives, FO 84/1684.
11. Liverpool Chamber of Commerce to Lord Granville, 8 October 1884, National Archives, FO 84/1690.
12. Lord Aberdare to Lord Granville, 28 February 1883, African No. 259 Confidential, National Archives, CO 879/20.
13. *Ibid.*
14. Sir Edward Hertslet, 'Memorandum on the Formalities necessary for the effective Annexation of Territory', 18 October 1884, National Archives, FO 84/1813.
15. Ronald Robinson & John Gallagher, *Africa and the Victorians: The Official Mind of Imperialism*, London: Macmillan, 1961.
16. H. P. Anderson, 'Memorandum by Mr Anderson on events connected with the West African Conference', 21 October 1884, National Archives, FO 84/1813.
17. *Ibid.*
18. Consul Hewett to Lieutenant & Commander Furlonger of HMS *Flirt*, 17 July 1884, quoted in Sir Claude MacDonald to Sir Eric Barrington, 11 January 1896, National Archives, FO 2/100.
19. H. P. Anderson, 'Memorandum by Mr Anderson on events connected with the West African Conference', 21 October 1884, National Archives, FO 84/1813.
20. H. P. Anderson, 'Memorandum by Mr Anderson on West African Conference', 14 October 1884, National Archives, FO 84/1813.
21. *Ibid.*
22. Ronald Robinson & John Gallagher, *Africa and the Victorians: The Official Mind of Imperialism*.
23. Julian Pauncefote, Foreign Office internal minute, 7 February 1885, National Archives, FO 84/1879.
24. T. V. Lister, 'Govt. of the Niger & Binué', 30 January 1885, National Archives, FO 84/1879.
25. J. C. Anene, 'The Foundations of British Rule in "Southern Nigeria" (1885–1891)', *Journal of the Historical Society of Nigeria*, Vol. 1, No. 4, December 1959.
26. Robinson & Gallagher, *Africa and the Victorians: The Official Mind of Imperialism*.
27. African Association, Liverpool, to Lord Iddesleigh, 7 December 1886, National Archives, FO 84/1880.
28. H. P. Anderson, 'Petition of Liverpool Merchants against the Royal Niger Co', 3 March 1887, National Archives, FO 84/1880.

29. Sir Cornelius Moloney, 'Minute by Governor Moloney in connection with his visit in April, 1888, to the present eastern limit of the Colony of Lagos', April 1888, National Archives, FO 84/1882.
30. Cherry Gertzel, 'Relations between African and European Traders in the Niger Delta 1880–1896', *Journal of African History*, Vol. 3, No. 2, 1962, Third Conference on African History and Archaeology: School of Oriental and African Studies, University of London (3–7 July 1961).
31. H. P. Anderson, Foreign Office internal minute, 24 October 1887, National Archives, FO 84/1828.
32. Foreign Office to Consul E. H. Hewett in Old Calabar, telegram, 12 April 1887, National Archives, FO 84/1828.
33. Anene, 'The Foundations of British Rule in "Southern Nigeria" (1885–1891)'.
34. Foreign Office internal note by H. P. Anderson, 24 June 1887, National Archives, FO 84/1828.
35. Acting Consul H. H. Johnston to Lord Salisbury, No. 18 Africa, 28 September 1887, National Archives, FO 84/1828.
36. *Ibid.*
37. Acting Consul H. H. Johnston to King Jaja, 19 September 1887, National Archive, FO 84/1828.
38. Acting Consul H. H. Johnston to Lord Salisbury, No. 18 Africa, 28 September 1887, National Archives, FO 84/1828.
39. Lord Salisbury, Foreign Office internal note, 25 October 1887, National Archives, FO 84/1828.
40. H. P. Anderson, 'Old Calabar Petition Consul Hewett', Foreign Office internal minute, 18 October 1887, National Archives, FO 84/1828.
41. H. P. Anderson, Foreign Office internal minute, 24 October 1887, National Archives, FO 84/1828.
42. Vice Consul H. H. Johnston, 'Memorandum by Vice Consul Johnston on the British Protectorate of the "Oil Rivers"; with suggestions as to its future government', 26 July 1888, National Archives, FO 84/1882.
43. *Ibid.*
44. Consul E. H. Hewett to Foreign Office, No. 34, 10 November 1888, National Archives, FO 84/1881.
45. H. P. Anderson, 'Old Calabar Petition Consul Hewett', Foreign Office internal minute, 18 October 1887, National Archives, FO 84/1828.
46. *Ibid.*
47. H. P. Anderson, Foreign Office internal minute, 24 October 1887, National Archives, FO 84/1828.
48. Foreign Office to Major C. M. MacDonald, No. 1, 15 December 1888, National Archives, FO 84/1881.

49. Foreign Office to Major C. M. MacDonald, No. 2, 17 January 1889, National Archives, FO 84/1940.
50. Scott R. Pearson, 'The Economic Imperialism of the Royal Niger Company', *Food Research Institute Studies*, Vol. 10, No. 1, 1971.
51. Consul E. H. Hewett to Foreign Office, No. 4, 12 February 1889, National Archives, FO 84/1941.
52. Consul E. H. Hewett to Foreign Office, No. 5, 15 February 1889, National Archives, FO 84/1941.
53. Consul E. H. Hewett to Foreign Office, No. 9, 30 March 1889, National Archives, FO 84/1941.
54. Foreign Office to Consul E. H. Hewett, 16 February 1889, National Archives, FO 84/1941.
55. Major C. M. MacDonald to Foreign Office, No. 7, 4 March 1889, National Archives, FO 84/1940.
56. Consul E. H. Hewett to Foreign Office, No. 8, 7 March 1889, National Archives, FO 84/1941.
57. Consul E. H. Hewett to Foreign Office, No. 12, 11 April 1889, National Archives, FO 84/1941.
58. Consul E. H. Hewett to Foreign Office, No. 22, 28 June 1889, National Archives, FO 84/1941.
59. Sir Claude MacDonald, 'Niger Coast Protectorate Annual Report for 1894–95', Old Calabar, 25 July 1895, National Archives, FO 2/84.

4. 'VERY BAD INDEED': CONSUL ANNESLEY IN THE OIL RIVERS

1. Major C. M. MacDonald to Foreign Office, No. 26, 7 September 1889, National Archives, FO 84/1940.
2. Scott R. Pearson, 'The Economic Imperialism of the Royal Niger Company', *Food Research Institute Studies*, Vol. 10, No. 1, 1971.
3. *Liverpool Mercury*, 'Amalgamation of African Traders', 18 June 1889.
4. Consul E. H. Hewett to Foreign Office, No. 30, 10 August 1889, National Archives, FO 84/1941.
5. Foreign Office file note, 7 September 1889, National Archives, FO 84/1941.
6. Foreign Office file note, 12 August 1889, National Archives, FO 84/1941.
7. Foreign Office telegram to Consular Agent at Bonny, 28 November 1889, National Archives, FO 84/1941.
8. Consul G. F. N. B. Annesley to Foreign Office, No. 1, 13 December 1889, National Archives, FO 84/1941.
9. *Annual Register*, July 1844.
10. *London Gazette*, 29 August 1884.

11. *Leeds Mercury*, 'Deaths', 31 August 1870.
12. *London Gazette*, 4 May 1888.
13. Consul G. F. N. B. Annesley to Foreign Office, No. 13, 27 February 1890, National Archives, FO 84/2020.
14. *Ibid.*
15. *Ibid.*
16. Consul G. F. N. B. Annesley to the United Presbyterian Mission, Old Calabar, 5 March 1890, National Archives, FO 84/2020.
17. Consul G. F. N. B. Annesley to Foreign Office, No. 15, 7 March 1890, National Archives, FO 84/2020.
18. *Ibid.*
19. Consul G. F. N. B. Annesley to Foreign Office, No. 16, 22 March 1890, National Archives, FO 84/2020.
20. *Ibid.*
21. *Ibid.*
22. Consul G. F. N. B. Annesley to Foreign Office, No. 23, 28 May 1890, National Archives, FO 84/2020.
23. Consul G. F. N. B. Annesley to Foreign Office, No. 13, 27 February 1890, National Archives, FO 84/2020.
24. *Birmingham Daily Post*, 28 May 1890.
25. Consul G. F. N. B. Annesley to Foreign Office, telegram, 10 November 1890, National Archives, FO 84/2020.
26. Major Sir Claude MacDonald to Foreign Office, 29 October 1895, National Archives, FO 2/85.
27. *The Times*, 19 January 1897.
28. J. U. Egharevba, *A Short History of Benin*, Ibadan: Ibadan University Press, 1968 (4th edition), p. 48.
29. *The Times*, 19 January 1897.
30. George J. Turner to Lord Salisbury, Old Calabar, 30 July 1891, National Archives, FO 84/2111.
31. Statement by George J. Turner, enclosed in Major C. M. MacDonald to Foreign Office, No. 12, 6 October 1891, National Archives, FO 84/2111.
32. Statement by Ekang, also known as Ekien Ranga, enclosed in Major C. M. MacDonald to Foreign Office, No. 12, 6 October 1891, National Archives, FO 84/2111.
33. George J. Turner to Lord Salisbury, Old Calabar, 30 July 1891, National Archives, FO 84/2111.
34. Statement by Ekang, also known as Ekien Ranga, enclosed in Major C. M. MacDonald to Foreign Office, No. 12, 6 October 1891, National Archives, FO 84/2111.

35. George J. Turner to Lord Salisbury, Old Calabar, 30 July 1891, National Archives, FO 84/2111.
36. Statement by Sergeant Edward Davies, enclosed in Major C. M. MacDonald to Foreign Office, No. 12, 6 October 1891, National Archives, FO 84/2111.
37. Statement by Ekang, also known as Ekien Ranga, enclosed in Major C. M. MacDonald to Foreign Office, No. 12, 6 October 1891, National Archives, FO 84/2111.
38. Consular Court, Old Calabar, 3 August 1891, enclosed in Major C. M. MacDonald to Foreign Office, No. 12, 6 October 1891, National Archives, FO 84/2111.
39. Old Calabar, 3 August 1891, enclosed in Major C. M. MacDonald to Foreign Office, No. 12, 6 October 1891, National Archives, FO 84/2111.
40. Major C. M. MacDonald to Foreign Office, No. 19, 17 October 1891, National Archives, FO 84/2111.
41. *Ibid.*
42. 'Statement by the Chiefs of Bonny', Grand Bonny, 10 August 1891, enclosed in Major C. M. MacDonald to Foreign Office, No. 19, 17 October 1891, National Archives, FO 84/2111.
43. 'Statements of the Aquetta Palaver', undated, enclosed in Major C. M. MacDonald to Foreign Office, No. 19, 17 October 1891, National Archives, FO 84/2111.
44. 'Statement by the Chiefs of Bonny', Grand Bonny, 10 August 1891, enclosed in Major C. M. MacDonald to Foreign Office, No. 19, 17 October 1891, National Archives, FO 84/2111.
45. Major C. M. MacDonald to Foreign Office, No. 19, 17 October 1891, National Archives, FO 84/2111.
46. 'Statements of the Aquetta Palaver', undated, enclosed in Major C. M. MacDonald to Foreign Office, No. 19, 17 October 1891, National Archives, FO 84/2111.
47. Sir Percy Anderson, Foreign Office file note, 14 December 1891, National Archives, FO 84/2111.
48. Consul G. F. N. B. Annesley to Foreign Office, No. 1 from Luanda, 5 August 1891, FO 84/2140.
49. Sir Percy Anderson, Foreign Office file note, 10 June 1891, National Archives, FO 84/2140.
50. Major C. M. MacDonald to Foreign Office, London, 7 May 1891, National Archives, FO 84/2111.
51. Major C. M. MacDonald to Sir Percy Anderson, 8 August 1891, National Archives, FO 84/2111.
52. *Ibid.*
53. *Ibid.*
54. Consul G. F. N. B. Annesley to Foreign Office, No. 9, 15 October 1891, National Archives, FO 84/2140.

55. Eric Barrington, Foreign Office internal note, 25 November 1891, National Archives, FO 84/2140.
56. Lord Salisbury, Foreign Office file note, undated, National Archives, FO 84/2140.
57. Consul G. F. N. B. Annesley to Foreign Office, Bad Thalkirchen, 20 February 1892, National Archives, FO 84/2224.
58. Sir Percy Anderson, Foreign Office file note, 22 February 1892, National Archives, FO 84/2224.
59. Foreign Office to G. F. N. B. Annesley, 14 June 1892, National Archives, FO 84/2224.

5. 'ALL QUIET IN RIVERS': MAJOR MACDONALD IN OLD CALABAR

1. Major C. M. MacDonald to Captain R. F. Synge, 6 June 1891, National Archives, FO 84/2111.
2. Major C. M. MacDonald to Foreign Office, telegram, 28 July 1891, National Archives, FO 84/2111.
3. Sir Claude MacDonald et al., 'The Land of the Ibibios, Southern Nigeria: Discussion', *Geographical Journal*, Vol. 44, No. 3, September 1914.
4. Major C. M. MacDonald to Sir Percy Anderson, 8 August 1891, National Archives, FO 84/2111.
5. 'Report by Major MacDonald of his Visit as Her Majesty's Commissioner to the Niger and Oil Rivers', 13 January 1890, Foreign Office Confidential Print, National Archives, FO 881/5913.
6. *Ibid.*
7. Cherry Gertzel, 'Relations between African and European Traders in the Niger Delta 1880–1896', *Journal of African History*, Vol. 3, No. 2, 1962, Third Conference on African History and Archaeology: School of Oriental and African Studies, University of London (3–7 July 1961).
8. *The Times*, 'The Niger Territories', 17 January 1890.
9. *The Times*, 'The Oil Rivers', 7 February 1890; *Liverpool Mercury*, 'African Oil Rivers', 17 February 1890.
10. *The Times*, 'House of Commons', 3 December 1890.
11. Major C. M. MacDonald to Foreign Office, 15 April 1891, National Archives, FO 84/2111.
12. Major C. M. MacDonald to Foreign Office, 23 May 1891, National Archives, FO 84/2111.
13. Major C. M. MacDonald to Foreign Office, 2 May 1891, National Archives, FO 84/2111.
14. Major C. M. MacDonald to Foreign Office, 13 June 1891, National Archives, FO 84/2111.

15. Major C. M. MacDonald, 'Memorandum by Major MacDonald on the Oil Rivers Establishment', Foreign Office Confidential Print, 23 December 1890, National Archives, FO 881/6107.
16. Major C. M. MacDonald to Foreign Office, 22 May 1891, National Archives, FO 84/2111.
17. *The Times*, 'The Oil Rivers Commissionership', 31 July 1891.
18. Major C. M. MacDonald to Sir Percy Anderson, 8 August 1891, National Archives, FO 84/2111.
19. *Ibid.*
20. Major C. M. MacDonald to Foreign Office, 1 September 1891, National Archives, FO 84/2111.
21. *Ibid.*
22. *Ibid.*
23. Major C. M. MacDonald to Foreign Office, 5 March 1891, National Archives, FO 84/2111.
24. Captain H. L. Gallwey, 'Report on visit to the Sobo and Abrakar Markets', 3 November 1891, National Archives, FO 84/2111.
25. *Ibid.*
26. Major C. M. MacDonald to Foreign Office, No. 30, 11 December 1891, National Archives, FO 84/2111.
27. Adogbeji Salubi, 'The Origins of Sapele Township', *Journal of the Historical Society of Nigeria*, Vol. 2, No. 1, December 1960.
28. Major Sir Claude MacDonald to Foreign Office, No. 15, 25 August 1893, National Archives, FO 2/51.
29. Captain H. L. Gallwey, 'Report on visit to Ubini (Benin City) the capital of the Benin Country', 30 March 1892, National Archives, FO 84/2194.
30. *Ibid.*
31. 'Treaty with King of Benin', 26 March 1892, enclosed with Major C. M. MacDonald to Foreign Office, No. 26, 16 May 1892, National Archives, FO 84/2194.
32. Captain H. L. Gallwey, 'Report on visit to Ubini (Benin City) the capital of the Benin Country', 30 March 1892, National Archives, FO 84/2194.
33. *Ibid.*
34. *Ibid.*
35. Major C. M. MacDonald to Foreign Office, No. 26, 16 May 1892, National Archives, FO 84/2194.
36. *Ibid.*
37. Captain H. L. Gallwey, 'Report on the Benin District, Oil Rivers Protectorate, for the year ending 31st July 1892', 31 July 1892, National Archives, FO 2/51.
38. *Ibid.*

39. *Ibid.*
40. Major C. M. MacDonald to Foreign Office, 12 January 1893, National Archives, FO 2/51.
41. Captain H. L. Gallwey, 'Report on the Benin District, Oil Rivers Protectorate, for the year ending 31st July 1892', 31 July 1892, National Archives, FO 2/51.

6. 'IN THE END YOU WILL ALL BE DESTROYED': ENFORCING BRITISH RULE IN THE NIGER DELTA

1. *The London Gazette*, Issue 26314, p. 4425, 5 August 1892.
2. *Hart's Army List*, 1895, p. 317.
3. R. D. R. Moor to Major Sir Claude MacDonald, 9 August 1892, National Archives, FO 84/2194.
4. *Ibid.*
5. Major Sir Claude MacDonald to Foreign Office, 8 December 1892, National Archives, FO 84/2194.
6. Major Sir Claude MacDonald to Foreign Office, 12 May 1893, National Archives, FO 2/51.
7. Major Sir Claude MacDonald to Lord Rosebery, 12 January 1893, National Archives, FO 2/51.
8. Consul G. F. N. B. Annesley to the chiefs of Opobo, 18 July 1890, enclosed with Annesley to Foreign Office, No. 31, 13 August 1890, National Archives, FO 84/2020.
9. *The London Gazette*, Issue 26403, p. 2835, 16 May 1893.
10. 'List of all Persons acting as British Vice Consuls or Consular Agents etc within the District of Her Majesty's Consul General at Old Calabar on 1st January 1893', 27 January 1893, National Archives, FO 2/51.
11. Major Sir Claude MacDonald to Foreign Office, No. 11, 23 June 1893, National Archives, FO 2/51.
12. *Ibid.*
13. Major Sir Claude MacDonald to Foreign Office, No. 15, 25 August 1893, National Archives, FO 2/51.
14. Major Sir Claude MacDonald to Lord Rosebery, 12 January 1893, National Archives, FO 2/51.
15. *Ibid.*
16. Major Sir Claude MacDonald to Foreign Office, telegram, 8 July 1893, National Archives, FO 2/51.
17. Obaro Ikime, 'Colonial Conquest and Resistance in Southern Nigeria', *Journal of the Historical Society of Nigeria*, Vol. 6, No. 3, December 1972.
18. Obaro Ikime, 'Chief Dogho: the Lugardian System in Warri 1917–1932', *Journal of the Historical Society of Nigeria*, Vol. 3, No. 2, December 1965.

19. R. Robinson, 'Non-European foundations of European imperialism: sketch for a theory of collaboration', in E. R. J. Owen & R. B. Sutcliffe, *Studies in the Theory of Imperialism*, London: Longman, 1972.
20. Captain H. L. Gallwey, 'Report on the Benin District, Oil Rivers Protectorate, for the year ending 31st July 1892', 31 July 1892, National Archives, FO 2/51.
21. R. D. R. Moor to Foreign Office, No. 17, 3 May 1894, National Archives, FO 2/63.
22. R. D. R. Moor to Foreign Office, No. 22, 6 August 1894, National Archives, FO 2/63.
23. *Ibid.*
24. Mr Coxon to James Pinnock, 1 July 1894, enclosed by Major Sir Claude MacDonald to Foreign Office, National Archives, FO 2/63.
25. *Ibid.*
26. R. D. R. Moor to Foreign Office, No. 22, 6 August 1894, National Archives, FO 2/63.
27. R. D. R. Moor to Foreign Office, No. 25A, 31 August 1894, National Archives, FO 2/63.
28. R. D. R. Moor to Foreign Office, telegram, 4 September 1894, National Archives, FO 2/64.
29. R. D. R. Moor to Foreign Office, No. 28, 5 October 1894, National Archives, FO 2/64.
30. *Ibid.*
31. *Ibid.*
32. R. D. R. Moor to Foreign Office, No. 35, 3 November 1894, National Archives, FO 2/64.
33. Major Sir Claude MacDonald to Foreign Office, telegram, 6 November 1894, National Archives, FO 2/64.
34. Major Sir Claude MacDonald to Foreign Office, telegram, 7 November 1894, National Archives, FO 2/64.
35. Major Sir Claude MacDonald to Foreign Office, No. 49, 13 December 1894, National Archives, FO 2/64.
36. Major Sir Claude MacDonald, 'Report on the Administration of the Niger Coast Protectorate', 16 August 1894, National Archives, FO 2/63.
37. *Ibid.*
38. Major Sir Claude MacDonald to Acting Vice Consul Roger Casement, No. 14, 20 November 1894, National Archives, FO 2/64.
39. Acting Vice Consul Roger Casement to Major Sir Claude MacDonald, 4 December 1894, National Archives, FO 2/64.
40. Major Sir Claude MacDonald to Foreign Office, telegram, 2 February 1895, National Archives, FO 2/86.

41. 'Report by Major MacDonald of his Visit as Her Majesty's Commissioner to the Niger and Oil Rivers', 13 January 1890, Foreign Office Confidential Print, National Archives, FO 881/5913.
42. Major Sir Claude MacDonald to Foreign Office, telegram, 5 February 1895, National Archives, FO 2/86.
43. *Ibid.*
44. T. N. Tamuno, 'Some Aspects of Nigerian Reaction to the Imposition of British Rule', *Journal of the Historical Society of Nigeria*, Vol. 3, No. 2, December 1965.
45. Major Sir Claude MacDonald to Foreign Office, No. 32A, 25 July 1895, National Archives, FO 2/84.
46. Major Sir Claude MacDonald to the chiefs of Brass, 13 February 1895, enclosed in MacDonald to Foreign Office, No. 11, 28 February 1895, National Archives, FO 2/83.
47. Major Sir Claude MacDonald to Foreign Office, No. 11, 28 February 1895, National Archives, FO 2/83.
48. Foreign Office to Major Sir Claude MacDonald, Telegram No. 9, 14 February 1895, National Archives, FO 2/86.
49. Major Sir Claude MacDonald to Foreign Office, Telegram No. 16, 18 February 1895, National Archives, FO 2/86.
50. Major Sir Claude MacDonald to Foreign Office, Telegram No. 17, 23 February 1895, National Archives, FO 2/86.
51. Major Sir Claude MacDonald to Foreign Office, Telegram No. 18, 25 February 1895, National Archives, FO 2/86.
52. Major Sir Claude MacDonald to Sir Clement Hill, private letter, 26 March 1895, National Archives, FO 2/83.
53. *Ibid.*
54. Foreign Office to Major Sir Claude MacDonald, Telegram No. 12, 26 March 1895, National Archives, FO 2/86.
55. Foreign Office to Major Sir Claude MacDonald, Telegram No. 15, 30 March 1895, National Archives, FO 2/86.
56. Major Sir Claude MacDonald to Foreign Office, Telegram No. 26, 9 April 1895, National Archives, FO 2/86.
57. Sir Clement Hill, Foreign Office file note, 10 April 1895, National Archives, FO 2/86.
58. R. D. R. Moor to Foreign Office, No. 29, 9 April 1896, National Archives, FO 2/100.
59. R. D. R. Moor to Foreign Office, No. 39, 12 September 1895, National Archives, FO 2/84.
60. Vice Consul Crawford to R. D. R. Moor, 16 August 1895, National Archives, FO 2/84.

61. *Ibid.*
62. R. D. R. Moor to Foreign Office, No. 39, 12 September 1895, National Archives, FO 2/84.
63. R. D. R. Moor to Major Sir Claude MacDonald, private letter, 9 October 1895, National Archives, FO 2/84.
64. Major Sir Claude MacDonald to Foreign Office, 29 October 1895, National Archives, FO 2/85.

7. 'THERE WOULDN'T BE A SINGLE SHOT FIRED': CONSUL PHILLIPS GETS HIMSELF KILLED

1. *London Gazette*, Issue 26706, p. 645, 4 February 1896.
2. *London Gazette*, Issue 26714, p. 1037, 21 February 1896.
3. R. D. R. Moor to Foreign Office, No. 13, 23 February 1896, National Archives, FO 2/100.
4. Foreign Office to R. D. R. Moor, No. 19, 5 March 1896, National Archives, FO 2/99.
5. R. D. R. Moor to Foreign Office, No. 50, 14 June 1896, National Archives, FO 2/101.
6. *Ibid.*
7. *Ibid.*
8. *Ibid.*
9. *Ibid.*
10. *Ibid.*
11. Sir Clement Hill, Foreign Office file note, 30 July 1896, National Archives, FO 2/101.
12. *Ibid.*
13. *Alumni Cantabrigienses*, Part II, Vol. 5, eds Venn & Venn, 1953, p. 112.
14. 'In Memoriam', *School Magazine*, Uppingham School, February 1897, p. 17.
15. Foreign Office to J. R. Phillips, 6 June 1896, National Archives, FO 2/99.
16. 'In Memoriam—J. R. Phillips', *School Magazine*, Uppingham School, February 1897, pp. 18–20.
17. H. D. Rawnsley, 'Acting Consul-General Phillips—An Appreciation', *School Magazine*, Uppingham School, November 1897, pp. 303–7.
18. Thomas Hughes, *Tom Brown's School Days*, 1857.
19. J. R. Phillips to Foreign Office, 14 June 1896, National Archives, FO 2/99.
20. R. D. R. Moor to Foreign Office, No. 58, 18 July 1896, National Archives, FO 2/101.
21. Foreign Office to R. D. R. Moor, No. 84, 30 July 1896, National Archives, FO 2/99.

22. Vice Consul P. W. Crawford to R. D. R. Moor, No. 10, 22 May 1896, National Archives, FO 2/101.
23. Sir Clement Hill, Foreign Office file note, 30 July 1896, National Archives, FO 2/101.
24. Captain H. L. Gallwey to Foreign Office, No. 71, 1 September 1896, National Archives, FO 2/101.
25. Captain H. L. Gallwey to Foreign Office, No. 90, 15 October 1896, National Archives, FO 2/102.
26. Captain H. L. Gallwey to Foreign Office, No. 93, 20 October 1896, National Archives, FO 2/102.
27. J. R. Phillips to Foreign Office, No. 102, 10 November 1896, National Archives, FO 2/102.
28. J. R. Phillips to Foreign Office, No. 103, 15 November 1896, National Archives, FO 2/102.
29. *Ibid.*
30. J. R. Phillips to Foreign Office, No. 105, 16 November 1896, National Archives, FO 2/102.
31. *Ibid.*
32. J. R. Phillips to Sir Clement Hill, private letter, 18 November 1896, National Archives, FO 2/102.
33. *Ibid.*
34. R. D. R. Moor to Foreign Office, 22 November 1896, National Archives, FO 2/102.
35. Sir Clement Hill, Foreign Office file note, 25 November 1896, National Archives, FO 2/101.
36. Sir Clement Hill, Foreign Office file note, 21 December 1896, National Archives, FO 2/102.
37. R. D. R. Moor to Foreign Office, 26 December 1896, National Archives, FO 2/102.
38. R. D. R. Moor to Foreign Office, No. 39, 12 September 1895, National Archives, FO 2/84.
39. R. D. R. Moor to Foreign Office, 26 December 1896, National Archives, FO 2/102.
40. *Ibid.*
41. *Ibid.*
42. Acting Governor Denton to Colonial Office, Lagos, No. 198, 4 January 1897, National Archives, CO 147/112.
43. Foreign Office to J. R. Phillips, No. 2, 9 January 1897, National Archives, ADM 116/87.
44. J. R. Phillips to Foreign Office, No. 119, 29 December 1896, National Archives, FO 2/102.

45. Alan Boisragon, *The Benin Massacre*, London: Methuen, 1897.
46. 'Diary of District Commissioner Burrows, showing Circumstances of Start of Expedition to Benin City', enclosed in R. D. R. Moor to Foreign Office, No. 2, 29 January 1897, National Archives, ADM 116/87.
47. *Ibid.*
48. Boisragon, *The Benin Massacre*, 1897, p. 70.
49. *Ibid.*, p. 68.
50. 'Diary of District Commissioner Burrows, showing Circumstances of Start of Expedition to Benin City', enclosed in R. D. R. Moor to Foreign Office, No. 2, 29 January 1897, National Archives, ADM 116/87.
51. *Ibid.*
52. Boisragon, *The Benin Massacre*, p. 73.
53. 'Diary of District Commissioner Burrows, showing Circumstances of Start of Expedition to Benin City', enclosed in R. D. R. Moor to Foreign Office, No. 2, 29 January 1897, National Archives, ADM 116/87.
54. *Ibid.*
55. Boisragon, *The Benin Massacre*, p. 92.
56. *Ibid.*, p. 92–3.
57. *Ibid.*, p. 100.
58. *Ibid.*, p. 100–1.
59. 'Diary of District Commissioner Burrows, showing Circumstances of Start of Expedition to Benin City', enclosed in R. D. R. Moor to Foreign Office, No. 2, 29 January 1897, National Archives, ADM 116/87.
60. Harrison at Brass to Foreign Office, telegram, 10 January 1897, National Archives, FO 2/125.
61. Foreign Office to J. R. Phillips, 6 June 1896, National Archives, FO 2/99.
62. J. R. Phillips to Foreign Office, No. 105, 16 November 1896, National Archives, FO 2/102.
63. Major C. M. MacDonald to Foreign Office, No. 26, 16 May 1892, National Archives, FO 84/2194.
64. R. D. R. Moor to Foreign Office, No. 39, 12 September 1895, National Archives, FO 2/84.
65. R. D. R. Moor to Foreign Office, No. 58, 18 July 1896, National Archives, FO 2/101.
66. Major Sir Claude MacDonald to Foreign Office, 29 October 1895, National Archives, FO 2/85.
67. J. R. Phillips to Foreign Office, No. 105, 16 November 1896, National Archives, FO 2/102.
68. Captain H. L. Gallwey to Foreign Office, No. 80, 24 September 1896, National Archives, FO 2/101.

69. Foreign Office to J. R. Phillips, No. 132, 27 November 1896, National Archives, FO 2/99.
70. Boisragon, *The Benin Massacre*, p. 63.
71. *Morning Post*, 'The Benin Disaster', 18 January 1897.
72. Captain H. L. Gallwey to Foreign Office, No. 1, 16 January 1897, National Archives, FO 2/121.
73. Obaro Ikime, 'Colonial Conquest and Resistance in Southern Nigeria', *Journal of the Historical Society of Nigeria*, Vol. 6, No. 3, December 1972.
74. Boisragon, *The Benin Massacre*, p. 83.
75. Geoffrey Rawson, *Life of Admiral Sir Harry Rawson*, London: Edward Arnold, 1914, p. 90.
76. Rear Admiral Harry Rawson to Admiralty, No. 9, 11 January 1897, National Archives, ADM 123/128.
77. Geoffrey Rawson, *Life of Admiral Sir Harry Rawson*, London: Edward Arnold, 1914, p. 104.
78. *The Times*, 'Latest Intelligence', 12 January 1897.
79. *Morning Post*, 13 January 1897.
80. *Manchester Guardian*, 'The Benin Massacre', 13 January 1897.
81. Foreign Office to Admiralty, 11 January 1897, National Archives, ADM 116/87.
82. Commander-in-Chief Mediterranean at Malta to Admiralty, telegram, 15 January 1897, National Archives, ADM 116/87.
83. Foreign Office to War Office, No. 2, 14 January 1897, National Archives, ADM 116/87.
84. Admiralty to Rear Admiral Harry Rawson, Telegram No. 7, 13 January 1897, National Archives, ADM 123/128.
85. Admiralty to Rear Admiral Harry Rawson, Telegram No. 9, 15 January 1897, National Archives, ADM 123/128.

8. 'OVERWHELMING FORCE': THE BENIN PUNITIVE EXPEDITION

1. Admiralty to Rear Admiral Harry Rawson, No. 30, 23 January 1897, National Archives, ADM 123/128.
2. *Ibid.*
3. *Ibid.*
4. Captain H. L. Gallwey to Foreign Office, No. 6, 21 January 1897, National Archives, FO 2/121.
5. Foreign Office to War Office, 14 January 1897, National Archives, ADM 116/87.
6. R. D. R. Moor to Foreign Office, No. 13, 8 February 1897, National Archives, ADM 116/87.
7. Captain H. L. Gallwey to Foreign Office, No. 6, 21 January 1897, National Archives, FO 2/121.

8. *Ibid.*
9. Captain H. L. Gallwey to Rear Admiral Harry Rawson, No. 8, 25 January 1897, National Archives, ADM 123/128.
10. R. D. R. Moor to Foreign Office, telegram, 7 February 1897, National Archives, ADM 116/87.
11. R. D. R. Moor to Foreign Office, No. 13, 8 February 1897, National Archives, ADM 116/87.
12. *Ibid.*
13. Rear Admiral Harry Rawson to Admiralty, Telegram No. 30, 16 February 1897, National Archives, ADM 116/87.
14. *Morning Post*, 'The Benin Expedition', 25 January 1897.
15. *Ibid.*
16. *Morning Post*, 'The Benin Expedition', 28 January 1897.
17. *Morning Post*, 'The Benin Expedition', 30 January 1897.
18. '"Malacca" Transport No 7, Hospital Medical Comforts, Wines, Spirits &c.', 20 January 1897, National Archives, ADM 123/128.
19. Admiralty to Rear Admiral Harry Rawson, G.339/525, 20 January 1897, National Archives, ADM 123/128.
20. Admiralty to Rear Admiral Harry Rawson, V.245/201, 20 January 1897, National Archives, ADM 123/128.
21. Rear Admiral Harry Rawson to Admiralty, 41/1268, 30 January 1897, National Archives, ADM 123/128.
22. *Ibid.*
23. Captain M. P. O'Callaghan to Rear Admiral Harry Rawson, 30 January 1897, National Archives, ADM 123/128.
24. *Ibid.*
25. Lieutenant & Commander E. D. Hunt to Captain M. P. O'Callaghan, 27 January 1897, National Archives, ADM 123/128.
26. Captain H. L. Gallwey to Rear Admiral Harry Rawson, No. 10, 28 January 1897, National Archives, ADM 123/128.
27. *Ibid.*
28. *Ibid.*
29. Captain M. P. O'Callaghan to Rear Admiral Harry Rawson, 'Notes and information', 30 January 1897, National Archives, ADM 123/128.
30. 'Notes taken from Private Adeshina, N.C.P. Force formerly a slave of Nana', enclosure in Captain M. P. O'Callaghan to Rear Admiral Harry Rawson, 30 January 1897, National Archives, ADM 123/128.
31. Rear Admiral Harry Rawson to Admiralty, 41/1268, 30 January 1897, National Archives, ADM 123/128.
32. Rear Admiral Harry Rawson to respective Captains, HM Ships & Vessels con-

cerned, 'General Orders for the information and guidance of the officers and men, who are about to be landed in the Benin Expedition', 30 January 1897, National Archives, ADM 123/128.

33. *Ibid.*
34. *Ibid.*
35. *Ibid.*
36. *Ibid.*, IV, 'General Remarks'.
37. *Ibid.*, section 17, 'Resisting Attacks'.
38. Rear Admiral Harry Rawson to Admiralty, Telegram No. 25, 4 February 1897, National Archives, ADM 116/87.
39. Commander R. H. Bacon, *Benin: The City of Blood*, London: Edward Arnold, 1897.
40. Rear Admiral Harry Rawson to Admiralty, 27 February 1897, National Archives, ADM 123/128.
41. R. D. R. Moor to Foreign Office, telegram, 7 February 1897, National Archives, ADM 116/87.
42. R. D. R. Moor to Foreign Office, No. 13, 8 February 1897, National Archives, ADM 116/87.
43. Rear Admiral Harry Rawson to Admiralty, 27 February 1897, National Archives, ADM 123/128.
44. Rear Admiral Harry Rawson to Admiralty, Telegram No. 25, 4 February 1897, National Archives, ADM 116/87.
45. Rear Admiral Harry Rawson to Admiralty, Telegram No. 29, 8 February 1897, National Archives, ADM 116/87.
46. R. D. R. Moor to Foreign Office, No. 13, 8 February 1897, National Archives, ADM 116/87.
47. Captain M. P. O'Callaghan to Rear Admiral Harry Rawson, 27 February 1897, National Archives, ADM 116/87.
48. *Ibid.*
49. Rear Admiral Harry Rawson to Admiralty, 27 February 1897, National Archives, ADM 123/128.
50. R. D. R. Moor to Foreign Office, No. 17, 24 February 1897, National Archives, ADM 123/128.
51. Bacon, *Benin: The City of Blood.*
52. Rear Admiral Harry Rawson to Admiralty, 27 February 1897, National Archives, ADM 123/128.
53. Bacon, *Benin: The City of Blood.*
54. Lieutenant-Colonel B. Hamilton to Captain G. Le C. Egerton, 21 February 1897, National Archives, ADM 123/128.
55. Rear Admiral Harry Rawson to Admiralty, Enclosure No. 1, 'List of Casualties

during the Benin Expedition', 27 February 1897, National Archives, ADM 123/128.

56. Bacon, *Benin: The City of Blood.*
57. *Ibid.*
58. Lieutenant-Colonel B. Hamilton to Captain G. Le C. Egerton, 21 February 1897, National Archives, ADM 123/128.
59. Bacon, *Benin: The City of Blood.*
60. Lieutenant-Colonel B. Hamilton to Captain G. Le C. Egerton, 21 February 1897, National Archives, ADM 123/128.
61. Bacon, *Benin: The City of Blood.*
62. Commander R. H. Bacon to Rear Admiral Harry Rawson, 55/1268, 27 February 1897, National Archives, ADM 116/87.
63. Bacon, *Benin: The City of Blood.*
64. Lieutenant-Colonel B. Hamilton to Captain G. Le C. Egerton, 21 February 1897, National Archives, ADM 123/128.
65. Bacon, *Benin: The City of Blood.*
66. Rear Admiral Harry Rawson to Admiralty, 27 February 1897, National Archives, ADM 123/128.
67. Bacon, *Benin: The City of Blood.*
68. Lieutenant-Colonel B. Hamilton to Captain G. Le C. Egerton, 21 February 1897, National Archives, ADM 123/128.
69. Bacon, *Benin: The City of Blood.*
70. R. D. R. Moor to Foreign Office, No. 17, 24 February 1897, National Archives, ADM 123/128.
71. *Ibid.*
72. Rear Admiral Harry Rawson to Admiralty, 27 February 1897, National Archives, ADM 123/128.
73. Bacon, *Benin: The City of Blood.*
74. Rear Admiral Harry Rawson to Admiralty, 27 February 1897, National Archives, ADM 123/128.
75. *Ibid.*
76. R. D. R. Moor to Foreign Office, No. 17, 24 February 1897, National Archives, ADM 123/128.
77. Captain G. Le C. Egerton, *General Orders*, 16 February 1897, National Archives, ADM 123/128.
78. Bacon, *Benin: The City of Blood.*
79. Lieutenant-Colonel F. W. B. Landin to War Office, 'Report on Benin Expedition', 29 May 1897, National Archives, WO 107/10.
80. Rear Admiral Harry Rawson to Admiralty, 27 February 1897, National Archives, ADM 123/128.

81. Bacon, *Benin: The City of Blood.*
82. Lieutenant-Colonel B. Hamilton to Captain G. Le C. Egerton, 21 February 1897, National Archives, ADM 123/128.
83. R. D. R. Moor to Foreign Office, No. 17, 24 February 1897, National Archives, ADM 123/128.
84. Commander R. H. Bacon to Rear Admiral Harry Rawson, 55/1268, 27 February 1897, National Archives, ADM 116/87.
85. Rear Admiral Harry Rawson to Admiralty, 27 February 1897, National Archives, ADM 123/128.
86. Bacon, *Benin: The City of Blood.*
87. *Ibid.*
88. Rear Admiral Harry Rawson to Admiralty, 27 February 1897, National Archives, ADM 123/128.
89. Bacon, *Benin: The City of Blood.*
90. *Ibid.*
91. R. D. R. Moor to Foreign Office, No. 17, 24 February 1897, National Archives, ADM 123/128.
92. Bacon, *Benin: The City of Blood.*
93. Rear Admiral Harry Rawson to Admiralty, 27 February 1897, National Archives, ADM 123/128.
94. R. D. R. Moor to Foreign Office, No. 17, 24 February 1897, National Archives, ADM 123/128.
95. Bacon, *Benin: The City of Blood.*
96. Lieutenant-Colonel B. Hamilton to Captain G. Le C. Egerton, 21 February 1897, National Archives, ADM 123/128.
97. Bacon, *Benin: The City of Blood.*
98. Rear Admiral Harry Rawson to Admiralty, Telegram No. 32, 22 February 1897, National Archives, ADM 116/87.
99. R. D. R. Moor to Foreign Office, No. 17, 24 February 1897, National Archives, ADM 123/128.
100. Lieutenant-Colonel B. Hamilton to Captain G. Le C. Egerton, 21 February 1897, National Archives, ADM 123/128.
101. Rear Admiral Harry Rawson to Admiralty, Telegram No. 32, 22 February 1897, National Archives, ADM 116/87.
102. Lieutenant-Colonel B. Hamilton to Captain G. Le C. Egerton, 21 February 1897, National Archives, ADM 123/128.
103. R. D. R. Moor to Foreign Office, No. 17, 24 February 1897, National Archives, ADM 123/128.
104. Rear Admiral Harry Rawson to Admiralty, Telegram No. 32, 22 February 1897, National Archives, ADM 116/87.

105. Rear Admiral Harry Rawson to Admiralty, 27 February 1897, National Archives, ADM 123/128.
106. R. D. R. Moor to Foreign Office, Telegram No. 9, 22 February 1897, National Archives, ADM 116/87.
107. Rear Admiral Harry Rawson to Admiralty, Enclosure No. 1, 'List of Casualties during the Benin Expedition', 27 February 1897, National Archives, ADM 123/128.
108. Rear Admiral Harry Rawson to Admiralty, Telegram No. 32, 22 February 1897, National Archives, ADM 116/87.
109. Bacon, *Benin: The City of Blood.*
110. Commander R. H. Bacon to Rear Admiral Harry Rawson, 55/1268, 27 February 1897, National Archives, ADM 116/87.
111. R. D. R. Moor to Foreign Office, No. 17, 24 February 1897, National Archives, ADM 123/128.
112. Dr Robert Allman to R. D. R. Moor, 13 March 1897, National Archives, FO 2/121.
113. Commander R. H. Bacon to Rear Admiral Harry Rawson, 55/1268, 27 February 1897, National Archives, ADM 116/87.
114. Bacon, *Benin: The City of Blood.*
115. R. D. R. Moor to Foreign Office, No. 17, 24 February 1897, National Archives, ADM 123/128.
116. Dr Robert Allman to R. D. R. Moor, 13 March 1897, National Archives, FO 2/121.
117. Bacon, *Benin: The City of Blood.*
118. R. D. R. Moor to Foreign Office, No. 17, 24 February 1897, National Archives, ADM 123/128.
119. Bacon, *Benin: The City of Blood.*
120. R. D. R. Moor to Foreign Office, No. 17, 24 February 1897, National Archives, ADM 123/128.
121. Bacon, *Benin: The City of Blood.*
122. Rear Admiral Harry Rawson to Admiralty, 27 February 1897, National Archives, ADM 123/128.
123. *Ibid.*
124. *Ibid.*
125. *Ibid.*
126. R. D. R. Moor to Foreign Office, No. 17, 24 February 1897, National Archives, ADM 123/128.
127. 'List of Kit lost by Lt Col. Hamilton in fire at Benin', 21 February 1897, Foreign Office, National Archives, FO 2/121.
128. R. D. R. Moor to Foreign Office, No. 17, 24 February 1897, National Archives, ADM 123/128.

129. Rear Admiral Harry Rawson to Admiralty, 27 February 1897, National Archives, ADM 123/128.

9. THE AFTERMATH

1. Commander R. H. Bacon, *Benin: The City of Blood*, London: Edward Arnold, 1897.
2. Captain Thomas MacGill to Rear Admiral Harry Rawson, 25 February 1897, National Archives, ADM 123/128.
3. Captain M. P. O'Callaghan to Rear Admiral Harry Rawson, 27 February 1897, National Archives, ADM 123/128.
4. Rear Admiral Harry Rawson to Admiralty, 27 February 1897, National Archives, ADM 123/128.
5. Rear Admiral Harry Rawson to R. D. R. Moor, 25 February 1897, National Archives, ADM 123/128.
6. Rear Admiral Harry Rawson to Admiralty, 27 February 1897, National Archives, ADM 123/128.
7. R. D. R. Moor to Foreign Office, No. 17, 24 February 1897, National Archives, ADM 123/128.
8. *Ibid.*
9. Lieutenant-Colonel F. W. B. Landin to War Office, 'Report on Benin Expedition', 29 May 1897, National Archives, WO 107/10.
10. R. D. R. Moor to Foreign Office, No. 17, 24 February 1897, National Archives, ADM 123/128.
11. Captain M. P. O'Callaghan to Rear Admiral Harry Rawson, 27 February 1897, National Archives, ADM 123/128.
12. Rear Admiral Harry Rawson to R. D. R. Moor, 25 February 1897, National Archives, ADM 123/128.
13. R. D. R. Moor to Foreign Office, No. 17, 24 February 1897, National Archives, ADM 123/128.
14. R. D. R. Moor to Foreign Office, Telegram No. 12, 5 March 1897, National Archives, ADM 116/87.
15. R. D. R. Moor to Foreign Office, Telegram No. 13, 12 March 1897, National Archives, ADM 116/87.
16. R. D. R. Moor to Foreign Office, No. 23, 18 March 1897, National Archives, ADM 116/87.
17. *Ibid.*
18. *The Times*, 'The King of Benin', 23 August 1897.
19. *The Edinburgh Gazette*, Issue 10899, p. 650, 9 July 1897.
20. *The Times*, 'The King of Benin', 6 October 1897.

21. Philip Igbafe, 'British Rule in Benin 1897–1920: Direct or Indirect?', *Journal of the Historical Society of Nigeria*, Vol. 3, No. 4, June 1967.
22. *The Times*, 'Latest Intelligence—Capture of Benin', 23 February 1897.
23. *The Times*, 'The Benin Expedition', 23 February 1897.
24. *Morning Post*, 'Capture of Benin—Flight of the King—The City Deserted', 23 February 1897.
25. *Morning Post*, 24 February 1897.
26. *Morning Post*, 'Arrival of Benin Troops', 20 March 1897.
27. *The Graphic*, 'The Taking of Benin', 27 February 1897.
28. *Morning Post*, 'Mr Goschen on Foreign Affairs', 25 February 1897.
29. *Ibid.*
30. *The Times*, 'Return of Mr Locke', 8 March 1897.
31. *Morning Post*, 'Arrival of Benin Troops', 20 March 1897.
32. *Morning Post*, 'Mr Chamberlain on Our Colonies', 1 April 1897.
33. *Ibid.*
34. *Ibid.*
35. *The Times*, 3 April 1897.
36. Admiralty to Rear Admiral Harry Rawson, Telegram No. 29, 19 February 1897, National Archives, ADM 123/128.
37. Admiralty to Rear Admiral Harry Rawson, Telegram No. 30, 25 February 1897, National Archives, ADM 123/128.
38. R. D. R. Moor to Foreign Office, No. 17, 24 February 1897, National Archives, ADM 123/128.
39. Admiralty to Rear Admiral Sir Harry Rawson, No. 268, 23 July 1897, National Archives, ADM 123/128.
40. Admiralty to Rear Admiral Harry Rawson, No. 192, 25 May 1897, National Archives, ADM 123/128.
41. *The Times*, 'Benin Honours', 26 May 1897.
42. *Morning Post*, 'New Books & New Editions', 23 September 1897.
43. *Morning Post*, 'Benin, the City of Blood', 25 November 1897.
44. *The Times*, 'Christmas books', 29 November 1897.
45. *The Times*, 'Christmas books', 14 December 1897.
46. *The Times*, 9 July 1897.
47. *Morning Post*, 'Memorial to Major Crawford', 20 November 1897.
48. *Morning Post*, 'Royal Military Tournament', 6 May 1898.
49. *The Times*, 'Royal Military Tournament', 20 May 1898.
50. *Ibid.*
51. *Ibid.*
52. R. D. R. Moor to Foreign Office, No. 24, 20 March 1897, National Archives, FO 2/121.

53. *The Times*, 19 May 1897.
54. Rear Admiral Harry Rawson to Admiralty, 2 March 1897, National Archives, ADM 123/128.
55. Admiralty to Rear Admiral Sir Harry Rawson, No. 202, 7 June 1897, National Archives, ADM 123/128.
56. Charles H. Read to Sir Edward Maunde Thompson, 17 March 1897, National Archives, FO 800/148.
57. Charles H. Read & Ormonde M. Dalton, *Antiquities from the City of Benin and from Other Parts of West Africa in the British Museum*, London: The British Museum Press, 1899.
58. Frank Willett, *African Art*, London: Thames & Hudson, 2002 (new edition).
59. Charles H. Read to Sir Edward Maunde Thompson, 17 March 1897, National Archives, FO 800/148.
60. Classified advertisement, *The Times*, 4 April 1898.
61. Annie E. Coombes, *Reinventing Africa: Museums, Material Culture and Popular Imagination in Late Victorian and Edwardian England*, New Haven: Yale University Press, 1994.
62. *Illustrated London News*, 'Spoils of Benin in the Horniman Free Museum at Forest Hill', 10 April 1897.
63. *The Times*, 'Benin Antiquities at the British Museum', 25 September 1897.
64. *The Standard*, 'The Benin Relics', 25 September 1897.
65. *The Times*, 'Benin Antiquities at the British Museum', 25 September 1897.
66. Read & Dalton, *Antiquities from the City of Benin and from Other Parts of West Africa in the British Museum*.
67. *The Standard*, 'The Benin Relics', 25 September 1897.
68. National Archives Currency Converter 1270–2017.
69. Henry Ling Roth, *Great Benin: Its Customs, Art and Horrors*, Halifax: F. King & Sons, 1903.
70. *Ibid*.

EPILOGUE

1. Sir Alan C. M. Burns, *History of Nigeria*, London: George Allen & Unwin, 1948.
2. *London Gazette*, Issue 27152, p. 145, 9 January 1900.
3. Bonny Ibhawoh, 'Stronger than the Maxim Gun: Law, Human Rights and British Colonial Hegemony in Nigeria', *Africa: Journal of the International African Institute*, Vol. 72, No. 1, 2002.
4. *Sanders of the River*, directed by Zoltán Korda, London Films, 1935.
5. *Zulu*, directed by Cy Endfield, Diamond Films, 1964.

6. Priyamvada Gopal, 'Redressing anti-imperial amnesia', *Race & Class*, Vol. 57, No. 3, 2016.
7. Audre Lorde, 'The Master's Tools Will Never Dismantle the Master's House', title of conference paper presented in New York on 29 September 1979, published in Audre Lorde, *Sister Outsider: Essays and Speeches*, Trumansburg, NY: The Crossing Press, 1984.
8. Thucydides, *History of the Peloponnesian War*, Book V, p. 89, translated by Rex Warner, London: Penguin, 1954.
9. Geoffrey Robertson, *Who Owns History?: Elgin's Loot and the Case for Returning Plundered Treasure*, London: Biteback, 2019, p. 177.
10. Neil MacGregor, *A History of the World in 100 Objects*, London: Allen Lane, 2010.

INDEX

INDEX

INDEX

INDEX

INDEX

INDEX

INDEX